Going Diverse:
Innovative Answers to Future Challenges

CW00606992

This publication is funded by the European Community's 6th Framework Programme for Research and Technological Development.

Carmen Leicht-Scholten
Elke Breuer
Nathalie Tulodetzki
Andrea Wolffram (eds.)

Going Diverse: Innovative Answers to Future Challenges

Gender and Diversity Perspectives in
Science, Technology and Business

Budrich UniPress Ltd.
Opladen & Farmington Hills, MI 2011

All rights reserved. No part of this publication may be reproduced, stored in or introduced into a retrieval system, or transmitted, in any form, or by any means (electronic, mechanical, photocopying, recording or otherwise) without the prior written permission of Barbara Budrich Publishers. Any person who does any unauthorized act in relation to this publication may be liable to criminal prosecution and civil claims for damages.

You must not circulate this book in any other binding or cover and you must impose this same condition on any acquirer.

A CIP catalogue record for this book is available from
Die Deutsche Bibliothek (The German Library)

© 2011 by Budrich UniPress Ltd. Opladen & Farmington Hills
www.budrich-unipress.eu

ISBN   978-3-940755-62-9

Das Werk einschließlich aller seiner Teile ist urheberrechtlich geschützt. Jede Verwertung außerhalb der engen Grenzen des Urheberrechtsgesetzes ist ohne Zustimmung des Verlages unzulässig und strafbar. Das gilt insbesondere für Vervielfältigungen, Übersetzungen, Mikroverfilmungen und die Einspeicherung und Verarbeitung in elektronischen Systemen.

Die Deutsche Bibliothek – CIP-Einheitsaufnahme
Ein Titeldatensatz für die Publikation ist bei Der Deutschen Bibliothek erhältlich.

Budrich UniPress Ltd.
Stauffenbergstr. 7. D-51379 Leverkusen Opladen, Germany

28347 Ridgebrook. Farmington Hills, MI 48334. USA
www.budrich-unipress.eu

Jacket illustration by disegno, Wuppertal, Germany – www.disenjo.de
Editor: Máiréad Collins

Printed in Europe on acid-free paper by Paper & Tinta, Warszaw, Poland.

Acknowledgements

The book would not have been realised without the fruitful discussions had within conference panels, without the presentations and the scientists and experts of enterprises there who shared their experience and knowledge, and who were willing to participate with their papers. And without my IGaD team, who supported and organised the conference. Here Elke Breuer and Nathalie Tulodetzki deserve special mention, as they not only coordinated the EU project, but were also responsible for collecting papers and coordinating the publication. And finally, I would like to thank the EU for supporting the conference and the publication of the results within the project TANDEM-plusIDEA.

I hope the readers can benefit from the diversity of the articles and get new ideas and insights in dealing with gender and diversity aspects in their own organisation. Additionally, I would be glad if we could foster the discussion and open it for a broader audience.

September 2010
Carmen Leicht-Scholten
RWTH Aachen University

Content

Preface

Over the years, the European Union's gender and research policies have been driven by dual concerns: the under-representation of women in research, particularly in decision-making positions, as well as the lack of awareness regarding the possible role of gender in many fields of research, and its consequent frequent absence in research content. These problems should be of general concern because they have a serious effect on how well science is carried out in Europe.

These concerns are also reflected in the recently adopted Communication from the Commission, the "Europe 2020" strategy. As President Barroso states in the Preface: "Europe 2020 shows how Europe has the capability to deliver smart, sustainable and inclusive growth". This strategy emphasises the important role of research innovation in smart growth and sets clear targets for 2020. How can Europe achieve the quality targets without a balanced participation of women in research? Shouldn't we use all our resources, and acknowledge that diversity plays a key part in innovation?

This publication is based on the achievements of the EU TANDEMplus-IDEA project, which have ranged from developing modular mentoring and personal development schemes for female scientists to bringing the gender dimension into scientific research. The project has also resulted in awareness-raising on the role of diversity management in human resources and the need to change the culture in universities and research organisations.

The articles in this publication in fact reflect the shift in focus for EU-funded activities in the field of women and science - a shift from an individual to an institutional-centred focus. By this we mean working to adapt the institutions and their structures to the skills and needs of individuals, and not the opposite, since there is a general consensus that the existing research system is far from perfect and needs modernising. It can surely be claimed that equality and diversity in research would result in better research quality.

The European Commission welcomes the publication of this book.

I am convinced that this collection of innovative articles on gender and diversity management will not only inspire the research community, scientists and human resource managers on diversity management, but will also help them to develop new and better ways of doing science.

Luisa Prista
(Head of Unit Scientific Culture and Gender Issues, European Commission)

Introduction

Organisations and institutions of higher education are faced with the challenges of current economic, social and political conditions; such as demographic change, globalisation or skilled labour shortage. Universities, as well as companies, will in the future have to compete for the most qualified staff to produce innovative solutions, better performance and a guaranteed competitive edge. To be successful, universities and employers need to acknowledge the diversity of their students and employees and foster a creative and respectful environment that supports the potential of the entire workforce, regardless of gender, age, ethnicity or sexual orientation. This is where gender and diversity management starts, and why it is becoming more and more important to integrate gender and diversity perspectives as important elements of organisational and human resources development of an institution.

This anthology picks up these topics and discusses them in the special focus of natural sciences, engineering and the business sector. It considers organisational change and human resources development, issues of work life balance as well as other perspectives on diversity management. In particular, it tries to answer the following questions: What are the benefits of gender and diversity-oriented policies for an organisation and its staff? What is the role of human resources development measures, for example mentoring, dual career and work-life balance concepts, regarding the increase and acknowledgement of diversity in the workforce? How can gender and diversity concepts be institutionalised in science, technology and business?

The contributions here are borne from the international conference "Going Diverse: Innovative Answers to Future Challenges. International Conference on Gender and Diversity in Science, Technology and Business" that took place in October 2009 at RWTH Aachen University. The conference was the final event of the project TANDEMplusIDEA and, as such was organised in cooperation with the partner universities of the IDEA League network, Imperial College London, TU Delft and ETH Zurich. Financed for three years, between 2007 and 2010, by the 6th Framework Programme of the European Commission, the project TANDEMplusIDEA contained the conception and implementation of a modular mentoring and personal development scheme for female scientists, as well as its scientific evaluation and the development of a best practice model of an international mentoring programme. The conference presented the results of the project and put them into the broader context of gender and diversity management in human resources and organisational development. A special emphasis of the conference was on the exchange between academia and companies. International representatives from renowned firms and universities presented their concepts and studies on workforce diversity and gender mainstreaming. The programme was complemented by speakers from the European Commission and the United Nations Alliance of Civilizations, as well as by diverse poster presentations. In ten parallel sessions 170 conference participants discussed various topics of gender and diversity management, for example, academic human resources development and intercultural trainings. One conclusion reached was on the importance of integrating gender and diversity aspects into science and business, as well as into all political decisions. This publication collects selected contributions from the conference, focusing in particular on the academic point of view. It gives international experts the opportunity to discuss recent theoretical research and practical approaches, highlights different perspectives of gender and diversity management, and contributes to the latest scientific discussion. In particular, it presents the international mentoring programme TANDEMplusIDEA as a model of best practice in the context of gender-oriented human resources and organisational development.

The publication is structured into six main chapters. In the first section, Teresa Rees and Katharina Schiederig consider the framework of the topic and give an insight into the overall conditions of the gender and diversity agenda. Teresa Rees reflects on research results and on her personal experience at a major European university to explore the patterns of gender segregation, and the causes and consequences of the loss of women to scientific careers. She particularly focuses on the efforts made by the European Commission's Research Directorate-General during the last ten years, and proposes to link equality with an "excellence" agenda to ensure that quality rather than gender is rewarded. Katharina Schiederig adds to this political view the role of International Framework Agreements (IFAs) as external factors for gender and diversity-oriented human resources management in large transnational corporations. She explains that the 80 IFAs signed in recent years commit the corporations to respect the ILO core labour standards, and, thus, contribute to the elimination of all forms of discrimination in employment. She argues that IFAs, and more generally the union movement, are, therefore, playing an important role in institutionalising diversity.

In the following chapters, the publication focuses on different aspects of gender and diversity management. Organisational and cultural change, perspectives on diversity management, gender in academic careers and work-life balance are important facets in this thorough discussion of the conditions and desiderata of gender and diversity in academia and business. Verena Bruchhagen and Iris Koall consider the potential for cultural change through gender and diversity management. They relate the concept to theoretical and methodological resources of gender research such as system theory to describe problems of complexity and contingency. Carmen Leicht-Scholten explains the institutional integration of a comprehensive gender and diversity management strategy at the technical university RWTH Aachen that was an essential element of the Institutional Strategy within the framework of the German Excellence Initiative. In particular, she concentrates on measures in organisational development, and describes the establishment of the scientific unit "Integration Team – Human Resources, Gender and Diversity Management" (IGaD) as the key actor in this change process. Susanne Ihsen, Victoria Hantschel and Sabrina Gebauer complement this chapter with their description of gender and diversity activities at TU Munich, also implemented in the aftermath of the German Excellence Initiative.

Different diversity perspectives are addressed in the next chapter. Junko Takagi elaborates on diversity as a concept, its challenges and categorisations. She uses gender as an exemplary diversity element and refers to two studies presenting the case of France. Asli-Juliya Weheliye discusses diversity as a strategy to induce and further equal opportunities, and especially highlights the role of the individual in these change processes. In this context she pays particular attention to diversity training as a useful instrument to change attitudes and perceptions of individuals, and, thus, to promote cultural change within an organisation. Thomas Köllen contributes his research on the diversity category of sexual orientation. He shows that the most important condition for attracting and retaining homosexual employees is the perceived working climate for gays and lesbians. Based on an empirical analysis conducted in 2008 in Germany, he presents the nine most implemented measures in diversity management regarding the dimension of sexual orientation.

A further contribution to the multifaceted topic of the publication is made by Ann-Kathrin Vaske and Martin K.W. Schweer. Their article reflects on the psychological construction of implicit career theories that are used to reduce social complexity through structuring social perception and providing orientation. The article draws on empirical results gathered during an ongoing dissertation project on the implicit career theories of male and female employees, and shows the theories' importance for the construction of gender mainstreaming instruments in human resources development. Female careers in academia are also examined from the perspective of negotiation procedures by Heather Hofmeister and Julia Hahmann. Their article describes the inequality in resource allocation, based on a study of 40 negotiation records conducted with newly hired associate professors between 2005 and 2008 at RWTH Aachen University. Karin Schlücker explores diversity in academic careers from a methodological and theoretical perspective, and in particular considers intersectionality in diversity inquiries. She argues for the strategy of a theoretical sampling as it was suggested by the Grounded Theory. In her article on highly skilled female migrants at German universities, Andrea Wolffram explains that modern knowledge societies cannot afford to ignore the potential of migrant women against the background of globalisation, increasing mobility and demographic changes. She discusses the career barriers and supportive factors for their career progression and shows the situation of migrant women scientists at German universities from an intersectional perspective.

Work-life balance is another strong factor for a successful gender and diversity management strategy. Londa Schiebinger presents findings gathered at Stanford University on the issue of academic dual career couples. She describes couple hiring as an important institutional objective of excellence and diversity and gives recommendations in this matter to all universities. Sara Connolly, Stefan Fuchs and Claartje Vinkenburg analyse the relationship between work-life balance and the careers of men and women in academia. They focus on the question what universities can do regarding work-life balance preferences and policies in order to stem any loss of talent through the so-called "leaky pipeline".

The publication concludes with practical examples of gender and diversity management, among them the final report on the mentoring programme TANDEMplusIDEA. Elke Breuer and Carmen Leicht-Scholten give an overview on the project that was funded by the European Commission between 2007 and 2010 and describe the results of its scientific evaluation. They present the programme in the context of gender-oriented human resources development and as a model of best practice, and develop recommendations for future international mentoring schemes. Jennifer Dyer, Peter Main, Saher Ahmed and Katherine Hollinshead give an insight into another approach to enhance the number of women in natural sciences. They introduce the JUNO Code of Practice, developed by the British Institute of Physics to promote the careers of women in higher education specifically in Physics. By describing the content and objective of the programme, they show how university boards can have a major impact in promoting gender equality. Alexia Petersen and Stephan Petersen concentrate on the intercultural perspective. In their paper, they identify some of the special challenges of transferring key intercultural communication skills to specific target groups in science, engineering, and business administration, and discuss potential risks for internationally-oriented universities in relying on uncoordinated training efforts.

This publication deals with various questions and in each chapter tries to combine the different perspectives on gender studies and diversity management. The disciplines represented at the conference – such as gender studies, diversity studies, sociology, political science and economics – are brought together and add their particular input to the topic. In doing so, the publication contributes to fostering interdisciplinary exchange and supporting new theoretical and practical findings on gender and diversity management. As with the conference, the book addresses a diverse audience, ranging from human resources and organisational development, over academia and science management, to the business world as well as the interested public. We want to contribute to the strengthening of the awareness of the importance of gender and diversity management, the variety of its approaches and its potential for creating a solution for future global challenges in the working world.

Women and Science in the European Union

Teresa Rees

Despite considerable research, published statistics, conferences and reports, the vexed issue of why there are so few women in senior roles in science, engineering and technology has still not been satisfactorily resolved. Gender remains a highly significant variable in the organisation of science. This chapter draws upon both research and personal experience as a leader in a major European research-intensive university to explore the patterns of gender segregation, and the causes and consequences of the loss of women in particular to scientific careers. The European Commission's Research Directorate-General has played a significant role in focusing attention on the issue over the last ten years, and we are in a much better position to understand some of the key tensions in the system that lead to so few women in top scientific positions. However, progress in the academy is slow and uneven. Linking equality with an 'excellence' agenda may be helpful in seeking to ensure that quality rather than gender is rewarded.

1. Introduction[1]

This chapter draws upon my own and others' research on the vexed question of why there are so few women in science, engineering and technology. Why do so few enter these areas of work? Why do they drop out of scientific careers, disproportionate to their numbers in the pool? Why are there so few women in lead positions in laboratories, in the private or the public sector? Is it the case that patronage and nepotism still play a role in the academy? Is gender as a dimension properly taken into account in the conduct of research? To what extent is it true to say that the concept of 'scientific excellence' is socially constructed, with a gendered dimension? There are more personal issues in women's careers in science too that are beginning to be explored. What are the 'chill factors' experienced by some women (but denied by others) as they progress through their careers? Why does the scientific infrastructure of funding bodies, journal boards and appointment panels remain so male dominated? What could universities and research institutes do to make them more welcoming employers? How do experiences differ in different sciences, or in different countries? Historically, many European and indeed

---

1 This chapter summarises my keynote address at the conference.

American universities excluded women from taking degrees altogether; some, including Cambridge University, as recently as 60 years ago. This exclusion has been replaced by clearly delineated patterns of vertical, horizontal and contractual gender segregation within the academy. Why do such patterns remain so rigid, within and across the member states of the European Union?

I have been engaged in these issues both as an individual researcher but also as a long term expert adviser and rapporteur for the European Commission's Research Directorate-General[2]. The Commission's Women and Science Unit[3] began to play a leading role in collecting statistics, commissioning research and organising activities, networks and events more than ten years ago. It has also addressed the treatment of gender as a variable in the research that it funds and the gendered construction of scientific excellence. The Directorate-General has succeeded in achieving a better gender balance in its own scientific committees and sought to mainstream gender equality in the Framework Programme Projects (although not with much success).

The chapter also draws upon my own experiences, as a Pro Vice Chancellor in a major research-intensive European University, firstly with the portfolio of Staff and Students (2004-7) and secondly for Research (2007-10). The Vice Chancellor, senior colleagues and I have sought to introduce good practice aimed at enhancing our recruitment, retention and promotion of women academics. This has been 'framed' under a strategy to promote excellence, by not allowing ascriptive characteristics, such as gender, to intervene in the allocation of positions, resources and opportunities. It is not always the equality policies that have most effect. More transparency is proving to be clearly related to both promoting equality – and promoting excellence.

The chapter begins with a contextual summary of the work of the European Commission's Research Directorate-General, which, in 2009, celebrated ten years of activity in the field of women and science with a conference in Prague.

2. The European Commission's Directorate-General for Research

The focus on women and science in the Research Directorate-General, it can be argued, came about due to concerns about the economic competitiveness of the European Union (EU) in the late 1990s. If the use made of human

---

2   Now known as the Directorate-General for Research, Science, Economy and Society.

3   Now known as the Scientific Culture and Gender Issues Unit.

resources was to be critical in competitiveness in the global economy, in particular for creativity and innovation within Research and Development (R&D), then the 'leakage' of women from scientific careers was a cause for concern. EU Ministers agreed to seek to ensure that member states were investing 3% of Gross Domestic Product in R&D by 2010: this would create a demand for many more researchers. While the goal is not likely to be achieved by the end of 2010 nor in the near future, it galvanised a series of research reports and activities on women and science. Indeed, the Research Commissioner, Edith Cresson, announced a commitment to research reports *by, for and about* women and science (Cresson 1999: 10). Nicole Dewandre, the civil servant heading the Women and Science Unit, set up a European Technology Assessment Network (ETAN) commissioned to review the position of women in science in Europe and to make recommendations for the Commission itself, the members states, universities, research institutes and the whole scientific infrastructure of funding bodies, learned societies and so on (Osborn et al. 2000). The ETAN group was chaired by Mary Osborn and made up of distinguished women scientists from across Europe. As rapporteur for the group, I witnessed how members became more convinced by the growing evidence that much needed to be done to challenge the ways in which women were, in effect, excluded from successful academic careers, even in the 'liberal, meritocratic' arbour of the European university or research institute.

The ETAN report showed how irrespective of subject, country or the extent to which a discipline was numerically feminised, women dropped out of academic careers in disproportionate numbers at every stage in the academic hierarchy. 'Waiting for equality' would not work. Equally, a political arithmetic of research funding bodies, scientific committees, prize committees and learned societies illustrated that the decision-making senior echelons of the scientific infrastructure included very few women. For many bodies, such as learned societies, entry was not transparent. Existing members recruited new people behind closed doors.

Three approaches to tackling the issue were proposed: equal treatment, positive action and mainstreaming gender equality (Osborn et al. 2000; see also Rees 2007). Equal treatment recommendations included ensuring that women had the same rights and opportunities as men. While the equalities legislation in the 1970s had addressed some equal treatment issues, problems remained. The scandal at MIT, where women professors discovered their salaries and laboratories were smaller than those of their male colleagues, would have led to a class action had the institution's President not addressed the issue. Positive action was still needed to address specific blockages. Recommendations were made for earmarked funding for research grants, ensuring all conferences had speakers of both genders, mentoring schemes, networking and so on. However, the main suite of recommendation was for

gender mainstreaming, that is, ensuring that all policies, processes and practices paid attention to the gender dimension. This would mean having gender
disaggregated statistics and equality indicators, gender impact assessments, a
gender balance on committees, gender monitoring, gender budgeting and
'visioning' to ensure that existing policies did not, however inadvertently,
discriminate against one gender or another. The Commission engaged with
the recommendations, and introduced many that were targeted at its own activities, such as introducing gender action plans into the Framework Programme, targets for gender balance on committees (40%), and commissioning gender studies on women and science. It also pursued an exploration of
the extent to which gender had been addressed as a variable in the Fifth
Framework programme, and organised a workshop on the gendered construction of scientific excellence (European Commission 2004). The 'mainstreaming communication' had already been adopted by the Commission and by
the Directorate as a way of working (Commission of the European Communities 1999), so the recommendations fell into an accepting culture.

The ETAN report was launched at about the time that the Women and
Science Unit set up the Helsinki Group, a network of national representatives
from the (then) 15 member states and those countries that could be partners
in EU projects – the latter comprising of another 15 countries, mostly from
Eastern Europe but including Malta, Cyprus and Israel. The review *National
Policies on Women and Science* (Rees 2002) was the beginning of a benchmarking exercise which allowed countries to compare and contrast policies
and statistics on women and science. It was evident that the development of
Women and Science committees and units within the countries helped to focus attention on the agenda and to mobilise activities. Many member states,
for example, the UK, had already, or soon after the formation of the Helsinki
Group, conducted their own reviews of the issue (Greenfield et al. 2002). A
recent update of the EU-wide exercise of benchmarking policy measures
concluded that women and science units in government departments, targets,
quotas, mentoring, earmarked funding and paternity leave all make a difference (Ruest-Archambault 2008). In addition, gender budgeting works. However, while all these policies may indeed make a difference, the major challenge remains of changing the culture and the gendered organisation of
science.

The Women and Science Unit also commissioned studies of women in
the central and eastern European countries and the Baltic region (the 'Enwise' report) (Blagojević et al. 2003), and on women in industrial research
(Rübsamen-Waigmann et al. 2003; European Commission 2009b), as well as
publishing various good practice guides for industry. It organised a 'networks
of networks' of women in science, as well as a series of conferences. These
were attended both by women working in science, many of whom were sceptical about the need for 'special' attention or measures on the issue, and

social scientists (gender experts), whose data suggested that action was indeed necessary if gender was not going to continue to be a major organising principle in the academy. The European Platform of Women in Science galvanised lobbying of the European Parliament and acted as a focus for networking. The connectivity between women in the European Commission, the Parliament and those who lobby it, as well as women in science and those who study women in science provided an interesting example of what Woodward (2004) has called 'golden triangles' of actors who can combine to progress feminist agendas.

The lack of gender disaggregated statistics for benchmarking was addressed by the Helsinki Group, which has since 2002 (Rees 2002), regularly generated statistics and indicators on women and science, published as *She Figures*[4] by the Research Directorate-General. The statistics show that a 'scissors diagramme' characterises each country, whereby women begin as a majority of well performing school leavers, but result as a small majority of the professoriate. While the crossing point of the two blades may come in different places, and while the size of gap between the blades may vary, nevertheless, the scissors shape remains universal.

Women are now the majority of undergraduates in all but a few of the European Union member states. They constitute 45% of all new PhD students. And yet fewer than 20% of professors and 30% of board members of science and funding organisations in the European Union are women. Women comprise fewer than 10% of University Rectors in 16 member states. The current 'glass ceiling index' for academic institutions in Europe is 1.7 (it would be 1.0 if gender did not make a difference)[5].

The figures underline the extent to which gender is still making a difference. Understanding why this is the case and what the consequences are for European science, as well as for aspiring women scientists remains a challenge. There has been a growth in the extent to which social scientists, in particular gender experts, have addressed the issue over the last ten years. Some of this work has been funded by the European Commission, either directly as consultancy or through Framework Programme Research Projects, where women and science has been identified as a theme.

---

4   http://ec.europa.eu/research/science-society/index.cfm?fuseaction=public.topic&1d=27.
5   All figures from European Commission (2009): She Figures 2009 Women and Science Statistics and Indicators. Brussels.
    http://ec.europa.eu/research/science-society/index.cfm?fuseaction=public.topic&1d=27.

3. Causes and consequences

So why does gender remain so significant in the organisation of science? One challenge is clearly the conflict between science, as an engrossing and time hungry activity, in universities and research institutes, which in themselves are characterised by a long hours culture, and individuals' desires and need for a work life balance. It is no coincidence that much of the 'leakage' of women from academic careers occurs during the years when professional women are likely to be engaged with childbearing and early years of child-rearing. While many institutions have sought to address this issue, from providing childcare to policies for flexible working, the underlying issue of the long hours culture has not successfully been addressed.

Even when women do not have children, assumptions may be made that they are likely to do so during the early thirties, which may mean they are regarded as 'at risk' as an employee. Indeed, in my mid 20s, I was asked to sign a clause in a three year research contract that I would not 'get myself pregnant' during the course of the project! Even if new fathers commit time to child rearing, the assumption will not necessarily be made that they are likely to be a 'bad risk' as employees because of stereotypes that inform understandings about the domestic division of labour.

These assumptions that inform the decisions made by decision makers are what Valian has referred to as 'gender schemas' – implicit hypotheses about gender differences based upon stereotypes. They accumulate to advantage men and advantage women. Valian has conducted laboratory and field studies that illustrate how gender schemas inform opinions and perceptions, however unintentionally (Valian 1997). Similarly, Foschi (2004) has shown how both men and women are more likely to associate men with competence.

Rising scholars are encouraged to spend part of their early professional years abroad: unfortunately this period in the academic career tends to coincide with childbearing and the early years of child rearing. The European Commission recognised this in its Marie Curie scheme, and, unusually, will cover the cost of childcare. However, international collaboration as well as presenting material at conferences abroad demands the ability and flexibility to travel at a difficult time in the lifecycle. Again, this is not simply about whether scholars find travel difficult at this time in the lifecycle, there is also the issue of assumptions being made on their behalf by gatekeepers to these opportunities.

Wenneras and Wold (1997) famously described their experiences of discovering what they described as 'patronage and nepotism' in the Swedish Medical Council. Here, in the midst of a peer review mechanism, the gendering of networks and linking of 'competence' with men were playing a role in the allocation of funding. While the Council immediately took remedial action, the example shows some of the more subtle associations between 'excellence' and gender in decision making.

The consequences of these processes whereby gatekeepers draw upon 'gender schemas' to assume limited availability and commitment of women and to associate excellence with men include not simply the patterns of gender segregation in science described earlier, but also in a gendered construction of scientific excellence. What is deemed excellent is so because individuals whose views are respected because of their position in the academic hierarchy deem it to be so. A political arithmetic of who sits on prize committees, promotion committees, journal boards, funding bodies demonstrates the role of gender in decision making: it is overwhelmingly men in these positions. The increase in the numbers of women playing a role in the academy has not been reflected as much as one might expect in the senior echelons of the scientific infrastructure. Indeed, many highly prestigious prizes are awarded exclusively by men to men (Osborn et al. 2000). Equally, those guarding the portals of learned societies tend overwhelmingly to be male, informed by their knowledge of the research community through their networks. Academic networks have a gendered dimension. How do the members of learned societies get there? The recruitment to these bodies is not always transparent or based on evidence of having reached appropriate benchmarks. Indeed, criteria for selection are not always clearly articulated.

Getting at the roots of the gendered construction of scientific excellence is highly challenging (European Commission 2004). While statistics are now more readily available, and some processes are becoming more transparent, the 'underbelly' or informal culture of the scientific culture can throw out messages about 'fitting in' or being 'part of the team'. Indeed, the paucity of women in senior academic roles in science raises the issue of 'looking the part'. The expectation, held by men and women based on their experience, that senior positions tend to be held by men focuses attention to how a senior woman dresses, behaves and commands authority. I have fallen foul of 'not looking the part' on more than one occasion, for example when meeting a visiting Minister from a train, who assumed my young junior male assistant must be the Pro Vice Chancellor rather than me – a gender stereotype taking precedence over age! Any gathering of senior women academics will be able to furnish such examples of not 'looking the part', and other 'chill factors' that can make life uncomfortable, the female downside of the 'male bonus'.

The European Commission's Research Directorate commissioned a review of the extent to which the gender dimension had been addressed in the Fifth Framework Programme research (see Laurila / Young 2001 *inter alia*). In fairness, the vade mecum for the Programme had not insisted upon such a requirement. But good research should, where appropriate, take account of all significant variables and certainly in many areas, such as research on health, gender may well be relevant. For example, the large clinical trials that found a positive association between taking an aspirin and heart disease were only conducted on men. When prescribed to women, in whom heart disease is different, an aspirin caused some contra-indications. The reviews of projects in the Fifth Framework Programme found no such attention had uniformly been paid and the conclusion was that in cases the research was compromised as a consequence. The Sixth Framework Programme had a requirement for a gender action plan and a breakdown of the gender of the research team. However, this has not proved to be a successful means of gender mainstreaming and the requirement has been dropped in the Seventh Framework programme. Part of the problem has been a lack of gender awareness among the research community in the conduct of their science. This poses questions about the need for a 'gender audit' of the curriculum to increase awareness of the role of gender for all students, but particularly in the training of postgraduates who will go on to do research.

4. Cardiff University

Cardiff University is in the capital city of Wales, and a member of the Russell Group of top UK research-intensive universities. It is the 9th largest university in the UK, with 26,500 students, 6,000 staff and two Nobel Prize winners. There is commitment at a senior level both to promoting excellence and to promoting equality. These twin aims are interlinked, as promoting excellence, in my view, requires having robust equality policies. The strategic plan highlights the mission and the equality values of the organisation.

The academic promotion system has been made far more transparent, with more emphasis on identifying benchmarks for candidates, who are then required to produce evidence to demonstrate that they have achieved them. It is interesting to note that women's success rates in promotion are now at or near 100%, higher than the male averages (although there are far fewer of them). The criteria for promotion now include reference to the strategic plan's mission to promote equality, making work such as mentoring visible and valued. A gender audit of committees demonstrated the lack of women on senior decision-making committees, especially those to do with the allocation of finance. The gender balance of committees is now taken into account when new members are recruited. A women professors' network has been running for four years, which has provided a comfortable and confidential space in which concerns can be raised and solutions found for some of the challenges identified. Mentoring is provided both for those who request it but also by some of the women professors for non promoted women. The University is also a member of Women Universities Mentoring Network, which matches mentors and mentees (support staff as well as academic staff) across all the universities in Wales.

The University was awarded a Leadership Foundation for Higher Education project to embed equality and diversity in the university (see Rees / Young 2007). This enabled us to collect baseline data, identify good practice and develop some strategy options for embedding and building capacity. The new Pro Vice Chancellor for Staff and Diversity, Prof Terry Threadgold, has led on the University's ambition to improve practice for women in science, engineering and technology and last year we were one of 19 UK universities awarded a 'Bronze' by Athena Swan, a national organisation which recognises activities and commitment by universities on women and science. Needless to say that by continuing to instigate good practice, the aim is to achieve gold for the university as a whole and for its individual departments (indeed, one has been awarded a silver this year).

5. Conclusion

My experience as a leader in a university, based on my knowledge of the research on women and science careers in Europe, is that transparency in systems of allocating resource, funding and opportunities, based on benchmarks and evidence, serves women particularly well. Of course, excellent men have nothing to fear from transparency! It also leads me to believe that being excellent is not enough. It is important for women to participate in networks and conferences and to be part of the informal culture of their specialism. Young researchers, men as well as women, need to be socialised into the academic culture within which they work. For women in science in the European Union, more transparency, networking and mentoring may reduce the impact that gender currently has in shaping scientific careers.

References

Blagojević M. / Bundale, M. / Burjhardt, A. / Calloni, M. / Ergma E. / Glover, J. / Grōo D. / Havelková, H. / Mladenič, D. / Olesky, E.H. / Sreten o-va, N. / Tripsa, M. F. / Velichová, D. / Zvinkliene, A. (2003): Waste of Talents: Turning private struggles into a public issue. Women and Science in the Enwise countries. Brussels.

Commission of the European Communities (1999): Communication from the Commission "Women and science". Mobilising women to enrich European research. COM (1999) 76 final of 17.02.1999. Luxembourg.

Cresson, E. (1999): Introductory address. In: European Commission (Eds.): Women and Science: Proceedings of the Conference Brussels April 28-29 1998. Luxembourg, 9-11.

European Commission (2004): Gender and Excellence in the Making. Brussels.

European Commission (2009a): The Gender Challenge in Research Funding: Assessing the European national scenes. Brussels.

European Commission (2009b): Women in Science and Technology: Creating sustainable careers. Brussels.

Foschi, M. (2004): Blocking the use of gender-based double standards of competence. In: European Commission: Gender and Excellence in the Making. Brussels, 51-56.

Greenfield, The Baroness Susan / Peters, J. / Lane, N. / Rees, T. / Samuels, G. (2002): Set Fair: A report on Women in Science, Engineering and Technology from The Baroness Susan Greenfield to the Secretary of State for Trade and Industry. London.

Laurila, P. / Young, K. (2001): Gender in Research: Gender Impact assessment of the Specific Programmes of the Fifth Framework Programme: An overview. Brussels.

Osborn, M. / Rees, T. / Bosch, M. / Ebeling, H. / Hermann, C. / Hilden, J. / McLaren, A. / Palomba, R. / Peltonen, L. / Vela, C. / Weis, D. / Wold, A. / Mason, J. / Wenneras, C. (2000): Science Policies in the European Union: Promoting excellence through mainstreaming gender equality. Report from the ETAN Network on Women and Science. Luxembourg.

Rees, T. (2005): Reflections on the uneven development of gender mainstreaming in Europe. International Journal of Feminist Politics, Vol. 7, No. 4, 555-574.

Rees, T. (2007): Pushing the Gender Equality Agenda Forward in the European Union. In: Danowitz Sagaria, M. A. (Ed.): Women, Universities and Change: Revisioning Gender Equality in the European Union and the United States. Basingstoke.

Rees, T. / Young, H. (2007): Embedding equality and diversity in the university. In: Marshall, S. (Ed.): Strategic Leadership of Change in Higher Education: What's New? London.

Rübsamen-Waigmann, H. / Sohlberg, R. / Rees, T. / Berry, O. / Bismuth, P. / D'Antona, R. / De Brabander, E. / Haemers, G. / Holmes, J. / Jepsen, M. / Leclaire, J. / Mann, E. / Needham, R. / Neumann, J. / Nielsen, N. C. / Vela, C. / Winslow, D. (2003): Women in Industrial Research: A wake up call for European industry. Brussels.

Ruest-Archambault, E. (2008): Benchmarking Policy Measures for Gender equality in Science. Brussels.

Smith-Doerr, L. (2004): Women's Work: Gender equality vs. hierarchy in the lifesciences. Boulder, CO.

Valian, V. (1997): Why So Slow? The advancement of women. Cambridge MA.

Wenneras, C. / Wold, C. (1997): Nepotism and sexism in peer review. Nature, Vol. 347, 341-343.

Woodward, A. (2004): Building Velvet Triangles: Gender and Informal Governance. In: Piattoni, S. / Christiansen, T. (Eds.): Informal Governance and the European Union. London.

Institutionalising Diversity in Transnational Companies: Trade Unions and International Framework Agreements

Katharina Schiederig

The paper discusses the potential of International Framework Agreements (IFAs) to influence the transfer of gender and diversity policies throughout global production networks. IFAs are agreements concluded between a Transnational Corporation and a Global Union Federation. The 80 IFAs signed in the past years engage the corporations to respect the ILO core labour standards in their global production and supply networks, and, thus, to eliminate all forms of discrimination in employment. It will be argued that IFAs and, more generally, the union movement have an important role for institutionalising diversity, but that this potential has been largely untapped so far. Thus, the paper might provide first insights into how external actors might shape the transfer of gender and diversity-oriented HRM practices in large transnational corporations.

1. Introduction

The internationalisation of business increases the diversity of the workforce within Transnational Corporations (TNCs). Although some studies have demonstrated a potentially positive effect of a diverse workforce on economic performance and the high cost of discrimination (e.g. Robinson / Dechant 1997), inequalities persist and are continuously exploited in the global value networks. Women are more likely to work at the lower end of the hierarchy and in informal or precarious employment, and their incomes and career opportunities tend to be lower. At the same time, their risk of harassment is higher (Pearson 2007). Other groups that suffer from discrimination or have special needs might be elderly employees, people with a handicap, ethnic minorities or non-heterosexual employees. Feminist scholarship has shown how these different categories of difference like gender, race and class might add up and interact in an intersectional (Crenshaw 1989) and hierarchical manner and, thus, need to be considered within their specific context.

In regard to gender and diversity[1], TNCs have a double role when relocating and outsourcing their labour-intensive business operations: on the one hand they benefit from the "comparative advantage of women's disadvantage" and that of other marginalised groups in developing countries (Kabeer 2000) and undermine national standards when undertaking "regime shopping"; on the other hand they might contribute to the emergence of norms in the host country, if higher standards from the home country are transferred (Geppert / Matten / Walgenbach 2006).

Increasingly, large companies strive to integrate equality aspects in their human resources management (HRM). However, these practices are not only determined by efficiency considerations within the company, but also influenced by external actors: national and supra-national political institutions, civil society movements and organised labour.

Different legal regulations exist to counter discrimination at work. The Convention 111 of the International Labour Organisation (ILO) obliges all ILO member states to take measures and adopt legislation against discrimination at work. The OECD Guidelines, the ILO MNE Declaration and the UN Global Compact all contain a non-discrimination clause. Especially the USA, and more recently the European countries, have introduced equal opportunities legislation; within Europe anti-discrimination and gender mainstreaming policies have been codified both at EU and national level. These political-legal institutions are complemented by an increasing number of private modes of regulation: company codes of conduct, corporate governance guidelines and multi-stakeholder-initiatives that often also reference non-discrimination (cf. Fuchs 2006; Greven / Scherrer 2005).

1.1 International Framework Agreements: A New Channel for the Co-regulation of HRM?

International Framework Agreements (IFAs)[2] are a new instrument initiated by the labour movement in its search for strategy development against a perceived lack of effective regulation at transnational level (cf. Schmidt 2007).

---

1   The term "gender and diversity" is used here as a descriptor of variety, as a policy approach and in reference to theories of difference and multiple social identities. In this perspective, diversity, originating form the U.S. civil rights movement, goes beyond a HR management approach. The coupling "gender and diversity" underlines the specific nature of the category gender, which concerns a relatively large number of the population and is connected to a history of struggle, theorising and organisational strategies.

2   The term "International Framework Agreements" is used because of its frequency in the literature and the practicability of the abbreviation IFA. With regard to substance, the term "Global Agreement" would be more appropriate, since IFAs are not concluded between states. The business world also uses the term "Transnational Corporate Agreement" (TCA).

IFAs are written agreements concluded between a TNC and a Global Union Federation (GUF)[3] to guarantee minimum labour standards and allow organising in companies' global production and supply networks (cf. Egels-Zandén / Hyllman 2007; Eurofound 2008; Fichter / Sydow 2008; Riisgaard / Hammer 2008). Central reference of almost all 80 agreements concluded so far[4] are the core labour standards of the International Labour Organisation (ILO): the prohibition of child labour and forced labour, freedom of coalition and the right to collective bargaining, as well as the elimination of discrimination in respect of employment and occupation (ILO Convention 111). ILO Convention 111 explicitly bans "any distinction, exclusion or preference made on the basis of race, colour, sex, religion, political opinion, national extraction or social origin, which has the effect of nullifying or impairing equality of opportunity or treatment in employment or occupation". Three quarters of IFAs also make reference to ILO Convention 100 that stipulates equal remuneration for men and women workers for work of equal value, and some agreements contain further clauses on equal opportunities and positive discrimination policies.

Although IFAs are "soft law", the social partners negotiate them jointly, and they contain more advanced standards than unilateral codes as well as specifications on their implementation, dissemination and the application throughout the production and supply networks. Many IFAs establish some form of monitoring and audit system, and, to varying degrees, this is also extended to the suppliers. Some companies threaten to end business relationships with suppliers and sub-contractors that do not respect these principles, and some include respect within performance criteria in the evaluation of their managers, creating monetary incentives. Other than that (and pressure by trade unions and consumers), there are no formal sanction mechanisms installed through IFAs.

---

3   A Global Union Federation (GUF) is a transnational federation that groups national and regional trade unions by industry sector or occupational group. With the 2002 renaming and reorientation process of the former International Trade Secretariats, many of the GUFs have focused on gaining negotiation status for the trade union movement at a global level and concluding International Framework Agreements (IFAs), besides training, networking and campaigning (cf. Schmidt 2007). Five GUFs (UNI, BWI, ICEM, IMF and IUF) account for 75 of 80 IFAs. In around 75% of cases national unions and/or employee representatives (e.g. European works councils) were involved in the negotiations in addition to the GUFs.

4   Different figures circulate on the number of IFAs concluded, depending which criteria are applied. The database set up for the IFA research project at Freie Universität Berlin contains 80 agreements concluded by unions with a TNC that have global scope and contain the core labour standards. Of these, 72 are concluded by one of the GUFs and are still in force. The large majority of IFAs has been concluded since 2000.

1.2 Line of Argument

Given the fact that IFAs establish unions as negotiation partners at trans-national level and that these documents contain non-discrimination clauses applying to all operations worldwide, it can be asked whether IFAs can be regarded as a new example for anti-discrimination rules within companies that might potentially have global impact. The following paper will analyse the potential of IFAs to influence the transfer of gender and diversity policies throughout the global value networks. It will review the provisions relevant for gender and diversity issues in all 80 IFAs concluded so far. The line of argument can draw on the extensive "varieties of capitalism" and IHRM literature (e.g. Esping-Andersen 1990; Hall / Soskice 2001; Streeck 1992; Walby 2007) that discusses convergence, divergence or hybridisation of practices. It will be argued that IFAs – as possible channels of influence on companies by external agents – and more generally the union movement have an important role for gender and diversity-oriented HRM (Fonow / Franzway 2007), but that this potential has been largely untapped so far. Thus, the paper hopes to provide first insights into how external actors might shape the transfer of gender and diversity-oriented HRM practices in large TNCs.

2. Analysing International Framework Agreements

There have been a few studies on International Framework Agreements (e.g. Eurofound 2008; Papadakis 2008; Riisgaard / Hammer 2008; Fichter / Helfen / Sydow forthcoming), but there has been no research to date focussing specifically on the non-discrimination clause that almost all of them include.

2.1 Methods

Data was collected through a database-driven content analysis of all IFA documents, 15 interviews with HR and diversity managers, GUF representatives and experts and one group discussion with GUF representatives on IFAs in general. The research is ongoing.

2.2 Content Analysis

The content analysis of IFA documents shows that almost all companies that have signed an IFA have committed themselves to non-discrimination policies (see Figure 1). 85% of IFAs include a reference to the non-discrimination clause and in many cases explicitly name the Convention 111 of the ILO. Around 60% list diversity categories such as sex/gender or ethnicity that might be a cause for discrimination, and some even list categories which go beyond the text of the convention (such as sexual orientation or marital status). 77% of analysed IFAs also make reference to ILO Convention 100 that stipulates equal remuneration for equal work for women and men. 19% of IFAs promise to act against sexual harassment at work. The UN Convention on the Elimination of All Forms of Discrimination Against Women (CEDAW) is referenced by one IFA.

Figure 1: Gender and Diversity-relevant contents in IFA documents

n=75[5]	Total number of IFAs including this clause	% of IFAs including this clause
Any form of reference	66	88,00
ILO Convention 111 (discrimination)	64	85,33
ILO Convention 100 (equal remuneration)	58	77,33
ILO Convention 156 (workers with family responsibilities)	2	2,67
Further provisions on gender equality	11	14,67
Further provisions on diversity	2	2,67
Further provisions on maternity protection	2	2,67
Further provisions on sexual harassment	14	18,67

Nine companies have not included any reference to gender, diversity or discrimination in their IFA. There is no significant relationship between ignoring gender and diversity issues and country of origin. However, French companies show a tendency to include stronger provisions on gender and diversity. It can be noted that the services and white collar union UNI is the

---

5   Of the 80 IFAs concluded as of June 2009, 75 have been included in the content analysis, due to a lack of availability of the remaining documents.

GUF with the highest number of IFAs concluded (27) but also that with the highest number of IFAs that do not include any non-discrimination clause (5 of 9 agreements without any reference have been concluded by UNI). This is probably linked to the quantitative instead of qualitative strategy UNI pursues in terms of IFAs, in the service industry where gender and diversity aspects are highly relevant.

Some documents also include further clauses against gender-specific discrimination and sexual harassment and for affirmative action. Already the first IFA, concluded in 1989 between Danone and the International Union of Food Workers (IUF), contained very specific provisions for an "Action Programme for the Promotion of Equality of Men and Women at the Workplace", providing for gender analysis, a working group with management and staff representatives, and an action plan with follow-up and evaluation. However, this strategy of a comprehensive "sustainability code" was not taken up by other GUFs in later IFAs. Here is a typical example for the non-discrimination and diversity clauses in more recent IFAs:

"We uphold and affirm equal opportunity among our associates, regardless of the color of their skin, race, gender, age, nationality, social origin, handicap, or sexual preference. We respect the political and religious convictions of our associates as long as they are based on democratic principles and tolerate those of different persuasions. (...) We observe the provisions of ILO Convention no. 100 with respect to the principle of 'equal remuneration for work of equal value." (Basic principles of social responsibility at Bosch, concluded with IMF, 2004)

In terms of further provisions, PSA Peugeot-Citroën and Brunel declare in their agreements, concluded with the IMF, their good intention for further diversity policies: "to apply and promote best practices beyond what is legally required and to fight racism, sexism, xenophobia and, more generally, intolerance of difference and to ensure respect for the personal lives of employees". Some companies (e.g. Statoil) declare that they will consider gender equality in recruitment, training and management. ENI and Rhodia commit themselves to affirmative action measures to increase the diversity of staff. The Lukoil and Rhodia IFAs also mention the ILO Convention 156, Lukoil promises to "pay[ing] special attention to defending rights of the working women, expectant mothers, nursing mothers and women with large families."

"Rhodia rejects any form of discrimination and is committed to respecting diversity and promoting equality of opportunity. The company is a signatory to the Diversity Charter in France and has made the provisions of ILO Convention 111 company policy. This convention rejects any infringement of equal opportunity or fair treatment in employment and the basis of race, sex, skin color, religion, political or trade union views, national origin or socioeconomic background. Rhodia will pay special attention to its employees with family responsibilities and in this respect will refer to measures in ILO Convention 156 given in chapter II - Article 1 1.1 of this agreement. This approach includes specific efforts to promote employee diversity." (Global Corporate Social Responsibility Agreement between Rhodia and ICEM, 2005/2008)

It is interesting to note that, unlike with other rights and monitoring procedures, there has not been a qualitative development towards stronger diversity clauses in IFAs.

An exception from this is again represented by Danone. In 2008, wishing to revitalise their earlier agreements, Danone management and the IUF concluded a "Convention on Diversity" that covers the areas of recruitment, training, career development, remuneration and conditions at work, and encourages the social counterparts in the different companies to negotiate application procedures and indicators adapted to local conditions.

2.3 Interview Results

Although the large majority of agreements contain some kind of non-discrimination clause or further provisions on paper, this has apparently had little practical relevance up to date. During the group interview, representatives of all GUFs stated that there has not been any complaint through IFA procedures on the grounds of discrimination. Discrimination has never been raised with the GUFs by any local union, while there have been many complaints for union rights. Still, most GUFs recognise gender and diversity as important issues, apart from some that do not see the relevance in their respective male-dominated industry (e.g. construction). However, they seem unsure of how to use IFAs as an instrument for enhancing equality. Several interviewees indicated the difficulty of realising equality in different countries in adverse cultural and legal contexts. In the case of those IFAs that contain further provisions on gender and diversity (e.g. French chemical company Rhodia) this happened on the initiative of management and in line with an existing gender and diversity policy within the company. Trade unionists said they pick up the issue "when there is negotiation space". These first results indicate barriers for further agenda setting of diversity issues within the IFA process on the trade union side: "It is our own people we have problems with at this stage", said one GUF representative.

3. Discussion: Transfer of Practices and the Role of Trade Unions

Despite some advancements and forerunners, the trade union movement has generally not been at the forefront of the gender and diversity agenda, as several studies have shown (Colgan / Ledwith 2002). In practice, but also in the Industrial Relations literature, gender issues remain marginal. Traditionally, unions have focussed on class as a category, and have mostly been patriarchal working-class organisations with a focus on male, blue-collar workers. This orientation is increasingly challenged by the forces of global restructuring and diversification of the workforce and internally by marginalised workers' groups. However, as Colgan and Ledwith show, unions are generally slow to adapt to this new reality, although traditionalism coexists with innovation and transformation, and many unions are slowly changing. Fonow and Franzway (2007: 173) underline the importance of mobilising women for renewing unions in a transnational perspective. They suggest the potential of International Framework Agreements for this: "IFAs (...) can be useful to feminists because they contain strong equity clauses, including protection for the rights of gays and lesbian workers." Unions tend to see organising workers as a priority, also in their IFA strategy, but diversity politics can be part of exactly this. Moreover, discrimination also concerns categories close to the heart of the trade union movement, such as discrimination on the grounds of political opinion and trade union membership. Nevertheless, trade unions are careful to adapt the diversity discourse that they perceive to be pushed by management, as opposed to the equal opportunities discourse. As Wrench (2005) and Kirton / Greene (2006) have outlined, unions are concerned that diversity might focus on the individual rather than social groups, replace the moral with the business argument, neglect discrimination, and marginalise the labour side in regard to social issues. Despite these reservations, IFAs could be an entry point for bringing unions back into the diversity discourse and reinforcing equal opportunities and anti-discrimination language and measures therein.

Can IFAs thus be regarded as a new example for anti-discrimination rules within companies that might potentially have global impact? Given the fact that these documents contain non-discrimination clauses applying to all operations worldwide and that IFAs establish unions as negotiation partners at transnational level, IFAs offer the potential to reinforce anti-discrimination rules and set diversity management on the agenda. Although unions focus on the capacity of IFAs as an instrument for organising and establishing union rights, IFAs might open a new channel for the co-regulation of other HRM practices at transnational level, since they establish an avenue for social dialogue between trade unions and management at local and global level. From the interviews we have seen that unions do not actively use the non-discrimination clause. It is included in IFAs because it is part of the ILO core labour standards. However, IFAs include written commitments to non-discrimination that in some cases link to existing gender and diversity policies within the corporation and might trigger a discussion between HR management and unions or employee representatives at global and local level.

The Diversity Agreement with Danone shows that a more proactive approach is possible, and both management and unions report that the agreement has been used to set up equality programmes, for example in the Polish companies. Other initiatives at national and European level point in the same direction: in Spain large companies are obliged to negotiate diversity agreements with the trade unions, in France such an obligation exists for the issue of elderly and disabled employees, and in Germany the Works Council Constitution Act represents a base for co-determination on gender and diversity issues and company agreements. These are complemented by diversity agreements between European Works Councils and corporations covering all operations in Europe, and the European equivalent of the International Framework Agreements, the European Framework Agreements that reference non-discrimination.

In this regard, it is interesting to note that 85% of the IFAs concluded so far have been with companies headquartered within Europe:

Figure 2: IFAs by country of origin of TNC (in %, n=80)

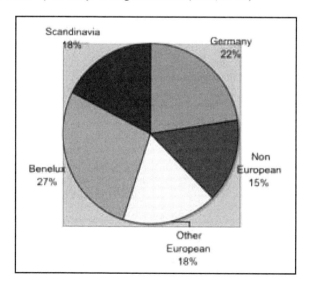

The concentration of IFAs in European TNCs suggests that the institutional setting in the European Union (EU) and the European culture of labour relations and social dialogue have laid the groundwork for the signing of such global accords (Rudikoff 2005). Also, the EU as the world's most integrated regional organisation and governance system beyond the national state is at the forefront in terms of institutionalising anti-discrimination and gender mainstreaming policies. To hope – in normative terms – for a transfer of diversity management practices from Europe to emerging and developing countries would be problematic, however. While Transnational Corporations actively foster such strategies, their profit is at the same time based on these same inequalities, both at local and global level. There is still the risk of "good practice" in the home country and "bad practice" at production sites worldwide, especially at supplier level, where the pressure exerted on prices is high. Moreover, although equality is a universal norm, its implementation is context-specific.

Thus, as a hypothesis, it is likely that convergence, divergence and hybridisation of practices coexist (e.g. Esping-Andersen 1990; Hall / Soskice 2001; Streeck 1992; Walby 2007; Özbilgin / Tatli 2008), depending on home and host country effects, sectoral effects, organisational and individual effects, trade union strategies and power, IFA contents, mimicry and discursive effects. This needs further research.

4. Conclusions

To conclude, IFAs can indeed represent a means for codifying a diversity approach within transnational corporations and for extending and democratising it. The top-down perspective that diversity often takes could be complemented through union involvement. For the time being, however, there are few indications that unions actively use this potential at global level, although it might be helpful for their representative renewal.

In the field of equal opportunities, we see two organisations – companies and trade unions – struggling with organisational change towards diversity. Both have their interests, both have their agenda, and diversity politics are not necessarily at the top of it. However, while the ethical argument and legal argument counts for both, for companies there is also the "business case" argument for diversity, and for trade unions there is the union democracy and representation argument. This should motivate both social partners in the future. Although for the time being, IFAs do not explore the gender and diversity issue fully, the first international Diversity agreement with Danone and numerous national agreements indicate that we will see further institutionalisation in the future. These kinds of agreements always bear the risk of window-dressing, but negotiating and concluding an agreement and publishing it also commits both management and trade unions to a new reality, slowly inducing organisational change. At the same time, the diversity concept with its management affinity could be a possible entry point and icebreaker for unions to enter into negotiations with otherwise reluctant management – the strategy pursued by the IUF in the Danone case.

IFAs thus represent an opportunity on paper that could be both fructified at global level and adapted to the specific circumstances at local level to strengthen gender and diversity policies within transnational companies.

References

Colgan, F. / Ledwith, S. (2002): Gender, Diversity and Trade Unions. International Perspectives. London / New York.

Crenshaw, K. W. (1989): Demarginalizing the Intersection of Race and Sex. In: University of Chicago Legal Forum.

Egels-Zandén, N. / Hyllman P. (2007): Evaluating Strategies for Negotiating Workers' Rights in Transnational Corporations: The Effects of Codes of Conduct and Global Agreements on Workplace Democracy. Journal of Business Ethics, 76 (2), 207-223.

Esping-Andersen, G. (1990): The Three Worlds of Welfare Capitalism. Cambridge.

European Foundation for the Improvement of Living and Working Conditions (2008): Codes of conduct and international framework agreements: New forms of governance at company level. Luxembourg.

Fichter, M. / Sydow, J. (2008): Organization and Regulation of Employment Relations in Transnational Production and Supply Networks. Ensuring Core Labour Standards through International Framework Agreements? Research Proposal.

Fichter, M., / Helfen, M. / Sydow, J. (forthcoming): Employment Relations in Global Production Networks - Initiating Transfer of Practices via Union Involvement. In: Human Relations, 63.

Fonow, M.M. / Franzway, S. (2007): Transnational union networks, feminism and labour advocacy. In: Schmidt, V. (Ed.): Trade union responses to globalization. Geneva, 165-175.

Fuchs, D. (2006): Privatwirtschaft und Governance : Transnationale Unternehmen und die Effektivität privaten Regierens. In: Schirm, S. A. (Ed.): Globalisierung. Baden-Baden, 147-168.

Gereffi, G. / Humphrey, J. / Sturgeon, T. (2005): The governance of global value chains. Review of International Political Economy, 12 (1), 78-104.

38 Katharina Schiederig

Geppert, M. / Matten, D. / Walgenbach, P. (2006): Transnational institution building and the multinational corporation: An emerging field of research. Human Relations, 59 (11), 1451-1465.

Greven, T. / Scherrer, C. (2005): Globalisierung gestalten. Weltökonomie und soziale Standards. Bonn.

Hall, P. A. / Soskice, D. (2001): Varieties of Capitalism: The Institutional Foundations of Comparative Advantage. Oxford.

Kabeer, N. (2000): The power to choose. Bangladeshi women and labour market decisions in London and Dhaka. London.

Kirton, G. / Greene, A. M. (2006): The Discourse of Diversity in Unionised Contexts: Views from Trade Union Equality Officers. Personnel Review. 35 (4), 431-448.

Krell, G. (2008): Chancengleichheit durch Personalpolitik. Gleichstellung von Frauen und Männern in Unternehmen und Verwaltungen. Rechtliche Regelungen, Problemanalysen, Lösungen. Wiesbaden.

Özbilgin, M. / Tatli, A. (2008): Global diversity management: an evidence-based approach. Basingstoke / New York.

Papadakis, K. (2008): Cross-Border Social Dialogue and Agreements: An Emerging Global Industrial Relations Framework? Geneva.

Pearson, R. (2007): Beyond Women Workers: gendering CSR. In: Third World Quarterly, 28 (4), 731-749.

Riisgaard, L. / Hammer, N. (2008): Organised Labour and the Social Regulation of Global Value Chains. DIIS Working Paper 2008/9.

Robinson, G. / Dechant, K. (1997): Building a Business Case for Diversity. The Academy of Management Executive, 11 (03), 21-31.

Rudikoff, L.P. (2005): International Framework Agreements: A Collaborative Paradigm for Labor Relations. Global Law Working Paper 01/05, Symposium "Transnational Corporations and Human Rights". New York.

Schmidt, V. (2007): Trade Union Responses to Globalization. A review by the Global Union Research Network. Geneva.

Streeck, W. (1992): Social Institutions and Economic Performance. Studies of Industrial Relations in Advanced Capitalist Economies. London.

Thomas, R. R. Jr. / Woodruff, M. I. (1999): Building a House for Diversity: How a Fable about a Giraffe & an Elephant Offers New Strategies for Today's Workforce. New York.

Walby, S. (2007): Introduction: Theorizing the Gendering of the Knowledge Economy: Comparative Approaches. In: Walby, S. et al. (Eds.): Gendering the Knowledge Economy. Comparative Perspectives. Houndmills, 3-50.

Wrench, J. (2005): Diversity Management can be Bad for You. Race and Class. 46 (3), 73- 84.

Managing Gender & Diversity Changes Organisations?!

Iris Koall, Verena Bruchhagen

The irritation of the dominant structure of logic, legitimacy and normalcy within personal and organisational life, affects the construction of inclusion and exclusion, discrimination and devaluation. Observing diversity practices as espoused theories and theories in use may stimulate a discussion about the manifest, as well as the latent capacities, in diversity practice and theory, related to organisational change.

This diversity approach uses paradoxes to describe how binary distinctions in organisations are covered. Paradoxes – according to the hypothesis - can be unfolded instead of avoided. Unfolding paradoxes makes it possible no longer to rely on gender binary, but to use the analysis of form, media and codes in communication processes in organisations.

We would like to develop and describe the consequences of the rise of complexity as the unfolding of paradoxes and the necessity to deal with contingency on a system level. This process is related to the capacity to observe the latency of action and communication. Further on, we would like to relate to theoretical and methodological resources of gender research to describe problems of complexity and contingency. Based on a systems theory approach, we describe how paradoxes enable complexity to become observable and manageable.

1. Managing Gender & Diversity – a mode to deal with complexity

Non-discrimination initiatives, dealing with Managing Gender & Diversity, seem to be in the mainstream of practical and political initiatives (V. Braunmühl 2009). Discourses of Managing Diversity are related to the promises of modernity: getting access to equal opportunities by processes of individualisation (Drumm 1989), or are related to "female" personnel potential (Meuser 2009) constituted and in demand in organisations – in combination with high social costs (Andresen / Koreuber 2009). Managing Diversity is criticised for being too close to neoliberal discourses of individual choices, and is becoming a part of the hegemonic cultural discourses (Bendl 2007). But if we observe the hard facts of discrimination of women in organisations, there are still structural constraints of chances of emancipation, e.g. a gender pay gap of 23% or the even more dramatic pension pay gap of nearly 44%[1]. The complexity of contemporary transformation processes of gender issues (Knapp 2009: 309) into concepts of Managing Gender & Diversity is observable between these *choices* (neoliberal individualisation) and *chances* (structural constraints).

(Pre)Modern organisations are characterised by gender stereotyping – embedded in structures and functions of division of labour and work-life-arrangements (Koall 2001). Gender stereotyping is following the functional imperatives of individualisation (Pasero 2004); at the same time engendering is coded by the postmodern hybrid constitution of subjectivity (Reckwitz 2006). There is the concomitance of gender stereotyping by hierarchical ordering as binary distinctions as well as deconstructing these gender differences in organisations (Kuhlmann / Kutzner / Müller / Riegraf / Wilz 2002; Wilz 2004). This challenges contemporary theoretical approaches, methodologies, action oriented approaches, disciplinary boundaries and social embeddedness in certain social systems: how to make social complexity observable and practically relevant (Aulenbacher / Riegraf 2009). In this chapter we would like to develop and describe the consequences of the rise of complexity as the unfolding of paradoxes and the necessity to deal with contingency on a system level. This process is related to the capacity to observe the latency of action and communication. This will depend on the "theory in use" or "espoused theories" to describe the processes of Managing Gender & Diversity. In doing so, we would like to relate to theoretical and methodological resources of gender research to describe these problems of complexity and contingency. Gender Studies are highly relevant for the diversity discourse and vice versa (Benschop 2006).

2. Managing Gender & Diversity: how to deal with contingency

Contingency describes the complex relationship of gender and organisation (Aulenbacher / Riegraf 2007) – as ambivalence of chances and choices or structural intertie and towards more open interpretation and constitution of discourses. In its long tradition, organisational theory[2] has focused on the

---

1   The average gender pension gap between women and men is 44% (Germany West 52%, Germany East 36%) Dec. 2008

2   Earlier contingency approaches of management theory were related to organisational structuring in turbulent environments; (Burns / Stalker 1961; Blau / Schoenherr 1971; Pugh / Hickson 1976). Structural inertia hinders change by limiting adaption to environmental demands (Hannan / Freeman 1989) by internal homogenisation. DiMaggio / Powell (1983)

contingency of organisational experiences and structuring (Kieser / Kubiceck 1992). However, Ortmann (2009: 32) relating to William Starbuck (1982: 3) criticised the contingency approach as reaching the status of "null finding". But he also states, the contingency approach has been able to overcome the paradigm of scientific management and its Tayloristic, mechanistic perspectives of organisations. Earlier contingency approaches tend to reduce complexity by figuring out "best practices". Rejecting a "one-best-way" for organisations means to deal with contingency and complexity in an irritating sense to produce "next practice" (Kruse 2009), and this is a chance to work with offending irritations in processes of interdependent constitution of stabilising and the systemic logic of enhancement (Ortmann 2009). Diversity Management might work as a mode and practice to raise social complexity, but at the same time is developing mechanisms and processes to reduce this complexity. This action described as moderation, rejection or pro-active, complexity-raising action and procedure (Thomas / Ely 2002) can be described as making a move between systems, as moving and shifting boundaries. Diversity Management prepares the conditions of its existence by itself[3], by producing and managing complexity. Culturally homogeneous organisations have no need to consider and invent Diversity Management. They tend to exclude complexity, rather than becoming more inclusive by explicit heterogeneous recruitment; mentoring, work-family-balance (Rapaport / Bailyn / Fletcher / Pruitt 2002). Managing Diversity needs to deal with the internal and the external side of the organisation. Managing Diversity is a form, which enables to observe the internal complexity of the organisation and its relevant complexity of the environment (Baecker 2007).

An interdependent enhancement of "best practices" and "business case" processes is preventing chances of development and leading to non-controllable and reversible connections of structures and functions. This constitutes path dependency of processes (Ortmann 2009: 35). Similarly, Diversity Management in organisations is following path dependent processes of development by being related to blocking "lock-ins" within hegemonic cultures, by following "rationally" oriented procedures as a business case, by being part of a competitive "rat race" using and positioning personal potential as human capital.

Thereby, discrimination and privileging does not appear as concurrency and interdependency of gender, class, race, political status, sexual orientation,

---

have developed the concept of isomorphism, a tendency of copying other organisations by adapting to trends. This is in counteracting diversity initiatives, which are related to genuine developments related to a unique workforce. Süss (2007) describes as isomorphic tendencies the capacity to copy diversity initiatives and enhance the spread of the concept.

3   "Perceiving and producing contingency produces best practices." ["Die Entdeckung der Kontingenz erzeugt dafür (für best practices, Anm.) den Bedarf und bereitet den Boden für die Bedarfsdeckung: das Terrain für die Entdeckung oder – kontingente! – Behauptung immer neuer one best ways. Die Proponenten solcher best practices sind Parasiten der Kontingenz"] (Ortmann: 2009: 31).

(dis-)ability, or religion[4], by constituting devaluation as path dependent and subsequent within processes of differentiation and institutionalisation (Walby 2007). But path dependent construction allows complexity to be tamed, or to organise pragmatic "log-ins" in business cases. This categorical connection of demographic attribute and social expectation is a subsequent construction, based on assumptions of "inherited" development in social systems. It gets its performativity by relating interaction to hegemonic social discourses (Foucault 1983; Koall 2001). However, a reflexive gender and diversity approach is related to organisational reality construction. Focusing breaking up with normalcy construction or "ab-normalities" as deconstructing and fluxionality of social distinctions, or: "doing difference" (West / Fenstermaker 1995)[5] by doing diversity.

Path dependency is related to structural inertia, which is stabilising organisations and organisational development in dynamic environments (Hannan / Freemann 1989). But, Managing Diversity offers a tendency of dynamisation by relating to different references of social systems, like political, legislative, educational, religious, cultural, economic, or ethical links. These connections enable to describe functional equivalents to widen the communicative and interactive contexts. Managing Diversity is broadening this systemic connectedness by not developing resistance towards the complexity of social relations in organisations. Anyhow, diversity initiatives are not related to one system relevance. Organisational discourses are more than business related by legitimating social interaction to the environment, but have the function to control division of labour and distribution of resources (Staehle 1992), for example as diversity initiatives or equal opportunity initiatives (e.g. Charta der Vielfalt). It will be interesting to observe the reaction to failure of intention and proclamations by comparing results on the level of structures or numbers and norms. The risk of de-legitimisation will be a driver for change.

In a reflexive sense, Managing Gender & Diversity is aspiring to deconstruct binary and to change binary structured distinctions and decisions. We want to ask for possibilities to observe more diverse and complex structures and their impact for practice. Managing Diversity implies an awareness of the rise of complexity. Paradoxes are a sign of complex systems; they might arise and show ambiguity and ambivalence, which is likely to be covered by reducing complexity in modern organisations. Paradoxes can also be unfolded instead of avoided. Based on a systems theory approach, we describe how paradoxes enable complexity to become observable and manageable. Managing Diversity enables to widen the frame of perception and to use paradoxes as useful irritations.

---

4   Relating to intersectional methodology of Gender Studies, (Winker / Degele 2009; Bruchhagen / Koall 2007)
5   Relating to the term not primary to the micro perspective.

3. Managing Gender & Diversity as a reflexive concept

Thus, we want to present the hypothesis that diversity is given as a part of most unobserved, partly unconscious or even undesirable realities. We do not have to "produce" diversity, but we have to manage it on a personal as well as an organisational level. In this approach a main issue of Managing Gender & Diversity is to question how the increasing complexity will be bearable for systems (person as well as organisation), particularly with regard to the irritation some of the intended deconstructions will evoke. In this situation we resist focusing on "best practice", which is prolonging contemporary organisational culture and structure. On the contrary we focus on "next practice" (Kruse 2007) in change processes. Relating to Argyris / Schön's (1996) distinction of *espoused theory* and *theory in use*, we would like to scrutinise on one hand how organisations as social systems attempt to invent inclusive and heterogeneous cultures and management procedures. On the other hand, related to constructivist psychodynamic approaches (Menzies 1960; Menzies Lyth 1988, 1989; Sievers 1991), we might consider the latent pattern (Luhmann 2002) and efforts not to talk about the provocative issues of Managing Diversity. This supports the rise of paradoxes within diversity processes. Furthermore, the coping management strategies of covering of paradoxes will affect the inherent discriminative capacity of organisations – and will powerfully oppress change.

In the following we want to outline three principal considerations, which seem to be important in this context of observing capacities of organisational and social change.

1. Logic and Latency
2. Paradoxes of diversity

3.1 Logic and Latency

According to Argyris / Schön's (1974) theory of action Diversity Management (DM) can be described and differentiated as *espoused theory* and *theory in use*. On the level of *espoused theory* Managing Diversity offers practical advise how to deal with issues of justice, valuation of differences. These practical assumptions can be described and espoused. *Espoused theories* make us believe we "live on the same planet". We are oriented within a certain semantic focus to perceive and interpret reality. On the other hand, there are *theories in use* (Argyris / Schön 1974), which are more related to the not espoused assumptions. Diversity Management, as an *espoused theory* – "which we call to speak of our actions to others" – is oriented towards business cases, best practices, developing strategies of profit- and non-profit organisations, affirmative action, non-discrimination due to emerging legislation and empowering personnel potential, challenges of heterogeneous work forces and team cooperation. Espoused Managing Diversity theories describe on the level of organisational behaviour (mostly us-approaches) how diverse teams are efficient structured and possible conflicts are moderated.

Theories in use are describing underlying patterns, which are most latent and not published. But these assumptions are governing actions, and seem to be the way of thinking (like grammar in use). They are cultivated as tacit structures. Theories in use have the function to avoid describing discrimination as inherent to organisational systems. Managing Diversity as theory in use has the function to avoid perceiving und discussing discrimination as inherent in profit-organisations. These discourses of human resource managers are analysed and criticised as ideology (Zanoni / Janssen 2003).

But why is there a need to distinguish what is done and what is to be talked about in social systems? These theories in use would probably destabilise the operation, as irritating by unfolding paradoxes. One track might be to have a look at deficits of legitimisation of private companies, described by Staehle (1992), a German management researcher acknowledged by the mainstream. Due to private wealth, public poverty, and state dependency on taxes, as well as private capital accumulation the influence of economic elites on political formation is strengthend. This de-legitimisation has to be covered by fostering control and non-solidarity among members of differentiated groups (gender, ethnicity). This needs to be supported by ideas of justice of inequality in benefits – according to differing quality of performance (manager/worker). Organisations regulate this control "necessity" through hegemonic cultures of homosocial recruiting, or by excluding standards of performance appraisal and regulating information and decisions through hierarchical processes, as well as many other regulatory processes.

In any case, this supports organisations, which are constructed much more as defence systems against anxiety, developed in order to avoid confrontation with "the other" and other such culturally suppressed irritations (Menzies 1960). Organisations use these defence systems to operate their inherent contradictions. The confrontation with complexity, insecurity, competition and a turbulent environment raises anxieties. The necessity to act forces the projection of these anxieties on others – either within the organisation or on external social groups (Ahlers-Niemann 2007). This perception, which is really a dark scenario, does not enable social entities to transform subjective efforts into collective performance.

Based on Argyris / Schön's distinction, we would like to describe Managing Diversity to become a *reflexive theory*, e.g. to analyse discriminative procedures. Managing Diversity as reflexive theory connects political (macro-approach) and business approaches (meso) by relating the interactional to societal relations (multi-level), e.g. as analysis and critique of individualisation of the work force (personnel management term; cf. Drumm 1989, Grieger 1998) or subjectivity of labour (sociological term). Second, there is the attempt to deconstruct the dominant (us-driven) business cultures in organisations, which act as an illusion of superiority and manageability of diversity (Adler 2008), or might be used to differentiate male identity (Miller / Katz 2002). Considering Managing Diversity on a reflexive level as complexity theory, research is dealing with challenges of change, perception and resistance against heterogeneity (Baecker 2003; Koall 2001; Knoth 2007).

Other considerations refer to external and organisational structures and procedures of inequality; these political-normative approaches are focusing on conditions of economic emancipation personnel management approaches. As a prescriptive approach they are suggesting and developing functional relevant alternatives to discrimination as descriptive, and analysing conditions of emancipation within political arenas of profit organisations (Bruchhagen et al. 2010).

Diversity Management has "the problem" of increased complexity in social systems, whereas most theories are very busy attempting to "reduce complexity". This tendency is related to ideas that organisations might not be able to deal with contingency and ambivalence, but need to produce rationality and control relating to management. Approaches that are enabling management and the organisation to deal with more than one hegemonic cultural reality, and, thus, unfolding paradoxes in social systems, are interesting. Paradoxes have the function to reduce complexity. They are guidelines to the development of a complex diversity theory (Özbilgin / Tatli 2008; Koall / Bruchhagen 2009).

3.2 Paradoxes of Diversity

Paradoxes are part of complex systems and learning about them depends on the capacity to unfold them (Lewis / Dehler 2000; Luhmann 1990; Baecker 2001). As we will see later, paradoxes are related to the necessity of complexity theory, which leads to work with multi-level approaches.

But now we will have a look at how paradoxes occur: Paradoxes occur in cases where an assumption or reality construction refers to a condition, which is contradicting the basic premises of its existence. Both, the intended and the opposite are claiming to be prevalent. A paradox is a form, which offers to see both sides of the complexity of reality – the manifest and the supplementary latent part. Standards of dominance are attempting to cover paradoxes to unfold and to reduce complexity by enabling congruence, stability, and de-cidedness. Seemingly negative phenomena might be helpful to reflect on diversity. Thus, one might observe how both sides of binary construction of reality – the good and the evil – are interdependently interwoven. Different forms of paradoxes might occur:

Paradox of categories or equality: Diversity is focusing differences by simultaneously expecting fair equity in organisational conditions. Differences are made relevant in a homogeneous context and are relative in contingent organisational settings. There is the need to describe the interaction of diffe-rences on organisational and personal level.

Paradox of tolerance: Diversity claims tolerance as appreciation of differences on a surface level (rhetoric of appreciation), but needs to under-stand that tolerance is a part of a hierarchical order of an excluding habitus (habitis) (Koall 2007). Managing diversity becomes relevant in a situation where it hurts one's own value system and conditions of identity construc-tion. However, conditions and structures of intolerance are still part of orga-nisational complexity avoidance and have certain functions by proceeding control, decisions and evaluations of performance. Intolerance is – as a blind spot – part of the construction of organisational reality – e.g. heteronormativ-ity and homophobic attitudes are part of the hegemonic masculinity construc-tion in management. Here, feminist critiques of gendered organisations (Acker 1990) describe the connection of masculinity, (Meuser 1998) and dominance in management processes (Collins / Hearn 1996). Also, analysing inequality regimes (Acker 2006) offers insights in the construction process and product of insiders and the tolerated outsiders. Focusing on more hybrid identity constructions (Hall 1999) becomes relevant to envisage frictions and change opportunities.

Paradox of strong culture: Diversity needs a strong cultural bond and commitment to be implemented, but strong cultures are promoting exclusion on the communicative and interactive level. Organisational cultures are not seen as fixed entities and construction can be analysed by relating to net-works of meaning and intentions (Czarniawska-Joerges 1992). Ethno-methodological (Frohnen 2005) and constructivist observations describe how cultures and professional identities are interdependently constructed – as an interplay of interaction and symbolic structuring. This ambivalence within hybrid cultural constructs in organisations offers opportunities for practical deconstruction (Fletcher / Bailyn / Blake-Beard 2008) and may lead to un-folding the paradox of strong culture. The way culture is perceived or dis-cussed depends on the perception of variety and sub-cultural aberrancy. Qualitative research, in particular, might be interested in not re-introducing dominant cultural representations, but instead looking at the functionality of sub-cultural micro-diversity in organisations (just like the Foucauldian sup-plementary logic).

Paradox of fit or inclusion and exclusion of otherness: Strong social bonds foster cooperation but are often related to the social dynamics of social categorisation theory (Tajfel / Turner 1986) or similarity-attraction theory (McCain / O`Reilly / Pfeffer 1983). These tendencies exclude constructed minorities, who are to be encouraged by Diversity Management; a concept that states it takes 7-9 years to include minorities in organisations by changing cultures and procedures (Cox 2002). Transformation of differences into inequality is related to organisational constructions like status beliefs (Ridgeway 2001) or convergence of social and organisational (gendered) hierarchies (Brewer 1996), or the powerful use of distinctions in processes of professionalization (Wetterer 2002). There is the tendency to relate the inclusive/exclusive debate to the inertia of opposing entities, like binary distinctions, but ethno-methodological work may show the fluidity of categorical constructions and connect it to organisational change processes,

Paradox of values: Diversity needs the knowledge of minorities to become successful, e.g. as marketing approach, but "outsiders" seldom acquire a powerful insider position. The hegemonic minority may avoid getting in touch with the painful experiences of "outsiders". Minorised employees almost always welcome diversity initiatives, whilst the members of the majority group tend to reject cultural change. Thereby, minorised personnel are in the position of the "token" and very often lack the "serenity" of insiders, which is essential for social acceptance (Moss Kanter 1977; Meyerson / Scully 2002). Research connecting the functional relatedness of organisations to environmental pressure and change patterns of distinction is highly relevant to this diversity issue.

4. Challenges of Reflexivity and Observing Competence

What do we get by unfolding paradoxes? The observation of ambivalence and contingency in the communication and cultural processes in organisations avoids and rejects a reliance on demographically related distinctions. This refers to anti-categorial intersectional methodology (Bruchhagen / Koall 2007). The analysis of the interconnectedness of micro, meso, and macro levels supports the idea of interdependence instead of structural inertia.

This diversity approach – which we developed in Dortmund - uses paradoxes to describe how binary distinctions in organisations are covered. Unfolding paradoxes make it no longer possible to rely on gender binary, but require the use of the analysis of form, media, and codes in communication processes in organisations.

Reframing Managing Diversity discourses is done by:

- understanding interpenetrative processes of subjective complexity and organisational functions, and understanding how gendered professional roles are functional or dysfunctional in gendered or gender-neutral organisational cultures.
- reconstructing the conditions of the possibility (Galtung 1978) of developing and changing organisations on the basis of self-organising processes, which is much more related to micro diversity, than to hierarchical forms of excluding diversity. The observation of diversity in interaction might support the fluidity of binary gender constructions and could be an opportunity to work with deconstructive modes of de-gendering in interactive processes.
- observing the inclusion in the form of the (de-) gendered person into the organisation, related to the functions and the autopoiesis of the system. There are possible junctions here to discourses about individualisation of workplace diversity or subjectivation of workforce possible (Pongratz / Voß 2003).

Managing Diversity is a management orientation concerning Human Resource Management and organisational change, thought out in terms of the advantages of dominant groups and the discrimination of the excluded others. Comparing espoused theories and theories in use enables the deconstruction of elitist standards of hegemonic groups and organisations.

In this sense Managing Diversity puts differences into perspective, strengthens them and focuses on the construction and use of social differences. It forces equal treatment of non-equity.

Managing Diversity follows the perspective that homogeneity and heterogeneity are interdependent system conditions to secure stability and enhance change. Systems (individuals and organisations) tend to reduce complexity to avoid irritation and ambivalence; in addition they prefer homogeneity in case their perception needs normalcy and security.

We consider that diversity change agents have to be enabled to observe and deal with complexity instead of mostly reducing it. Diversity managers are willing to focus on the personal variety rather than homogeneity, and are developing and using diverse personnel and organisational potential. Observing competence in managing diversity means:

- to describe the construction, the use, and function of social differences in espoused theories
- to observe and communicate the distinctions in use within theories in use
  - in professional experience (field studies)
  - in group dynamics (diversity in the group, team)

- to formulate alternatives to discriminatory structures as functional equivalents (Koall 2001).

The object of irritation is the dominant structure of logic, legitimacy, and normalcy within personal and organisational life, which affects the construction of inclusion and exclusion, discrimination and devaluation. Observing even diversity practices as espoused theories and theories in use may stimulate a discussion about the manifest, as well as the latent, capacities in diversity practice and theory, related to organisational change.

References

Ahlers-Niemann, A. (2007): Auf der Spur der Sphinx – Sozioanalyse als erweiterter Rahmen zur Erforschung von Organisationskulturen. Norderstedt.

Andresen, S. / Koreuber, M. (2009): Gender und Diversity: Alptraum oder Traumpaar? Eine Einführung. In: Andresen, S. / Koreuber, M. / Lüdke, D. (Eds.): Gender und Diversity: Alptraum oder Traumpaar? Interdisziplinärer Dialog zur Modernisierung von Geschlechter- und Gleichstellungspolitik. Wiesbaden, 19-34.

Argyris, C. / Schön, D. (1974): Theory in Practice: Increasing Professional Effectiveness. San Francisco.

Argyris, C. / Schön, D. (1996): Organizational learning II: Theory, method and practice. Reading/MA.

Aulenbacher, B. / Riegraf, B. (2009): Erkenntnis und Methode. Geschlechterforschung in Zeiten des Umbruchs. Wiesbaden.

Baecker, D. (2001): 'Why systems?' Theory Culture & Society, 18(2), 59-74.

Baecker, D. (2003): Organisation und Management. Frankfurt a.M.

Baecker, D. (2007): Studien zur nächsten Gesellschaft – Innovative Unternehmen. Frankfurt a. M.

Bendl, R. (2007): Betriebliches Diversitätsmanagement und liberale Wirtschaftspolitik – Verortung eines diskursiven Zusammenhangs. In: Koall, I. / Bruchhagen, V. / Höher, F. (Eds.): Diversity Outlooks – Managing Diversity zwischen Ethik, Profit und Antidiskriminierung. Münster, 10-28.

Benschop, Y. (2006): Of Small Steps and the Longing for Giant Steps – Research of the Intersection of Sex and Gender within workplace and Organization. In: Konrad, A. / Prasad, P. / Pringle J. (Eds.): Handbook of Workplace Diversity. London, Thousand Oaks CA, New Delhi, 273-298.

Blau, P.M. / Schoenherr, R.A. (1971): The structure of organizations. New York.

Braunmühl, C. v. (2009): Diverse Gender – Gendered Diversity: Eine Gewinn- und Verlust-Rechnung. In: Andresen, S. / Koreuber, M. / Lüdke, D. (Eds.): Gender und Diversity: Albtraum oder Traumpaar? Wiesbaden, 53-64.

Bruchhagen, V. / Koall, I. (2007): Loosing Gender-Binary? Winning Gender-Complexity! Intersektionelle Ansätze und Managing Diversity. In: Journal des Netzwerks Frauenforschung, 22, 32-42.

Burns, T. / Stalker, G.M. (1961): The Management of Innovation, London.

Czarniawska-Joerges, B. (1992): Exploring complex organizations: a cultural perspective. Newbury Park, CA.

DiMaggio, P.J. / Powell, W.W. (1983): The iron cage revisited: Institutional isomorphism and collective rationality in organizational fields. In: American Sociological Review 48, 147-160.

Drumm, H. J. (1989): Individualisierung der Personalwirtschaft. Grundlagen, Lösungsansätze und Grenzen. Bern, Stuttgart.

Fletcher, J. K. / Bailyn, L. / Blake-Beard, S. (2008): Practical pushing: Creating discursive space in organizational narratives. In: J. W. Cox /T. G. LeTrent-Jones /M. Voronov / D. Weir (Eds.): Critical management studies at work: Multidisciplinary approaches to negotiating tensions between theory and practice. Kidlington, Oxford, 82-93.

Foucault, .M. (1983):Der Wille zum Wissen. Sexualität und Wahrheit 1. Frankfurt a. M.

Frohnen, A. (2005): Diversity in Action – Multinationalität in globalen Unternehmen am Beispiel Ford. Bielefeld.

Hall, S. (1999): Kulturelle Identität und Globalisierung. In: Hörning, K. H. / Winter, R.(Eds.): Widerspenstige Kulturen. Cultural Studies als Herausforderung. Frankfurt a. M., 393-441.

Hannan, M. / Freeman, J. (1989): Organizational Ecology. Cambridge.

Kieser, A. / Kubicek, H. (1992): Organisationen. 3rd Edition. Berlin.

Knapp, G.-A. (2009): Intersectionality" – ein neues Paradigma feministischer Theorie? Zur transalantischen Reise von ‚Race, Class, Gender'. Feministische Studien, 23 (1), 68-80.

Knoth, A. (2007): Managing Diversity. Skizzen einer Kulturtheorie zur Erschließung des Potenzials menschlicher Vielfalt in Organisationen. Tönning.

Koall, I. / Bruchhagen, V. (2009): Twisting Paradoxes - Implications for Teaching and Learning Diversity. In: International Journal of Innovation in Education (IJIIE), special issue "Innovation in Education: Diversity in Teaching and Learning" (in print).

Koall, I. (2001): Managing Gender & Diversity – von der Homogenität zur Heterogenität in der Organisation der Unternehmung. Hamburg.

Kruse, P. (2007): nextexpertizer und nextmoderator: Mit kollektiver Intelligenz Veränderungsprozesse erfolgreich gestalten. In: Rank, S. / Scheinpflug, R. (Eds.): Change Management in der Praxis. Berlin.

Kuhlmann, E. / Kutzner, E. / Müller, U. / Riegraf, B. / Wilz, S. (2002): Organisationen und Professionen als Produktionsstätten von Geschlechter(a)symetrie. In: Schäfer, E. / Fritzsche, B. / Nagode, C. (Eds.): Geschlechterverhältnisse im sozialen Wandel – Interdisziplinäre Analysen zu Geschlecht und Modernisierung. Opladen, 221-249.

Lewis, M.W. / Dehler, G.E. (2000): Learning through Paradox: A Pedagogical Strategy for Exploring Contradictions and Complexity. Journal of Management Education, 24, 708-725.

Luhmann, N. (1990): Haltlose Komplexität. In: Luhmann, N. (Ed.): Soziologische Aufklärung 5. Konstruktivistische Perspektiven. Opladen, 58-77.

Luhmann, N. (2002): Entscheidungen in Organisationen. Opladen.

McCain, B.E. / O'Reilly, C. / Pfeffer, J. (1983). The Effects of Departmental Demography on Turnover: The Case of a University. Academy of Management Journal, 26 (4), 626-641.

Menzies, I. (1960): A Case Study in Functioning of Social Systems as a Defence against Anxiety: A Report on a Study of Nursing Service of a General Hospital. Human Relations, 13, 95-121.

Menzies Lyth, I. (1988): Contaming Anxiety in Institutions selected essays volume I. London.

Menzies Lyth, I. (1989): The Dynamics of the Social: selected essays volume II. London.

Meuser, M. (1998): Geschlecht und Männlichkeit. Soziologische Theorie und kulturelle Deutungsmuster. Wiesbaden.

Meuser, M. (2009): Humankapital Gender. In: Andresen, S. / Koreuber, M. / Lüdke, D. (Eds.): Gender und Diversity: Albtraum oder Traumpaar – Interdisziplinärer Dialog zur „Modernisierung" von Geschlechter- und Gleichstellungspolitik. Wiesbaden, S. 95-109.

Meyerson, D. E. / Scully, M. A (1995): Tempered Racialism and the Politics of Ambivalence and Change. Organizational Science, 6 (5), 585-600.

Moss Kanter, E. (1977): Men and Women at Work. New York.

Ortmann, G., (2009): Management der Hypermoderne – Kontingenz und Entscheidung. Wiesbaden.

Özbilgin, M. / Tatli, A. (2008): Global Diversity Management – An Evidence-based Approach. Palgrave.

Pasero, U. (2004): Frauen und Männer im Fadenkreuz von Habitus und funktionaler Differenzierung. In: Nassehi, A. / Nollmann, G. (Eds.): Bourdieu und Luhmann – ein Theorievergleich. Frankfurt a. M., 191-207.

Pongratz, H.J. / Voß, G. (2003): From employee to "entreployee": Towards a "selfentrepreneurial" work force? Concepts and Transformation, 8 (3), 239–254.

Pugh, D.S. / Hickson, D.J. (1976): Organizational structure and its context: the Aston Programme 1. Farnsborough.

Rapaport, R. / Bailyn, L. / Fletcher, J. K. / Pruitt, B. H. (2002): Beyond Work-Family Balance – Advancing Gender Equity and Workplace Performance. San Francisco.

Reckwitz, A. (2006): Das hybride Subjekt – eine Theorie der Subjektkulturen von der bürgerlichen Moderne zur Postmoderne. Weilerswist.

Sievers, B. (Ed.) (1991): Management - Was bedeutet es, wie kann man es verstehen, ausüben und gestalten? Arbeitspapier Nr. 153. Wuppertal.

Süss, S. (2007): Managementmode – Legitimitätsfassade – Rationalitätsmythos? Eine kritische Bestandsaufnahme der Verbreitung des Diversity Management in Deutschland. In: Koall, I. / Bruchhagen, V. / Höher, F. (Eds.): Diversity Outlooks, Münster, 440-456.

Staehle, W. H. (1992): Funktionen des Managements. 3rd Ed. Bern, Stuttgart.

Tajfel, H. / Turner, J. C. (1986): The social identity theory of intergroup behavior. In: Worchel, S. / Austin, W.G. (Eds.): Psychology of intergroup relations. Chicago, 7-24.

Thomas, D. A. / Ely, R. J. (2002): Making Differences Matter: A New Paradigm for Managing Diversity. In: Harvard Business Review on Managing Diversity. Boston, 33-66.

West, C. / Fenstermaker, S. (1995): Doing Difference. In: Gender & Society.1995 (9), 8-37.

Wetterer, A. (2002): Gender Mainstreaming und Managing Diversity als Strategie rhetorischer Modernisierung. Zeitschrift für Frauenforschung und Geschlechterstudien, 20 (3), 129-148.

Wilz, S. (2004): Relevanz, Kontext und Kontingenz – Zur neuen Unübersichtlichkeit in der Gendered Organisation. In: Pasero, U. / Priddat, B.P. (Eds.): Organisationen und Netzwerke. Der Fall Gender. Wiesbaden, 227-258.

Winker, G. / Degele, N. (2009): Intersektionalität – Zur Analyse sozialer Ungleichheit. Bielefeld.

Zanoni, P. / Maddy J. (2004): Deconstructing Difference: The Rhetoric of Human Resource Managers' Diversity Discourses. Organizational Studies, 25 (1), 55-74.

Meeting Global Challenges - Gender and Diversity as Drivers for a Change of Scientific Culture

Carmen Leicht-Scholten

Current economic, social and political conditions demand new strategies and innovative answers for future global challenges such as demographic change, globalisation, or skilled labour shortage. Technical universities, which are traditionally male-dominated, and where women and minorities are underrepresented in almost all areas, are facing these challenges with an increasing urgency. For excellent performance, these institutions need diverse people who are equally included and promoted within the educational system. The paper describes the institutional integration of a comprehensive gender and diversity management strategy at a technical university, with special focus on measures in organisational development. In this context RWTH Aachen University has established a strong scientific unit, the "Integration Team – Human Resources, Gender and Diversity Management" (IGaD), to support faculties, management and administration to implement this strategy and to actively pursue the desired change of organisational culture.

1. Introduction

In order to respond to complex worldwide developments, such as the growth of knowledge societies, the effects of globalisation, individualisation, demographic change, changing labour markets, and new arrangements of governmental structures, organisations must start to incorporate these trends into their decision-making processes. Institutions of higher education, such as universities, are challenged in a triple way. From a societal view, these developments foster on the one hand the constraint of mobility of high qualified employees. On the other hand there is an increasing skilled labour shortage due to demographic changes which forces organisations to act accordingly. These developments affect universities in the competition for the most qualified and excellent scientists and students. From an economic view, these processes entail universities having to act increasingly entrepreneurially, as they are places where knowledge must be produced, consumed and marketed. For that purpose universities need excellent scientists and students as well as economic resources. Yet, the education and labour market is characterised by a competition for personnel and economic resources. From a scientific point of view, innovations and creative solutions are needed in order to develop strategies to face global challenges like pollution or global warming, and corresponding societal consequences such as increasing migration. Institutions of higher education need diverse people with different perspectives in order to come up with new sources of creativity and innovation.

In order to cope with these challenges RWTH Aachen has developed a gender and diversity management strategy, which will be successively implemented all over the university within the next few years. The gender and diversity approach describes the entirety of all measures that lead to the acknowledgement and appreciation of diversity as a positive contribution to the overall success of an organisation. To ensure this, RWTH Aachen University is incorporating two different strategies, which, combined, could change the scientific culture and support excellent scientific performances to cope with these global challenges: Firstly, more women and people with diverse backgrounds will be involved and promoted at all levels of decision-making, and, secondly, gender and diversity aspects will be taken into account in human resources, organisational development, research and teaching. In terms of heterogeneity German universities in particular have to catch up with other European institutions of higher education (Luciak 2008). Their knowledge of diversity among the workforce and student body is still nascent. In this context, change processes have to be initiated. An efficient organisational development is crucial when introducing comprehensive change processes like gender and diversity management to an organisation. Therefore, an organisational development, which strives to initiate a change of organisational culture from within, is being implemented at RWTH Aachen University in the framework of the overall gender and diversity strategy. RWTH Aachen University is actively dealing with these issues by being one of the first universities in Germany to establish a gender and diversity unit. Located at the president's office and situated between management and science, the scientific unit, "Integration Team – Human Resources, Gender and Diversity Management" (IGaD), develops concepts to integrate gender and diversity aspects in all areas of the university. More specifically, the fields of activity are human resources and organisational development, research, and teaching. The unit supports faculties and university administration in developing a coherent gender and diversity policy in order to attract and retain people from diverse and underrepresented groups, and to integrate diversity management in the culture of the organisation. Thus, RWTH is at the cutting edge of the integration of diversity management by establishing IGaD as an institutional model in Germany. Its strategy emphasises a dynamic and constructive tension between theory and practice and, thereby, also enriches the area of learning and teaching at the university.

In this contribution, firstly we describe the institutionalisation of gender and diversity through the establishment of a scientific support unit, which is located at the president's office and situated between management and science. This is then contextualized conceptually based on academic research, derived from the academic fields of Gender Studies and diversity research, as well as from the two approaches of gender mainstreaming and diversity management. Finally, I will discuss how the programme was implemented by presenting concrete measures that have been implemented at RWTH Aachen University in the area of organisational development and how it will be evaluated.

2. Integration Team - Human Resources Gender and Diversity Management

RWTH Aachen University is one of the leading European universities, and highly regarded for its excellent engineering programme. More than 30.000 students are educated in 260 institutes and nine faculties. However, contrary to the excellent position of the technical university in national and international rankings, the university has not succeeded in attracting and retaining women and people from diverse backgrounds in science.

In order to be perceived as an attractive location of work and study in the future and to maintain and foster an atmosphere of education that is characterised through openness and respect, RWTH Aachen University has implemented a comprehensive gender and diversity management strategy. Additionally, the need to integrate gender and diversity aspects at all levels of decision-making got further incentives through the Excellence Initiative by the German Federal and State Governments. Universities were requested to develop an "Institutional Strategy to promote top-level university research"[1] that could be funded, and which was supposed to include a gender concept. With the funding of the institutional strategy the universities could gain the title of a university of excellence. In the course of the successful participation of RWTH Aachen University in the Excellence Initiative[2] in 2007, the university has initiated a comprehensive re-organisational process in order to implement the strategy "Mobilising People", formulated within the Institutional Strategy (RWTH 2007: 49). Within this strategy, RWTH Aachen University considered the implementation of a proactive gender and diversity policy as a central part of this re-organisational process, which integrates these perspectives into the mainstream of the university (cf. figure 1). Accordingly, RWTH Aachen University has established the scientific unit "Integration Team – Human Resources, Gender and Diversity Management"

1   For more information please visit: http://www.dfg.de/foerderung/programme/exzellenzinitiative/index.html
2   For more information please visit http://www.bmbf.de/en/1321.php.

(IGaD) within its institutional strategy. Located at the president's office, and situated between management and science, the unit's main objective is to contribute to the successful implementation of diversity and equality in teaching, science and administration at all levels of decision-making and to accompany related change management processes at the university.

The integration of gender and diversity aspects into all levels of decision-making requires both the consideration of the peculiarities of the university structure as well as its overall strategy. Only if gender and diversity come to the fore of decision-making processes within this system is a cultural change possible.

Figure 1: Overview of all measures at RWTH Aachen University

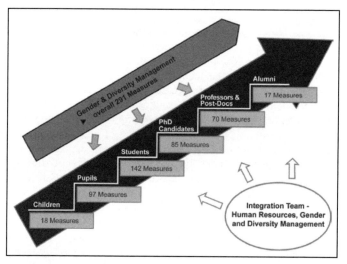

Source: IGaD 2009, in reference to the Institutional Strategy of RWTH Aachen University, p. 48

In order to apply a coherent organisational and human resources development concept, all existing measures and activities of the university have to be scrutinised, e.g. specific measures and activities to promote discriminated groups, curricula, further education, recruiting, and public relations. In this context five main fields of activity can be identified: university management, human resources development and promotion of junior scientists, research, teaching and studies, and social conditions (Kahlert 2003, Macha / Fahrenwald 2007, Leicht-Scholten / Wolf 2007). In particular, the development and arrangement of human resources management strategies, which incorporate aspects of gender and diversity, and also focus on the strengthening of central and peripheral employee responsibility, contribute to the realisation of structural equality as a mainstream task. Next to measures to enhance the percentage of women and minorities on various academic levels, gender and diversity aspects are integrated in teaching, research, and human resources development. One central task in this strategy is the sensitisation of different stakeholders at the university, who need to be supported, advised and accompanied in carrying out a successful gender and diversity strategy. In the following, organisational development, as one central area of activity, will be described in more detail; having presented the theoretical approach of the gender und diversity unit (Leicht-Scholten / Weheliye / Wolffram 2009).

3. Gender and diversity management at a technical university – theoretical contextualisation

RWTH Aachen University's gender and diversity policy combines gender mainstreaming and diversity management into a joint approach by capitalising on the strengths of both and by referring to the theoretical approach of Gender Studies and Diversity Studies. Whereas Gender Studies and Diversity Studies scrutinize attributes such as gender, age, ethnicity, disability etc. as categories of social construction and inequality on the scientific level, gender mainstreaming aims to institutionalise gender justice in organisations, with diversity management striving to achieve equality for minority groups in organisations. While in Germany there is an active discussion on the relationship between Gender Studies and the strategy of gender mainstreaming, a comparable discussion between Diversity Studies and diversity management is still in its beginning. Within the current debate, it is considered that the strategy of gender mainstreaming combined with Gender Studies is well suited to be a radical re-organisational approach with regard to gender equality, if this strategy does not confine itself to its descriptive and normative means. Gender mainstreaming, as an organisational management approach, can become radical if it aims at the consequent reorganisation of the whole organisation at all hierarchical levels in combination with the theoretical basic assumptions of Gender Studies. Consequently, the gender question will be considered as crucial criteria for the overall output of an organisation, and in science the development of new research questions and projects which integrate the gender question will be rendered possible (Leicht-Scholten / Wolffram 2010).

Thus, the category gender is being understood as a core element also determining other diversity dimensions without ignoring the interdependence of single attributes (Krell 2009). In addition, whereas Gender Studies in Germany are already institutionalised as an independent discipline, Diversity

Studies are still at the beginning of being recognised as an integrating and multi-/interdisciplinary research discipline. This trend is influenced by the diversity management approach which has become increasingly importa in the business sector in Germany since the late 1990s. While, in the context of the business sector diversity is an objective, because of its presumed economic advantages, the connecting frame of Diversity Studies is the socio-political meaning of diversity in the context of the human-rights-movements in particular in the United States. The striving of minority groups for equality in the United States resulted in the fact that companies and public institutions started to implement and establish programmes to promote people from minority backgrounds, which exceeded existing law requirements, such as Affirmative Action or Equal Opportunity. So, even though the diversity approach is not legally required, law enforcement still paved its way. Krell et al. (2007) point out that, in Germany the implementation of several antidiscrimination laws within the scope of the EU and the General Equal Treatment Act (based on the European anti-discrimination directives) have, likewise, been important drivers for Diversity Studies. Both the critical perspective and emancipatory potential of Gender Studies and Diversity Studies complement the pragmatic and managerial perspective of gender mainstreaming and diversity management, and, therefore, allow the development of synergies and new perspectives. With the concept of gender and diversity management RWTH Aachen University combines the two approaches into a complex model by focusing on the corresponding synergies (Leicht-Scholten / Weheliye / Wolffram 2009). Such efforts have allowed the university to, hereby, enter new grounds in the scientific field of Gender and Diversity Studies.

The gender and diversity strategy of RWTH Aachen University pursues as a top-down approach, both equality between women and men and the acknowledgement of differences and similarities between organisational members, which exceed the gender dimension (e.g. ethnicity, skin colour, age, religion or sexuality). Processes involving innovation, creativity, or complex-problem-solving are particularly important in institutions of higher education. According to various studies, diversity can improve these processes and lead to more productivity and better results in organisations (European Commission 2005). Thus for RWTH Aachen University, diversity among the work or student body is seen as an asset and economic advantage (Leicht-Scholten / Weheliye / Wolffram 2009). Additionally, the growing diversity of employees, customers and business markets force organisations to act more flexibly according to the needs of their stakeholders and the market (Cox 1993, Thomas 1991). To successfully face these challenges, old behavioural patterns in organisations have to be questioned and most probably changed in order to profit from the advantages of diversity (Cox / Blake 1991). This is in particular a challenge for homogeneous and monocultural organisations in which a dominant group defines the values, rules and norms for every organisational member and occupies most of the executive positions (Vedder 2007). Since these characteristics are prevalent at RWTH Aachen, women and other minority groups are underrepresented in all areas of the university. However, the university acknowledged these conditions and decided to proactively change structural inequalities within the university system. A comprehensive gender and diversity strategy seemed to be most suitable in pursuing these kinds of change processes. In this context, measures such as mentoring programmes, coaching offers, awareness workshops or interdisciplinary lectures have been developed and implemented with an aim to change prevailing monocultural conditions at the university (Leicht-Scholten / Weheliye / Wolffram 2009). At the same time, all measures that existed beforehand have to be compiled and evaluated regarding its effects on the integration of gender and diversity (see below).

4. Gender and diversity-oriented organisational development

RWTH Aachen University understands the realisation of equal opportunities as a leadership responsibility and, therefore, as an important part of the overall strategy of the university. One focus lies in the establishment of a gender and diversity-oriented organisational development, formulated in the profile of RWTH Aachen University and on the institutionalisation of equality at all levels of decision-making in research, teaching and administration. In order to obtain this goal RWTH, Aachen University includes equality in monetary and structural control systems.

One main objective of organisational development is to encourage social change in organisations (Schein 2000, Gairing 2002). All members of an organisation are involved in this process and asked to prepare the organisation for new requirements from within. At RWTH Aachen University these change processes have been initiated through the successful participation in the German Excellence Initiative, seeking to proactively meet future global challenges. In detail these challenges encompass the sharpening of the scientific profile of the institution as an integrated, interdisciplinary, and international university of technology as well as global competition and the promotion of top-level research at German universities. To this end, RWTH Aachen University has initiated a complex process of re-orientation and re-focussing involving every member of the university. One crucial component in this change process is the incorporation of gender and diversity aspects in all areas of the university (cf. figure 1).

This fundamental restructuring process started with the identification of all existing measures, projects and resources for the development of a coherent organisational development concept regarding gender and diversity (RWTH Aachen University 2007) and the development of a catalogue, which compiles all existing activities of the university. The IGaD has identified altogether 291 activities presenting the total of offers for all status groups at the university – "from children to alumni" (cf. figure 1). This is the first step of a gender and diversity audit. In a next step, these measures have to be compiled and evaluated in terms of their gender and diversity focus. The evaluation serves as the basis for an identification of insufficiencies and will facilitate the development of additional measures regarding gender and diversity. Furthermore, examples of good practice can be identified and transferred to other facilities or departments. This research project funded by the DFG within the Excellence Initiative is one of the central projects within the measure "Mobilising People".

The evaluation of all measures and activities is based on the theoretical framework of the gender and diversity strategy at RWTH Aachen University (see above). The starting point is the acknowledgement of already existing measures, which are either not identified as gender and diversity-oriented or have not been properly evaluated yet. Therefore, a comprehensive and precise analysis and evaluation of these activities is crucial in order to determine their efficiency in terms of gender and diversity aspects. The analysis will comprise crucial aspects of the two theoretical approaches, while combining new parameters such as the scrutiny of intersectional aspects in all measures. In a first step all measures are classified according to their target group, general objectives, budget, and duration. The target groups at RWTH Aachen University are divided as follows: children, pupils, students, PhD candidates, professors, postdocs, and alumni. The systematisation of projects and measures according to content-related aspects with a gender and diversity focus is a prerequisite for the determination of the scope of action and the relevance of these measures. After the development of these indicators, it is possible to focus on the crucial determinants of the evaluation, namely necessity, cost-efficiency, and satisfaction. The category "necessity" of measures focuses on the general motivational reasons behind the implementation of an activity and scrutinizes any overlapping or repetition within the single measures. This is necessary in order to determine whether it is expedient to combine, to centralise, or discontinue with certain offers at the university. Consequently all measures have to be assessed according to their cost-effectiveness, by combining the general interest of participation with the general costs of the activity and its funding. In this context it would also be possible to estimate the costs per person and then decide if the measure is effective in terms of time-cost-effectiveness regarding the necessity and satisfaction of participants.

Thus a general satisfaction inventory will be conducted into this matter. The estimation of the necessity and costs give only information on external indicators. They do not give any information on how the specific measure was successful in terms of professional support, motivation or promotion of single participants. Therefore, this determinant has to be assessed as well. Appraisals and evaluations of single activities will be used as a source. Furthermore responsible project managers will be interviewed and specific questionnaires will be distributed to members of the target groups, e.g. at the beginning and end of the studies.

The final evaluation of the catalogue seeks to improve the coordination of existing activities inside and outside the university and will show possible shortfalls. The analysis of the current situation in administrative and academic facilities will subsequently be accomplished and complemented with single action plans specifically designed for every faculty and facility. Agreements on objectives complete the process, and the scientific gender and diversity unit will support the implementation of these measures through process consultation and attendance at the different faculties and facilities of the universities. Here the scientific gender and diversity unit works in close cooperation with the departments of planning, development, controlling and human resources as well as with all faculties and administrative facilities.

To further the establishment of gender and diversity aspects in organisational development with fixed agreement on objectives, the scientific gender and diversity unit developed an equality concept (Leicht-Scholten et al. 2009). This concept, which was approved by the president's office, comprises target agreements on the basis of a balanced score card. These objectives make it possible to establish equal and sustainable structures at the university. The concept has recently been awarded, by a nationwide expert committee, an inclusion within the framework of the "Female Professorship Programme" by the Federal Ministry of Education and Research. For the first round of the programme 113 universities applied, of which 79 were evaluated positively. RWTH Aachen now receives up to 450.000 Euro p.a. over the next five years in order to increase the proportion of female professors at the university.[3]

Finally, monitoring of diverse students and employee groups was hitherto not present in the controlling processes of most German universities (Bakshi-Hamm / Lind 2008). In other European universities diversity monitoring is already institutionalised and used as an instrument to assess the needs of underrepresented groups. In the framework of RWTH Aachen's gender and diversity strategy a possible diversity monitoring programme was discussed. The importance of the recognition of data, which exceed the category gender was identified; correspondingly a first data collection will follow on a voluntarily basis in 2010. Students will then have the opportunity to specify their

---

3   For more information please visit http://www.bmbf.de/de/494.php.

backgrounds (e.g. ethnic/migrational background or disability) during the enrolment process at the university.

5. Conclusion

With its strong engagement on gender and diversity issues, RWTH Aachen University takes on the role as a precursor among German universities. As a technical university it is male-dominated due to the subjects, and so the necessity to integrate gender and diversity perspectives in the organisational strategy of the university is evident (Leicht-Scholten 2007, Leicht-Scholten / Weheliye / Wolffram 2009).

With the establishment of the scientific gender and diversity unit, RWTH Aachen University breaks new and innovative grounds. Following research in gender and diversity, and based on corresponding studies, the IGaD works scientifically and is application-oriented, and, therefore, operates within a permanent tension.

As a top-down strategy, "Gender and Diversity Management" is integrated within the organisational logic of the German system of higher education, taking into account the main five areas of university (see above). The successes achieved within the last two years confirm the approach.

However, in combination with the bottom-up approach, such a unit is faced with the risk of being usurped by different players within the university. The possibility for other faculties to ask the IGaD to give advice regarding the integration of gender and diversity aspects, for example in research proposals, is often noted, and demonstrates the high acceptance of the new institution. Due to the scientific expertise of the unit, staff members of the university hope to get rid of actively dealing with the issue by instead referring directly to the IGaD for direction. Here such a unit has to maintain and secure its independence.

Critical self-reflection, as well as discussions within the scientific community of Gender Studies and Diversity Studies are necessary to reflect the own position. If gender and diversity management is not seen as an overall strategy but instead reduced to the tasks only realised by one unit, the critical potential of the system is lost. Therefore the unit has to sharpen its scientific profile by realising independent research projects and cooperating with other experts in the scientific community. In doing so, the tension in which the unit works can remain very productive and innovative, and perhaps may lead to developing a best practice example for organisations in higher education within the coming years.

References

Bakshi-Hamm, P. / Lind, I. (2008): Migrationshintergrund und Chancen an Hochschulen: Gesetzliche Grundlagen und aktuelle Statistiken. In: Lind, I. / Löther, A. (Eds.): Wissenschaftlerinnen mit Migrationshintergrund. Cews Public No.12, 11-24.

Cox, T., / Blake, S. (1991): Managing Cultural Diversity: Implications for Organizational Competitiveness. Academy of Management Executive, 5 (3), 45-56.

Cox, T. (1993): Cultural Diversity in Organizations: Theory, Research & Practice. San Francisco.

European Commission (2005): Business Case for Diversity – Good Practices in the Workplace. Luxembourg.

Gairing, F. (2002): Organisationsentwicklung als Lernprozess von Menschen und Systemen. Weinheim.

Kahlert, H. (2003): Gender Mainstreaming an Hochschulen – Anleitung zum qualitätsbewussten Handeln. Opladen.

Krell, G. / Riedmüller, B. / Sieben, B. / Vinz, D. (2007): Einleitung - Diversity Studies als integrierende Forschungsrichtung. In: Krell, G. / Riedmüller, B. (Eds.): Diversity Studies. Grundlagen und disziplinäre Ansätze. Frankfurt a. M., 7-16.

Krell, G. (2009): Gender und Diversity: Eine 'Vernuftehe' - Plädoyer für vielfältige Verbindungen. In: Andresen, S. / Koreuber, M. / Lüdke, D. (Eds.): Gender und Diversity: Albtraum oder Traumpaar? Interdisziplinärer Dialog zur "Modernisierung" von Geschlechter- und Gleichstellungspolitik. Wiesbaden, 133-153.

Luciak, M. (2008): Diversity Management an europäischen und US-amerikanischen Institutionen höherer Bildung. In: Iber, K. / Virtbauer, B. (Eds.): Diversity Management. Eine transdisziplinäre Herausforderung. Göttingen, 39-52.

Leicht-Scholten, C. / Wolf, H. (2007): Gender Mainstreaming – Mehr als nur ein Papiertiger? – Wie viel Gender ist im Mainstream der Wissenschaften. In: Leicht-Scholten, C. (Ed.): Gender and Science – Perspektiven in den Natur- und Ingenieurwissenschaften. Bielefeld, 19-35.

Leicht-Scholten, C. et al. (2009): Gender and Diversity Management-Gleichstellungskonzept RWTH Aachen. Kurzfassung. Aachen: RWTH Aachen.

Leicht-Scholten, C. / Weheliye, A.-J. / Wolffram, A. (2009): Institutionalisation of Gender and Diversity Managament in Engineering Education. European Journal of Engineering Education, 34 (5), 447 - 454.

Leicht-Scholten, C. / Wolffram, A. (2010): Managing Gender and Diversity Mainstreaming an Hochschulen im Spannungsfeld zwischen Theorie und Praxis. Gender (forthcoming).

Macha, H. / Fahrenwald, C. (Eds.) (2007): Gender Mainstreaming und Weiterbildung. Organisationsentwicklung durch Potentialentwicklung. Opladen.

Thomas, R. (1991): Beyond Race and Gender: Unleashing the Power of Your Total Work Force by Managing Diversity. New York.

RWTH Aachen University, der Rektor (2007): Proposal for the Establishment and Funding of the Institutional Strategy to Promote Top-Level Research. In: RWTH Aachen University (Ed.): RWTH 2020 – Meeting Global Challenges. Aachen.

Schein, E. (2000): Prozessberatung für die Organisation der Zukunft. Der Aufbau einer helfenden Beziehung. Köln.

Vedder, G. (Ed.) (2007): Managing Equity and Diversity at Universities. München.

Gender and Diversity concepts as drive for institutional change in scientific institutions

Susanne Ihsen, Sabrina Gebauer, Victoria Hantschel

Diversity management as a strategy is becoming more and more common. It means that enterprises respond to the fact that their employees are diverse. Hence the strategy is to be applied to the working environment: Thus, the aim of the diversity management approach is for these people to work together without stereotypes and by accepting existing differences and equality, as well as by changing cultural and structural frameworks equalise modifiable differences. But for these changes to take place, many different measures have to be taken, which start at different points of the organizational culture. Gender mainstreaming and diversity management have to influence the administrative structure, but they also change teaching patterns, working conditions, public performance, the organisational culture and the minds of university managers as well as their employees, and, of course, the minds of the students. The culture in technical universities, in particular, is still male-dominated. That is the reason why scientific institutions are also challenged to change their organisational culture in a gender and diversity-oriented way.

By being successful in the German Excellence Initiative with a future concept that includes gender issues as a main field, TUM as an institution is changing. Within the excellence initiative many different measures at several levels of university were invented, they started to work in the last two years and will be accompanied scientifically.

1. Introduction

Diversity management[1] as a strategy has found its way into Germany's enterprises. There are many different measures that can be subsumed under the title diversity management, for various cases there are various main focuses. But there are certain key outstanding foci: Tolerance and appreciation of difference and synergy of diversity and equality. Thereby concepts for greater integration of foreign and older workers and the promotion of equality between women and men in working life for example can change attitudes of

---

1   The term "Diversity Management" means that handling personal variety in organisations is a managerial function. The term Diversity can be seen as diversity as differences vs. diversity as differences and similarities (comp. Krell / Wächter 2006).

employees and open the culture of a company. Many of these measures are not new, but come under the principles of non-discrimination established for many years. Under the label of diversity management, they were extended to a new concept, which focuses on the productivity and additional benefit of diversity (see Döge 2008).

Looking at the economical oriented organisations in comparison to universities as an organisation, it becomes clear that integration of diversity management is not only of hight interest within Organisational and Human Resource Development (Krell 2006). The question is how his new concept and the cultivated standardisation in Human Resource Management get along. HR departments define processes, arrange consistent criteria and deviate statistics and operation instructions that make personnel recruiting and development transparent and comparable. How can the diversity approach be adequately considered? Moreover, what criteria can be developed to especially consider the differences in the workforce?

Universities and other scientific institutions differ in their HR Development in some cases from enterprises: the criteria of searching for personnel is not transparent, from one institution to another there are a lot of different ways of approaching HR – from more industry-oriented down to nothing. Even in appellate proceedings for professorships some parts of the process are transparent, while others differ along the disciplines with a lot of "hidden" rules being implemented. Most of the persons who are responsibly involved are not trained for recruitment. In the scientific context the real challenges are the models, theories of the single scientific disciplines, and the interpretations. Depending on the scientific direction different goals are tracked. Interdisciplinary research projects especially experience a negotiation process which realises diversity management. So the question arises: Which differences are help to respect and integrate, and for what differences are measures needed to get a long lasting balance? Here the feminist equality and difference debate of the 1980s moves in tandem with today's Diversity Concept: The question arises then how stereotypes can be debunked. This includes the consideration of individual association with varying requirements in diverse social roles and the rules (open or secret) organisations have to promote and to limit equality and diversity.

2. Diversity management and Gender Mainstreaming at Technical University Munich (TUM)

Twenty years ago, TUM set out its aim to be Germany's most attractive technical university for women. Meanwhile, gender mainstreaming as a strategy has entered the structures of university and has become more and more part of the university system. Gender sensibility and gender justice are seen as necessary competencies that are to be lived and conciliated in university. Gender mainstreaming and diversity management influence the administrative structure, but they also change teaching patterns, working conditions, public performance, the organisational culture and the minds of university managers and of their employees and, of course, their students. However, the engineering professional culture has hardly changed for decades; the culture in technical universities, especially, is still male-dominated. 85% of the professorships are held by men and there are still very few female students enrolling for technical study programmes. In 1980 the number of female professors was even lower, at about 8% (cp. Destatis 2007). Also the number of female engineers is low in Germany (12%) and women are under-represented at every level of technical scientific research (see figures 1 and 2).

"Technology Universities all have a special challenge in common: in particular, it is due to their focus on engineering and science subjects that they continue to be perceived as a male domain. It is time to overcome traditional prejudices and modernize academic cultures" (Prof. Dr. Dr. h.c. mult. Wolfgang A. Herrmann, president of TUM, TUM 2007).

In 2009 TUM had a proportion of 32% studying women, 26% women in scientific personnel, 55% non-scientific and about 12% women hold a professorship.

Engineering sciences, in particular, are male dominated and have a strong male culture. To get more women into these fields, this culture must change. Organisations are only able to change their cultural identity by an internal demand because they are almost "blind" to external influence, so called autopoietic[2] systems. That means that although scientific institutions, especially technical universities, are challenged to change their organisational culture in a gender and diversity-oriented way by society and industry, they need internal mentors for the initiation. To initiate sustainable changes an external accompanying party is likewise needed to reflect the conflicts back to the system or organisation. In this process the specific culture and identity of the organisation has to be kept in mind and the existing power structures have to be included in the changing process (see Ihsen 1999).

At TUM the executive committee started the change management approach together with the women representatives, administrative offices, department members and gender research persons as a top-down strategy to control and implement changes in structures, processes and cultures.

---

2   Autopoiesis means self-creation and self-preservation of a system (Maturana / Varela 1987).

Figure 1: Proportions of men and women in a typical academic career in science and engineering, students and academic staff, EU-27, 2002/2006

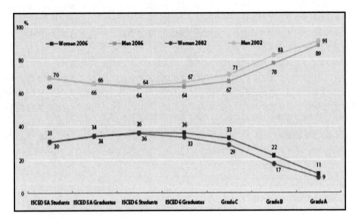

Source: She Figures 2009

Figure 2: Relative share of women and men in a typical academic career

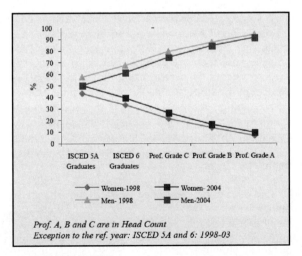

Source: European Commission 2008

3. The influence of the Excellence Initiative

The Excellence Initiative of the German federal government and the state governments promotes excellence in research in German universities. The aim is to support top-level university research and improve its international visibility, create excellent conditions for young scientists at universities, deepen cooperation between disciplines and institutions, strengthen international research cooperation, promote equal opportunities for men and women in research and intensify scientific and academic competition, and improve the general standard of science and universities in Germany. In an extensive and internationally reviewed process universities could apply for funding.

The Excellence Initiative is conducted by the German Research Foundation (DFG) and the German Council of Science and Humanities (WR). It includes three lines of funding:

1. Graduate Schools, to foster young researchers
2. Clusters of Excellence, for the promotion of top-level research
3. Institutional Strategies, to advance top-level university research.

TUM was successful in all three funding lines of the 2006 Excellence Initiative. By being successful with a future concept that includes gender issues as a main field, TUM as an institution is changing. One outstanding feature of the proposal was the integration of gender issues. Accordingly a "Gender Board" was set up in 2006 for creating the specific gender programme under the management of one of the Vice Presidents. It was the vital step for the "Entrepreneurial TUM" towards realising these gender issues. The committee meets regularly to monitor the development and implementation of TUM's gender concept.

A Gender Consulting Office was established during the course of the Excellence Initiative. This is an advisory service for all matters related to gender mainstreaming in the different departments: It also deals with the promotion of gender awareness concepts in research, study programmes and administration. Several new funds[3] were also set up:

- the "Family Care Structural Fund" to help scientists with children or dependents at home
- the "Gender Issues Incentive Fund" to support gender-oriented departmental measures involving structural changes
- the "Vocational Training Fund", set up to finance refresher courses following periods of parental leave

---

3   The use of these funds is recorded. Departments or individuals can apply, but there is a short review-process about the correct use of the money.

- the "Parental Leave Compensation Fund" which provides funds to bridge periods of maternity leave (Ihsen / Gebauer / Buschmeyer 2008).

The Munich Dual Career Service aims at promoting careers in science. It is a collaborating office cooperating with the Max-Planck-Society in Munich and the Helmholtz-Society in Munich. Its goal is to help the partners of new professors and post doc scientists to find jobs nearby. Thus, it is a contact point for all matters of career advice and relocation.

Another main focus lies on creating integration between work and life: work-life-balance. The professional and the private life of employees should ideally co-exist and complement each other to form a meaningful whole. Therefore, several additional measures have been intensified, for example the improvement of the child care facilities, the possibilities to work from home, and part-time studies.

A core event in integrating gender and diversity issues is the annual symposium regarding this topic. It is named Liesel-Beckmann-Symposium after the first female professor in economics in Germany and at TUM. In 2007 the first symposium took place with the topic "Gender and diversity in the technical culture". It is organised by the IAS – Institute for Advanced Study at Technical University Munich and promoted from funds of the Excellence Initiative because of the wish to integrate the gender constituent in teaching. The symposium can be seen as a pilot project with concrete impact on seminars held by "Gender Studies in Science and Engineering". Experienced and young researchers as well as students came together for two days to discuss gender and diversity aspects in research, technology development and in enterprises. They developed new ideas to implement gender and diversity into future projects (ibid.). In the meantime two more symposia took place, the topic in 2008 was "Gender and diversity in medicine", and in 2009 "Gender in education".

As a future concept it is intended to become "the entrepreneurial university". Entrepreneurial thinking means to invest, to risk new ventures, and to develop sustainable strategies. In the context of top research this means a maximum of individual freedom connected with a science-friendly administration. One important requirement to reach this goal is to include Gender and Diversity in the whole process.

In this context, in 2007 the activities in diversity orientation started: TUM became the first university in Germany to sign the federal government's Charter of Diversity[4]. The fundamental principles of this Charter are to respect and make allowances for the different needs, talents and interests of both employees and customers of both sexes. TUM hopes that, by signing the Charter, it will also become internationally recognised as a university that promotes and actively implements equal opportunities.

---

4   http://www.diversity-charter.org/

Figure 3: TUM Future Concept: The concept of the "Entrepreneurial University"

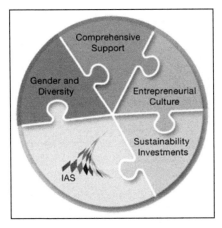

Source: http://portal.mytum.de/tum/exzellenzinitiative/zukunftskonzept

4. Gender and Diversity in Engineering Education

The change of paradigm discussed here concerns Engineering Education as a whole. It includes implementing process-oriented, interdisciplinary engineering courses. They would also improve communication and application-oriented cross-disciplinary skills relevant for the engineering profession. In the long run, these specific educational processes may have an impact on the existing engineering profession and the engineering professional culture (see Ihsen 2005). To teach students of engineering studies on diversity issues as part of the curriculum in engineering programmes is an essential approach of preparing the students for their professional life. By teaching them what this is and what it means for their (professional) lives makes them aware of their greater responsibility. The idea is to connect diversity issues with technical subjects.

Ihsen, Hanny and Beuter (2008) identified two levels at which the concepts of diversity and gender mainstreaming can be included into the study designs:

- at the level of overall organisational goals and measures related to a certain study programme

- and at the level of the educational goals of the study programme itself by defining learning outcomes that reflect diversity and gender-oriented competencies (Ihsen / Beuter / Hanny 2008).

The research team of Gender Studies in Science and Engineering has developed the core elements of a new "soft skills" curriculum for electrical and mechanical engineering, which gives, to both female and male students, the possibility to get new kinds of information and practical experiences about their future engineering profession. Specific non-technical aspects are an integrated part of the Bachelor's and several Master's curricula. A new challenge for the next years will be to integrate gender and diversity elements into the new TUM School of Education.

In the future the following questions have to be integrated into the study programmes to include gender and diversity elements (see Ihsen / Beuter / Hanny 2008):

- Do these curricula, their educational methods and structures, and the university regulations reflect the gender and diversity related elements?
- Have the different professional groups and stakeholders been taken into consideration when the educational programmes have been designed?
- Do the study programmes take into consideration the different student groups in developing their individual qualities?
- Are sufficient resources available to develop the specific gender and diversity competencies of the students?

For this issue a research project runs until 2011, together with the Technical Universities of Dortmund and Braunschweig and with Leuphana University Lüneburg.

It is essential to integrate gender and diversity aspects into the educational aims of the courses. The special aim of Gender Studies in Science and Engineering is the combination of active teaching and learning for getting to know what gender, diversity and equality mean. In this way the engineering graduates acquire specific skills (besides technical knowledge), which will help them to get along in their jobs where they will have to deal with new gender and diversity aspects. These aspects will be part of their work when they develop new products and technical solutions. They also have an impact on their everyday lives when they are communicating and collaborating with other people.

In different seminars like "presentation and communication for engineers" or "successful through teamwork" gender and diversity are but two topics discussed alongside others, which makes it much simpler to talk about the issues with the predominantly male student-group. Students learn to self-organise their learning processes, moderate discussions and work in small groups. They learn more self-awareness and reflect about their own and their colleagues' behaviour and self-representation. They practice giving and receiving personal feedback in a protected laboratory setting. "Teamwork, Presentation and communication for engineers" prepares the students for giving professional presentations. The students do several exercises of forming, moderating and working in groups where they have to solve small tasks together. They then analyse their group roles and become aware of communication processes and group dynamics. In their engineering curriculum the students hardly ever have an opportunity to practice presentations or lectures in front of a crowd until their final bachelor- or master speech. Hence, here they not only learn the theoretical basics of presenting but also practice it, see other students doing the same and discuss the rights and wrongs of giving a presentation.

In other seminars and lectures on "interdisciplinary aspects of the engineering profession", "job application", and "career planning" students learn about gender and diversity as part of their future professional skills. The diversity aspect that students have not been confronted with before in their studies is integrated throughout all the tools the students have to work in.

Furthermore, we have developed an interdisciplinary course programme dealing with gender and diversity in organisational development. Here, students from different subjects like business administration, electrical engineering and consumer science come together to learn about several topics of organisational development from a gender and diversity perspective. The main focus of the seminar lies in diversity management and customer-oriented product development. The students have to point out the interaction between these two topics and the consequences for personnel development and organisational structures. They learn about the idea that diverse teams are more liable to create customer-oriented products than homogeneous teams and at the same time can experience this in the seminar. In addition to this, they see that the economic aspect of customer-oriented product development is not the only one highlighted. From the manifold feedbacks of the students, we learned that they have started to be more sensitive to invisible power structures and more aware of how to work successfully in diverse teams themselves. Concerning the feedback and proposals of the students we always try to rethink and improve our seminars.

Other topics of "Gender Studies in Science and Engineering" are research projects on the further development of the German Excellence Initiative at TUM, continuing adjustment to the gender and diversity concepts of companies but also a lot of surveys on several groups depending on engineering education and profession.

5. Conclusion

It can be stated that changes in engineering culture and organisational structures of technical universities are long overdue. The German educational system is under considerable strain because of the shortage of highly skilled employees, especially due to lack of engineers. It needs to maintain and strengthen the political and economic position of the high-technology country Germany within the global economy. For this goal, qualified personnel especially in engineering has to be educated. Germany has to invest particularly in women, in order to not waste their qualities and experiences. Gender mainstreaming and diversity management have to influence the administrative structure, but they also change teaching patterns, working conditions, public performance, the organisational culture and the minds of university managers as well as of their employees and students. Technical universities, like the TUM, are challenged to enter the complex process to become, in itself, a learning organisation. This is why the diversity concept of the TUM is still changing. The next step is to identify new target groups and develop target agreements and measures. In terms of the idea of lifelong learning, one particular working field in scientific institutions will be the elderly. An important topic is the re-entry of men and women after parental leave or elder care. Nowadays, it is difficult to return to the scientific community after being out of academia for a while, because of enduring technical and scientific changes. But for these changes to occur many different measures have to be taken starting at different points of the organisational culture.

References

Destatis (2007): Frauenanteil bei Professoren steigt auf 15%. Press Release No. 27 (July 11th, 2007).

Döge, P. (2008): Von der Antidiskriminierung zum Diversity-Management. Ein Leitfaden. Göttingen.

European Commission (Ed.) (2008): Benchmarking Policy Measures for Gender Equality in Science. Brussels.

Ihsen, S. (1999): Zur Entwicklung einer neuen Qualitätskultur in ingenieurwissenschaftlichen Studiengängen. Ein prozessbegleitendes Interventionskonzept. Köln.

Ihsen, S. (2005): Engineering culture in changing processes – Gender Studies as one cross road. In: Cagdas, S. / Yavuz, Y. (Eds.): Engineering Education at the Cross-Roads of Civilizations, SEFI Annual Conference '05, 317-322.

Ihsen, S. (2007): Technik ist doch neutral: Genderorientierte Veränderungs-ansätze in den Ingenieurwissenschaften. In: Dudeck, A. / Jansen-Schulz, B. (Eds.): Zukunft Bologna!? Gender und Nachhaltigkeit als Leitideen für eine neue Hochschulkultur, Frankfurt a. M., 235-246.

Ihsen S. / Beuter, I. / Hanny, I. B. (2008): Gender and Diversity as structural Components of Quality in new (engineering) Study Programs. SEFI Deans Conference Berlin.

Ihsen, S. / Gebauer, S. / Buschmeyer, A. (2008): Gender motivated institu-tional changes at Technische Universität München and its influence on engineering education. Book of abstracts: Annual SEFI Conference. Aal-borg.

Krell, G. / Wächter, H. (2006). Diversity Management. Impulse aus der Per-sonalforschung. München / Mering.

Krell, G. / Riedmüller, B. / Sieben, B. / Vinz, D. (Eds.) (2007): Diversity Studies. Grundlagen und disziplinäre Ansätze. Frankfurt a. M., New York.

Maturana, H. R. / Varela, F. J. (1987): Der Baum der Erkenntnis. Bern, Mün-chen.

TUM (2007): Women at Technische Universität München, Brochure for the Liesel-Beckmann-Symposium.

The Challenge of Diversity: examples from France

Junko Takagi

In this paper, I address the challenges facing diversity as a concept. The assumption that diversity is a clearly defined concept can be questioned at several levels. First, recent accounts of diversity have emphasised the importance of contextualising diversity and the difficulty of standardising diversity initiatives. To illustrate this point, I present a comparative study of the meaning of diversity between France and the U.S. to illustrate this approach. Second, Harrison and Klein (2007) have formulated a categorisation of diversity to distinguish between different diversity phenomena. When diversity is disparity according to this categorisation, perceptual differences between stakeholders can diverge such that diversity issues are interpreted differently. I use the example of gender as a diversity element and present a qualitative study of perceptions of gender in French firms in which I identify incongruities between the perceptions of different actors. While the paper does not present an exhaustive list of challenges facing diversity and the implementation of diversity initiatives, it raises questions around the utility of the concept itself.

1. Introduction: multiple facets of diversity and the challenge of finding a common understanding

The diversity management literature has significantly expanded in volume and the term "diversity" has become an umbrella term for management issues including workplace discrimination, inequality, equal opportunity, and the business case for diversity. The past decade has generated attempts to conceptualise the concept into something more systematic and universal. Two recent examples of attempts to conceptualise diversity have, however, brought to the surface the complexity of the term and the challenges of developing a coherent body of research around the concept.

These discussions of diversity in the management literature highlight the importance of understanding diversity issues in a contextualised setting (Nishii / Özbilgin 2007), and also the utility of clearly distinguishing between different types of diversity phenomena (Harrison / Klein 2007). Both research streams underscore the complex nature of diversity with the fundamental assumption that diversity cannot be understood as a universal concept. In this paper, I illustrate the complexity of developing a coherent argument around diversity issues with examples of two studies carried out in France.

I argue that the lack of a common understanding of the issues will hinder the effectiveness of diversity initiatives.

The literature on global diversity management emphasises the importance of a "situated" approach to implementing diversity policies across countries (Agocs / Burr 1996; Nishii / Özbilgin 2007; Sippola / Smale 2007; Sub / Kleiner 2007; Syed 2007). Studies which address this point focus either on case studies of particular firms and their diversity practices across countries, or are country-specific and describe the implementation of diversity practices across firms in a particular country. The former investigate the different ways in which firms try to adapt to country-specific conditions for implementing diversity policies, and the latter identify similarities in diversity practices across firms. While both types of studies contribute to a better understanding of the challenges facing the implementation of global diversity policies, they do not address the more social aspect of diversity management as a practice embedded in a social and cultural context in which understanding meanings becomes critical to successful cross-cultural implementation of management practices. In this paper, I first present a comparative qualitative study of the meaning of diversity between France and the U.S. to underscore the importance of the "situated" approach and the necessity for firms to take into account differences in the meaning of diversity across countries in order to effectively implement diversity policies.

Harrison and Klein (2007) have developed a categorisation that distinguishes between different diversity phenomena. For example, in considering global diversity management, the available literature addresses global diversity both in terms of cross-national differences in work populations (e.g. Agocs / Burr 1996; Egan / Bendick 2003; Sippola / Smale 2007; Suss / Kleiner 2007), and also in terms of cultural diversity where there is intercultural interaction of employees and organisations (e.g. Barinaga 2007; Earley / Gibson 2002; Barkema et al. 2002; Salk / Brannen 2000). The former addresses local diversity issues and their variation across countries, while the latter investigates individual and group interactions in multicultural teams and international project groups. The two applications refer to conceptually different social phenomena and should not be confused under one umbrella term (Harrison / Klein 2007). The authors define diversity as one of three potential social phenomena: diversity as disparity concerns differences in the concentration of valued social assets or resources such as pay or status; diversity as separation concerns differences in position or opinion among group members; and diversity as variety indicates differences in kind or category, primarily of information, knowledge or experience among group members (Harrison / Klein 2007). This stream of research emphasises the confusion that can be generated by using an umbrella term that covers different phenomena. For example, there has been a gradual shift overtime in the management literature from discussions around inequalities to a business case for diversity, which has been facilitated by the introduction of the diversity concept. This shift is perceived by critical analysts as diluting key management issues and bringing diversity into the business discourse (Benshop 2010; Greene / Kirton 2010). While increasing diversity efforts center around promoting diversity in the name of the business case, inequalities persist in firms. The different categorisations existing within the diversity concept as identified by Harrison and Ford (2007) provide the basis for different understandings of diversity issues for different stakeholders leading to difficulties in implementation of diversity initiatives. In this paper, I discuss the case of gender as one such diversity element, and show that differences exist between different actors concerning their definition of diversity in relation to gender leading to problematic implementation of diversity initiatives in firms.

The objective of this paper is to present examples of distinctions in the meaning of diversity due to contextual issues and differences in the understanding of diversity issues on the part of stakeholders. The examples help to illustrate the complexity of diversity and the difficulties in creating a common understanding and put into question the utility of diversity as a management concept.

First, I present findings from a comparative study of the meaning of diversity in the U.S. and France. The study shows that diversity is interpreted very differently from one country context to another. Next, I present findings from a qualitative study of women in the workplace, which indicate that there are gender differences in the perception of causes of gender inequalities. Both studies support the existing conceptual literature on diversity with findings that show the complexity of the diversity concept.

2. Contextualising diversity: a comparative study of the meaning of diversity in France and the U.S.

Diversity, a relatively new concept in French society, addresses "differences" within the population, which is in contrast to the more traditional republican principle. Discussions around what constitutes diversity and its effective management remain embryonic. While there is general agreement that discrimination needs to be tackled, divergent views concern the object of discrimination (e.g. the person as opposed to their experiences) and how to establish equality. Regarding the latter, there is a preference toward focusing on "competencies" as opposed to "differentiating elements" (e.g. ethnic background). Although discussions on diversity since 2005 increasingly concern ethnic minority issues, most of the diversity initiatives in firms in France continue to focus on gender and people with disabilities. The current situation in France maybe described as "emergent" and, thus, an interesting phenomenon to observe.

In order to address the need to contextualise diversity and to provide a general overview of the focus of current diversity discussions in France, Takagi and Gröschl (2007) conducted a comparative study of newspaper articles on diversity. This study compares how diversity is discussed in France, an example of a Continental European country that continues to rely on non-differentiating concepts regarding the management of its increasingly complex and diverse workforce, and the U.S., a country in which diversity is well-established as a concept and which is the source of most diversity management initiatives. The study was carried out on press articles between 2001 and 2006. Results suggest that this type of comparison of meanings is useful to understanding contextual differences in the meaning of diversity with consequences for the development and application of diversity initiatives.

In terms of volume, the study identified a general increase in articles discussing diversity in the French press during the period between 2001 and 2006, while U.S. articles on diversity decreased slightly. The use of the term "diversity" gradually increased in France during the study period. As in the case of the general volume of articles on diversity, it was necessary to look into the content of each article identified in order to understand these trends and to determine the similarity or differentiation in terms of meaning.

For example, it became quickly apparent during the coding of the study that the term diversity is used very explicitly in the U.S. press to apply to clearly identified minority groups and minority issues. These findings reflect Litvin's (1997) observations that diversity discourse in the U.S. serves to identify and specify membership categories, and to distinguish between these categories. For example, an article in Business Week on corporate diversity discusses a "...view of diversity – in gender and racial terms..." (21/5/2001). In an article entitled "Diversity is about to get more elusive, not less" (Business Week, 7/7/2003), not only does the article talk about minorities, but clearly specifies "...Hispanics, African-Americans, Asians, and Native Americans...." and compares them to "...Caucasians....". In fact, a majority of the U.S. articles on diversity apply specifically to race and ethnicity, and a significant number of these articles specify the category "black" or "African-American" as the target of their discussion regarding diversity.

In comparison, it was much more difficult to code the French articles in both the weekly journals and the business press into categories of indicators. First, articles on diversity cover a much larger range of diversity indicators, including not only ethnic and gender differences, but also differences in family composition, educational establishments, clientele and product choice, as well as workplace, housing, and professional diversity, some of which are indirectly related to "cultural" or "population" diversity. In addition, until very recently, articles that talk about ethnicity in particular have been comparatively indirect in their approach, rarely specifying any particular ethnic group(s) but rather using individual names ("...je m'appelle Yamina!..."[1] from "Faire du cinema n'est pas evident pour une femme"[2] L'Express, 19/9/2002) or styles of clothing (e.g. "costard-cravates" as opposed to "djellabas"; L'Express 2004) to evoke such differences. The race category also includes articles that discuss populations from "quartiers sensibles" (sensitive areas) and "quatiers difficiles" (trouble areas), "milieu defavorizé" (underprivileged backgrounds), and ZEP (zone d'education prioritaire – education priority zones) and ZUS (zone urbaine sensible – sensitive urban zones). These terms are synonymous with geographical areas that are highly ethnic and are another way of addressing ethnic differences. Compared to the U.S., the French articles also include more categories in their discussion of diversity such as people with disabilities, the elderly, and the obese.

The results from this qualitative study on the meaning of diversity show not only that there are differences in the meaning of diversity in the two contexts, but also indicate that in the U.S., the term is established with a meaning that is clear and shared, whereas in France, there is an evolution in the use and the meaning of the term in the press over the period of the study, and the meaning remains vague and non-specific. A contextualised study identifies significant differences in the understanding of what constitutes diversity and what issues are more or less easily tackled by diversity initiatives. It is evident that the field of diversity management in the French context is in the process of structuration, which may hinder effective implementation of diversity practices, but which creates opportunities for different actors in the field to influence its evolution.

As mentioned previously, currently in France, most of the diversity initiatives are based around issues of gender and people with disabilities. Both are diversity categories clearly identified by law as objects of discrimination which need to be rectified. With the implementation of a legal quota in the workplace for people with disabilities, and laws protecting equal opportunities for women, many firms have started to invest in these issues. Ethnic background remains a thorny issue and firms and anti-discrimination institutions alike are trying to build mechanisms specific to the French context to try to deal with this issue. For the time being, different diversity categories are treated separately generating different sets of initiatives, and we can say that diversity has not become as yet an all encompassing term. Rather it highlights the variety of differences that may (or may not) be perceived and is a means of increasing awareness particularly at the firm level.

---

1 "..my name is Yamina..."
2 " It's not easy for women to be film-makers"

3. A qualitative study of gender diversity: the difficulty of dealing with diversity as disparity

The discussion of gender diversity in the workplace and other professional settings is not particularly a new subject. Gender is different from other diversity categories in that women are not a minority in society, and have long been present in the workforce. At the same time, firms have tried to promote women in recent years to overcome gender discrimination and equal opportunity biases in the workplace.

In France, for example, firms are encouraged by a solid legal framework and governmental legislation on the topic, such as the creation of *"La Charte de l'Égalité"* (8/3/2004), and a Label Égalité rewarding companies whose practices are effective in eliminating gender biases, or the more recent law on equality in salaries (23/3/2006) that is currently being tackled by many firms. Despite such initiatives, although some managers claim that it is no longer an issue, gender equality in the workplace continues to be problematic.

Some concrete examples show that the gender gap is still present and requires justification. In 2007, we carried out a management study on perceptions of gender and the impact of gender-related initiatives in a sample of three French firms. Despite being diversity champions in France for their contribution to the development of the diversity domain through membership in diversity networks and obtaining the Equality Label, in one firm, 13% of upper-level managers are women although women constitute approximately 50% at entry-level for managers, with only 2 women on the 20-member executive committee. At another firm, the Board is composed of 18 administrators of whom one is a woman. The 15 members of the Executive Committee are men. At yet another firm, the balance in the executive committee is 2 women out of 13 members, 3 women are directors out of 39 in a particular branch, and there are only 3 female members on the administration board. This trend has also been identified by the McKinsey reports on women in management (Women matter, 2007; Women matter 2, 2009) in which they observe not only that women continue to be significantly underrepresented in upper-level management positions, but also that this is likely to continue. For firms, this observation is increasingly problematic as European countries lean towards adoption of gender quotas for executive committees. The French government passed a draft law to this effect at the beginning of 2010.

In order to better understand this under-representation of women in upper-level management positions, we carried out twenty-five interviews with both human resources managers and managers from other functions in the three firms. The interviews with human resources managers enabled us to draw a global picture of the companies' policies and corporate vision concerning the gender issue and its challenges. The interviews with the other managers allowed us to have the perspectives of women within the firms at different levels of the hierarchy as well as those who had left the firm, and also to understand the perspectives of male managers. Study participants were asked about the situation of women in their firm and their personal experiences of working with women, their observations regarding the management styles of men and women, company programs to encourage women in the workplace, and their perceptions of obstacles for women in the firm.

The interviews supported us in our observation that, despite gender having been on the agenda for a long time (particularly compared to other diversity initiatives), the need for significant efforts remains. Women interviewees often expressed the opinion that *"male chauvinism clearly exists in the generation of men holding top management today"*. For some, the dilemma of maintaining a balance between private and professional life is problematic: *"To reach a high level of management, you need to make huge sacrifices in your personal life"*. To others, again, this is seen as a fatality to be accepted that will not change: *"To have more gender balance in top management, mentalities and culture would have to change. This is not the trend. It would not be accepted by all"*.

A similarity that showed up in all three case studies was that recruitment at entry level was relatively fair, and both male and female young professionals were being recruited in equal numbers. The formalisation of recruitment processes was seen as effective in ensuring the fair evaluation of potential candidates at the entry point for managerial positions. However, as employees climbed up the hierarchy, the risk of bias increased as processes were less structured and the promotion criteria became opaque. In some cases, interviewees observed that the main criteria for promotion reflect a somewhat masculine culture, and that men usually feel more comfortable building a network, inside visibility, and getting into the fighting arena for career development. According to some, it is easier for men to become known inside the firm, implicitly coached by eminent figures so as to be co-opted by upper-level managers. This is a phenomenon that has been modelled by Athey et. al. (2000) who identify mentoring as a significant determinant of career progression.

From an HR perspective, several factors were seen as generating the gender gap in promotions. The first element pointed out by HR managers is maternity. Maternity plays a major role in women's lives, particularly for those in the 30 to 40 age group. They are often perceived as having to make sacrifices which considerably slow down their career path. This is due in part to the fact that in most French firms, 30 to 40 is also the age range within which most companies identify their high potentials. Women often miss or refuse opportunities at this critical moment since their life cycle is not adapted to this company practice. This idea was prevalent in all the interviews.

The perception of self-censorship also seems to be a well-spread female characteristic according to HR managers. Here is one quotation among many to illustrate this perception: *"When confronted with an opportunity for example, women tend to question their abilities and seek reassurance. That's a behaviour a man wouldn't have."* This observation is supported by findings from the McKinsey report in which it is noted that: *"Only 15% of highly qualified women aspire to positions of power, against an average of 27% of men."*

Evaluation criteria, when they are not formally specified as seems to be the case for internal promotions, are perceived to rely on the masculine culture that has developed over time in most companies. These criteria are generally not perceived to be adapted to women's ways of working and act to create a bias in managers' perceptions of female performance on the job. They differ from company to company according to the business and culture, but they often include being more "visible", being able to "sell" and "show" oneself better. This was often mentioned in our interviews with HR managers.

Finally, one of the most important factors identified by HR professionals is the lack of role models. Here is a quotation from an interview with a HR manager: *"It is all the more difficult for women to project themselves at a top position if no woman has ever been there".*

The managerial perspective greatly reflects the perceptions of HR managers. Both women and men perceive that women focus more on their family life. For example, a female interviewee observed that: *"I think women care more about bringing up their children, being there for them, they do not have the same objectives than men."* Women are also generally perceived to lack ambition: as a woman put it: *"I do not project myself in the future. I have an interesting job, that's all I care about".* Also, female managers are perceived to be less interested in some fields, such as science or technical fields, or in particular strategic positions. As one interviewee stated: *"Some positions and fields constitute springboards to high responsibility jobs. Women are less sensitive to those kind of things."*

In our interviews with male and female managers, a particularly interesting point raised was the perception of female role models in upper-level management positions. In one firm in particular, there was a strong sentiment among women in middle-management positions that they did not want to move up to upper-level management since they did not want to become like the women in upper-level positions. The women who had "succeeded" acted as anti-role models to other women and were attributed negative characteristics such as not having a life outside of work, acting like men, being single, becoming tokens etc. As one interviewee put it: *"They (women) have become like men. They don't make us dream anymore, they have masculine behaviors, they have lost their female sensitivity".* These statements suggest that the "glass ceiling" effect is not only due to structural factors and others' expectations, but also to female non-identification with potential role models and less perhaps to low female self-expectations as may be imagined.

Finally, a reason that came up frequently in the interviews was the fact that there were few educated women when the current top management was hired. There is a general perception that it is necessary to change the guard and that it is a question of time for significant changes to take place.

The factors identified in our case studies are well-known in the gender literature. The striking point is that they continue to be identified by HR managers, female managers and male managers alike. The remark regarding the changing of the guard may be particularly important in taking into account the time factor. However, it may be too simplistic to leave things to time. We also found from our interviews that men and women perceive different factors which impact on the career evolution of women in firms. Male interviewees tended to attribute the current situation of women in their firms to individual and social factors (e.g. lack of ambition, family roles), while female interviewees systematically cited organisational factors (e.g. organisational culture, promotion mechanism). This tendency was consistently observed throughout our sample. Women who experience discrimination in the workplace are more likely to identify external factors to explain their lack of promotion while men are more likely to make internal attributions for the same outcome. The difficulty in having a shared interpretation of the problematic between men and women hinders the creation and implementation of solutions. Women expect more from organisations, whereas men expect more from women to change their behaviour or to accept traditional social roles. Even for well-established diversity categories such as gender, it continues to be important to take into account the differences in perceptions and expectations of stakeholders in order to have a better understanding of and to effectively tackle diversity issues.

This study reinforces past findings that gender is an example of diversity as disparity. Women and men do not have the same social capital in firms for career evolution, based on personal choices, self- and other-expectations, life cycles, self- and other-perceptions, and organisational culture and practices. It also identifies gender as a cause of separation in firms since, on the topic of gender, men and women tend to have different perspectives and understanddings of the problems. At the same time, the management discourse around diversity in general, and gender in particular, portrays differences as a positive element that (should) lead to increased creativity and performance.

Harrison and Klein's (2007) categorisation helps to formulate the complexity of the gender issue. First, the management discourse does not fit with the reality of gender as disparity and separation. The management focus attempts to reap the benefits of diversity, but it lacks a realistic foundation. Second, due to the differences in perspectives between men and women, the reasons for disparity are not likely to be addressed effectively due to lack of consensus on the necessary actions. The separation perspective also helps us to observe the asymmetric motivation for promoting gender initiatives.

4. Conclusion

Recent attempts to categorise and contextualise diversity help to clarify what are the diversity elements that are activated in a particular context, and the type of diversity that needs to be addressed. The diversity concept has tended to pool together all kinds of differences in the same pot with consequences on the implication of differences and on diversity policies. The pooling of different meanings has diluted or camouflaged important inequalities and perceptual differences in the management discourse. The conceptual frameworks discussed in this paper allow us to make distinctions between different diversity phenomena and help management discourse to distinguish between diversity as equal rights and diversity as a direct source of enhanced performance. In light of this discussion on the complexity underlying diversity, it is possible to question the utility of the diversity concept. While it is difficult to determine whether the concept has in fact increased interest and knowledge on issues that previously existed, such as gender inequality for example, we have seen that it has also had insidious consequences. In contexts where the concept has been imported, there is much work that is required to clarify the sense and the utility of the concept bringing in the perspectives of different stakeholders.

References

Agocs, C. / Burr, C. (1996): Employment equity, affirmative action and managing diversity: Assessing the differences. In: International Journal of Manpower, 17(4/5), 30-45.

Athey, S. / Avery, C. / Zemsky, P. (2000): Mentoring and diversity. In: American Economic Review, 90(4), 765-786.

Barinaga, E. (2007): 'Cultural diversity' at work: 'National culture' as a discourse organizing an international project group. In: Human Relations, 60(2), 315-430.

Barkema, H.G. / Baum, J.A. / Mannix, E.A. (2002): Management challenges in a new time. In: Academy of Management Journal, 45(5), 916-930.

Benshop, Y. (2010): The dubious power of diversity management. Paper presented at the ESSEC Diversity and Performance Chair Conference, Paris.

McKinsey & Company (2007): Women Matter. Gender diversity, a corporate performance driver. Available from: http://www.mckinsey.com/locations/paris/home/womenmatter/pdfs/Women_matter_oct2007_english.pdf.

McKinsey & Company (2009): Women Matter 2. Female leadership, a competitive edge for the future. Available from: http://www.mckinsey.de/downloads/publikation/women_matter/Women_Matter_2_brochure.pdf

Earley, P. / Gibson, C. (2002): Multinational work teams PR: A new perspective. Mahwah, NJ.

Egan, M. / Bendick, M. (2003): Workforce diversity initiatives of US multinational corporations in Europe. In: Thunderbird International Business Review, 45(6), 701-727.

Harrison, D. / Klein, K. (2007): What's the difference?: Diversity constructs as separation, variety, or disparity in organizations. In: Academy of Management Review, 32(4), 1199-1228.

Kirton, G. / Greene, A.M. (2010): The dynamics of managing diversity: A critical approach. Oxford.

Litvin, D. (1997): The discourse of diversity: From biology to management. In: Organization, 4 (2), 187-209.

Nishii, L. / Özbilgin, M. (2007): Global diversity management: towards a conceptual framework. In: International Journal of Human Resource Management, 18(11), 1883-1894.

Salk, J. / Brannen, M.Y. (2000): National culture, networks, and individual influence in a multinational management team. In: Academy of Management Journal, 43(2), 191-202.

Sippola, A. / Smale, A. (2007): The global integration of diversity management: a longitudinal case study. In: International Journal of Human Resource Management, 18(11), 1895-1916.

Suss, S. / Kleiner, M. (2007): Diversity management in Germany: Dissemination and design of the concept. In: International Journal of Human Resource Management, 18(11), 1934-1953.

Syed, J. (2007): 'The other woman' and the question of equal opportunity in Australian organizations. In: International Journal of Human Resource Management, 18(11), 1954-1978.

Takagi, J. / Gröschl, S. (2007): The Diversity of Diversity: Exploring Different Meanings of Diversity. Presented at EGOS Colloquium 2007, Vienna.

Changing minds, changing attitudes: The role of the individual in diversity change processes

Asli-Juliya Weheliye

The diversity approach is a strategy to induce and further change processes regarding the establishment of equal opportunities in organisations. Tackling and changing inequalities on a structural and personal level requires an overall cultural change. In this context corresponding practical measures, such as mentoring programmes, employee networks, etc. are often implemented by organisations. However, most of them fail to accomplish a real organisational change since they ignore important parts of organisational culture that have to be taken into account while dealing with changes. In particular the role of the individual is often ignored in the implementation process (employees, managers, executives and other stakeholders). Individuals determine formal and informal behavioural codes, norms and rules; they also define sublime power structures and hierarchies. If the diversity concept aims at changing traditional organisational cultures by opening them to members of minority groups, it has to break persisting normative values and rules. This paper will discuss change management processes in the framework of a diversity strategy by focusing on the crucial role of the individual. In this context awareness raising activities, in particular diversity training, will be portrayed in more detail and it will be discussed whether they are a useful instrument in changing attitudes and perceptions of individuals and, thereby, function as a driving force to promote cultural change within an organisation.

1. Starting Point

Diversity management is becoming a more and more common term in theory and practice around the globe. The concept aims at eliminating all forms of discrimination within an organisation and fostering an organisational culture of respect and open exchange. Dealing proactively and successfully with differences and equal opportunities in organisations comes with change processes that have to be properly managed. Since the implementation of a comprehensive diversity strategy requires essential changes within an organisation, affecting its culture, structures and individuals in equal measure, it becomes apparent that these change processes have to be professionally monitored and accompanied. However, in most diversity strategies the role of the individual stays somehow ignored; organisations are introducing all kinds of measures such as mentoring programmes, employee networks, diversity days or awareness campaigns, yet the question remains how these activities and programmes can positively affect individual attitudes and perceptions towards diversity and equal opportunities in general, in particular those persons who are in power.

Implementing a comprehensive diversity strategy includes the scrutiny and, most probably, change of old behavioural patterns in organisations (Cox / Blake 1991). Therefore the mere implementation of a diversity strategy with corresponding measures does not necessarily guarantee success, since change processes require more than just the simple introduction of several new activities that address diversity issues (Palmer / Dunford / Akin 2006). It will not substitute the need for a critical appraisal and fundamental alteration of organisational structures and the involvement of all members of an organisation. This could be, in particular, a challenge for homogeneous and monocultural organisations in which a dominant group defines the values, rules and norms for every organisational member and occupies most of the executive positions (Vedder 2007). In this context the implementation of diversity strategies will meet resistance and scepticism, since changing structures and organisational culture presupposes also the questioning and reallocation of power relations within an organisation.

The paper does not aim at providing a common solution for all organisations in this matter, but rather raises some important questions and offers insights into the topic. Furthermore, it will discuss the role of the individual in change management processes of diversity strategies by highlighting their connection to cultural change. Diversity workshops as instruments of awareness raising and personnel development will be used as examples of good practice on how to acknowledge the crucial role of the individual in this process and to induce change on a personal level, thereby affecting structural and cultural layers of an organisation as well.

2. Diversity Management - a successful concept to foster change processes?

The main objective of diversity management is to eliminate all forms of discrimination and to establish a culture of open exchange and appreciation where individuals can work to their fullest potential. According to Thomas (1991) diversity management is "(…) a comprehensive managerial process for developing an environment that works for all employees". The concept is an answer to changed economical, legal and cultural conditions, globalisation and individualisation of lifestyles, and is related to management practices that deal with changing demographics of employees and inequalities at the work-place (Gatrell / Swan 2009). It is a managerial concept which exceeds mana-gerial responsibilities; meaning that the elimination of all types of discrimina-tion constitutes a normative demand, which addresses the joint responsibility of every single member of an organisation. Therefore, diversity management begins with the identity and performance of an individual, is economically legitimised and legally not binding (Krell 2001b). One pragmatic goal of managing diversity is to capitalise on the strengths of a diverse workforce, eliminate discriminatory behaviour, decrease law suits and reduce interper-sonal conflict (Cox 1993). There are various different interests by multiple stakeholders regarding the objectives, meanings and outcomes of a diversity strategy and what defines, legitimises and categorises heterogeneity within organisations (Özbilgin / Tatli 2008). Therefore, an exclusive definition of diversity management is complicated, since its interpretations vary enor-mously depending on the context of an organisation and/or perspective of an interest group. These ambiguities have to be taken into account when imple-menting a diversity strategy, while the organisation has to define its own un-derstanding of diversity. In general promoting and realising a diversity stra-tegy within an organisation starts and ends with the support and consent of its members and thus highly depends on awareness raising among them. Hence, it becomes apparent that individuals play a central role in this change process and should be included as early as possible.

The concept of change management seems to be suitable in this context to observe how to increase change, in this case promoting equal opportuni-ties, within an organisation. If a diversity strategy is considered as a change management process within an organisation, it can also be defined as a stra-tegy of a planned and systematical change that originates in the inducement of organisational structure and culture as well as individual behaviour (Kraus / Becker-Kolle / Fischer 2004). Thus diversity management not only aims at changing the organisational culture but also its structure and the individual behaviour of its members – however, not in a normative way. Consequently a sustainable diversity approach in the context of change management should acknowledge the interdependency between individuals, groups, organisation, society, time and communication patterns, norms, values as well as power relations, which preside within the organisation (Kraus / Becker-Kolle / Fischer 2004).

Traditionally, the term *organisational culture* can be defined as basic as-sumptions, values and norms, which have developed in the course of time and are assertive for all members of an organisation (Schein 1984). The em-phasis on normative values and conduct in this definition contradicts the idea of valuing heterogeneity and differences in the diversity concept. Here, the focus lies on valuing differences and heterogeneity while focusing on the benefits of a diverse workforce (European Commission 2005). Accordingly the diversity approach aims at breaking down these patterns and opens up to diverse ideas, perspectives and perceptions. Consequently, the classical concept of organisational culture by Schein is not suitable in the framework of the diversity concept. If people bring different values, perceptions and behavioural styles to the organisation, it will become more difficult to find common ground regarding basic paradigms or working styles which are suitable for every member of the organisation. It becomes even more complicated if hitherto ignored interest groups are suddenly included in defining new paradigms and norms that are applicable for all members of the organisation.

As figure 1 points out, there are various interdependences between the elements that comprise an organisational culture. Johnson (1998) describes the culture of an organisation by using the model of a "cultural web" (Palmer / Dunford / Akin 2006). The "cultural web" thus presents an organisational culture consisting of seven essential elements (Johnson 1998; Palmer / Dunford / Akin 2006): The central element, the *paradigm*, is described as the collection of common assumptions dominant within an organisation regarding basic elements of business or organisational targets such as market, competitors, etc..

Figure 1: Gerry Johnson, 1998 Cultural Web

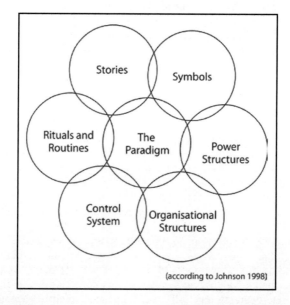

Rituals and routines refer to basic beliefs, behavioural rules and norms that members of an organisation (sub)-consciously share with each other.

Through *stories* the history, and often the myths and traditions of the organisation, are emphasised, communicated and passed on to new generations of employees. *Symbols* are used to impart crucial aspects of culture, such as corporate design, dress code or language, whereas *control systems* determine what is valued and sanctioned by the organisation. The *organisational structure* comprises the extent of formal and informal incorporation of assignments, while *power structures* address influential social groups who define rules and norms within the organisation. According to Johnson (1998) the mapping of aspects, which comprise organisational culture can be helpful to identify existing barriers to change as well as to question and analyse the status quo of the organisation, which is usually taken for granted. Furthermore the map of organisational culture can also serve as a basis for targeting the changes that need to occur in order to successfully pursue a new strategy and to eventually develop and implement new ideas.

Transferred to the diversity management concept the cultural web model represents a helpful visualisation of the main areas the diversity concept has to target for serious change of organisational culture. It makes lucid that it takes more than simple measures to change a whole organisational culture. Informal rules and norms, subtle codes and behavioural customs as well as unconscious and well established decision-making processes and power relations have to be scrutinised, questioned, modified or changed. The role and power of the individual and group has to be emphasised since the willingness for change is more likely to increase if there is consent on the reason for change, members of an organisation are included in the development of the change concept, the change is approved collectively and the change is made tangible (Schreyögg 2002). That is the most difficult and challenging objective in diversity management. Yet, most organisations fail to accomplish this goal, since they are not able to change attitudes, perceptions, bias and behavioural styles of their members. In this regard diversity workshops can be an efficient instrument to induce change on a personal level, starting at the individual perception of members of an organisation. They are often used to sensitise and educate individuals for gender and diversity issues and to give them an easy entrance into the topic.

3. Diversity Awareness Workshops – Helpful instruments to foster cultural change?

In general diversity training strives to underline, further and facilitate the overall objectives of diversity management such as eliminating discrimination, raising awareness for injustice, fostering equal opportunities or

94   Asli-Juliya Weheliye

emphasising the benefits of a diverse workforce (Medik / Sanchez 2004).
Addressing topics such as exclusion, discrimination or power relations within
an organisation is not an easy task, since these issues affect not only the professional lives of members of an organisation but also have a deep impact on
their personal lives and identities. Consequently there is an overlapping of
professional and personal roles, which cannot be seen as separated from each
other anymore. Experiences of discrimination and exclusion happen in both
spheres and influence people's behaviour extensively. Therefore, these topics
have to be addressed sensitively, with good instinct and professional support.
It should be acknowledged that people will no longer be able to separate their
personal from their professional experiences when dealing with these issues
and as a consequence might also refuse to reflect on certain opinions and
perceptions.

  Members of an organisation are often not aware of the existing diversity
within the workforce, and that discrimination and exclusion exist on the
grounds of certain individual traits. Therefore, workshops can be a useful
instrument to raise awareness on diversity issues in the workplace and to introduce the topic of diversity to members of an organisation through specific
exercises that evoke certain feelings regarding discrimination and prejudices
and that simulate real life scenarios of exclusion and discrimination. In diversity training people usually get information about the topics of minorities,
discrimination, privileges, exclusion and inclusion, which may reduce bias in
general (Fiske 1998). The main objective is to enhance the level of awareness
for injustices by addressing issues of discrimination and exclusion and dis-
playing and communicating the complexity of one's identity. Furthermore, it
is intended to create an understanding and awareness for differences among
members of an organisation and to show which role homogeneity and
adaptability play in the work environment. Cultural identity activities are
often used as a way to raise personal awareness; and to become sensitive of
one's own cultural assumptions and biases. Once people reflect on their own
role within society there is a chance that they also become aware of certain
power structures and the relations affecting the position of minority groups in
society and organisations.

  Even though the level of self-reflection is highly important in awareness
raising processes, it is even more crucial to convey to individuals the essential tools needed to transfer their knowledge to the level of positive action.
The conveyance of knowledge on diversity issues is just a prerequisite that
gives a person the ability to change his/her attitude or behaviour towards different groups of people but does not necessarily have to change their behaviour in general. As Rasmussen (1996) states, the workshop itself will not
change anything but rather the fact what people will do with their new
knowledge and skills afterwards. Accordingly, the actual knowledge transfer
to real behavioural change represents the crucial component while raising

awareness among members of an organisation. It becomes apparent that workshops alone will not make the crucial difference when striving for a culture of respect and open exchange. One objective of awareness raising should be then to develop individuals' skills regarding diversity related issues that succeed the level of sensitisation and actually give people helpful tools to convert their knowledge on diversity issues to positive action. The objective is to develop actual skills for the interaction in a heterogonous workforce, such as intercultural competence, conflict management, flexibility, or empathy. The conveyance of knowledge and skills can comprise specific thematic components like homophobia, racism, sexism, ageism, or islamophobia as well as practical tools on transparent performance appraisals, diverse recruitment strategies or successful intervention practices. Also specific common objectives can be developed together in a team and afterwards jointly pursued through an action plan if the objective is to improve teamwork.

However, there are also certain risks in raising awareness regarding diversity issues in an organisation. In particular training workshops can become a minefield when certain risks are ignored. There is a possibility that stereotypes can be reinforced in heterogeneous groups and some participants might feel excluded on the basis of their identity, or they can be taken as representatives of their identity group (if they are, for example, the only black person or woman). It can also occur that issues of minority groups differ too much from each other and that the topics cannot be covered in the same training, e.g. racism, sexism or homophobia. Consequently, the content of diversity workshops should be adapted to the needs of the group and target groups should be addressed differently; e.g. trainings with managers or trainees should have different objectives. Managers will more likely focus on their leadership skills and styles towards their team members, whereas training for trainees will have to focus more on the conveyance of key competencies to work in a diverse setting.

An emphasis on differences can lead to the reinforcement of stereotypes or to misunderstandings and tensions between groups or individuals rather than reducing stress and conflict. It should always be communicated that dealing with diversity issues does not necessarily imply to be preoccupied only with differences between individuals, but rather focuses on finding similarities among them. Another crucial point is a safe environment in which people feel free to express their feelings and points of view; if people are forced to reveal personal information such as stereotypes or identity issues, they might feel insecure and ashamed and will not be able to open up. In this case it has to be clearly communicated that every person has stereotypes and that it is important to be aware of them in order to change them. Also mandatory training can lead to resentment and rejection of the workshop, in particular if the objectives of the event were not properly communicated beforehand and if people feel that they are being punished for their behaviour. It is also quite common that only those members of an organisation attend a workshop that are already sensitive to and/or interested in the topic. Those persons who show ignorant tendencies often do not feel addressed by voluntary workshops. Hence, if an organisation intends to raise awareness comprehensively among the workforce, diversity issues should also be addressed in other human resources development measures apart from the "real" diversity workshops such as in leadership, management, or social skills seminars. Diversity issues could be addressed as a cross-sectional topic in various fields and, therefore, initiate a first contact with the topic and decrease scepticism. An organisation could also motivate its members to engage in the topic by offering incentives or other benefits.

The last important point to consider is the fact that people often participate in a training with the expectation that afterwards they will be free of stereotypes and prejudices – basically a perfect non-discriminatory human being. However that is not the case and it will never be; dealing with injustice and exclusion on a personal and organisational level is a life-learning process that has to be clearly communicated within the workforce.

If a workshop is professionally organised and the trainers are taking all possible risks into account, the results can be quite positive for the organisation. If professionally planned, monitored and accompanied (before and afterwards) diversity trainings can trigger a change of perception and behaviour towards differences and, consequently, reduce exclusive behaviour within an organisation. This can lead to the improvement of working conditions through better understanding of others and increase empathy among colleagues and employees. Accordingly, interpersonal relationships can improve and people might start to commit to diversity objectives and participate in developing and planning further actions in their team or department.

4. Conclusion

Change processes, in terms of the diversity concept, can be seen as complex and intangible. The objective to eliminate all forms of discriminations seems somehow quite idealistic and unattainable if one considers the actual work that needs to be done in order to accomplish this goal. Changing perceptions and attitudes of individuals is a mission that will affect personal as well as professional lives of individuals, in particular those persons who are in power. The change has to influence all parts of the organisation and its culture; e.g. power relations or rituals and routines have to be reconsidered, analysed and changed. It is crucial that change has to be induced on different levels of the organisation affecting both its structures and individuals at the same time. Additionally a cultural change has to be embedded in a strategy that combines the different interests of the various stakeholders. To this end, different interest groups have to be included in the change process and should have the opportunity to participate in articulating new objectives that seem reasonable to all of them. Consequently, this will lead to a culture of critical exchange as well as to a positive identification with the organisation.

Diversity workshops can have the capability to set off at different levels of an organisational culture and to further change by providing members of an organisation the opportunity to reflect on diversity issues from different perspectives, in particular on one's own identity as well as on power relations and inequalities within the organisation. However the effectiveness of these workshops is often questionable since variables of success differ enormously and behavioural changes are in general difficult to assess (Gieselmann / Krell 2001). Unfortunately, there is a paucity of empirical research on the effects of diversity training and its impact on interpersonal behaviour (Medik / Sanchez 2004; Larkey 1996). If an organisation decides to raise awareness through the offer of diversity workshops it should take into account certain facts. Firstly, trainings should not be limited to one day or a couple of hours and should not present single measures of a diversity strategy; moreover, they have to be part of an overall strategy which fosters equal opportunities within an organisation, e.g. training, policies, compensation, performance appraisals, monitoring, diversity evaluation (feedback), mentoring, interest groups, or employee networks. Secondly, it should be clear that developing diversity competence is a process which requires awareness, skill-building and positive action as well as a combination of both cognitive and organisational learning. Therefore, the actual transition of the knowledge takes place after the workshop at the workplace and within the team and represents, somewhat, the crucial part of change - the personal change. Workshops are not a universal remedy but they can be a starting point to induce a change of mind and eventually further cultural change in particular on an individual level, thereby affecting other important aspects of organisational culture.

References

Cox, T. (1993): Cultural diversity in organizations: Theory, research, and practice. San Francisco.

Cox, T. H. / Blake, S. (1991): Managing cultural diversity: Implications for organizational competitiveness. The Executive, 5(3):45-56.

Emmerich, A. / Krell, G. (2001): Diversity Trainings: Verbesserung der Zusammenarbeit und Führung einer vielfältigen Belegschaft. In: Krell, G., (Eds.): Chancengleichheit durch Personalpolitik. Gleichstellung von

Männern und Frauen in Unternehmen und Verwaltungen. Rechtliche Regelungen - Problemanalysen – Lösungen. Wiesbaden, 421-441.

Fiske, S. T. (1998): Stereotyping, prejudice, and discrimination. In: Fiske, S. T.,Gilbert, D. T. and Lindzey, G., (Eds.): The handbook of social psychology. New York.

Gatrell, C. J. / Swan, S. E. (2008): Gender and Diversity in Management: A Concise Introduction. London.

Johnson, G. (1998): Mapping and re-mapping organizational culture. In: Ambrosini, V./ Johnson, G. / Scholes, K., (Eds.): Exploring techniques of analysis and evaluation in strategic management New York.

Kraus, G. / Becker-Kolle, C. / Fischer, T. (2004): Handbuch Change-Management - Steuerung von Veränderungsprozessen in Organisationen. Berlin.

Krell, G. (2001a): Chancengleichheit durch Personalpolitik: Gleichstellung von Frauen und Männern in Unternehmen und Verwaltungen. Rechtliche Regelungen - Problemanalysen - Lösungen. Wiesbaden.

Krell, G. (2001b): Managing Diversity: Chancengleichheit als Wettbewerbsfaktor. In: Krell, G., (Ed.): Chancengleichheit durch Personalpolitik: Gleichstellung von Frauen und Männern in Unternehmen und Verwaltungen. Rechtliche Regelungen - Problemanalysen - Lösungen. Wiesbaden.

Larkey, L. K. (1996): Towards a theory of communicative interactions in culturally diverse workgroups. Academy of Management Review, 21(2):463-491.

Özbilgin, M. / Tatli, A. (2008): Global Diversity Management: An Evidence-Based Approach. New York.

Palmer, I. / Dunford, R. / Gib, A. (2006): Managing Organizational Change: A Multiple Perspectives Approach. New York.

Rasmussen, T. (1996): The ASTD Trainer's Sourcebook: Diversity. New York.

Sanchez, J. I. / Medkik, N. (2004): The effects of diversity awareness training on differential treatment. Group & Organization Management, 29(4):517.

Schein, E. H. (1984): Coming to a new awareness of corporate culture. Sloan Management Review, 26(Winter):3-16.

Schreyögg, G. (2000): Neuere Entwicklungen im Bereich des Organisatorischen Wandels. In: Busch, R., (Ed.): Change Management und Unternehmenskultur: Konzepte in der Praxis. München und Mering.

Thomas, R. (1991): Beyond Race and Gender: Unleashing the Power of Your Total Work Force by Managing Diversity. New York.

Vedder, G. (2007): Managing Equity and Diversity at Universities. München.

The contribution of diversity management to create a supportive working climate for gays and lesbians

Thomas Köllen

In the German speaking countries and on an international level, "sexual orienttation" is the most denied core dimension of workforce diversity in business research and practice (Krell et al. 2006; Tonks 2006). For employers, the most important parameter for attracting and retaining homosexual employees is the perceived working climate for gays and lesbians. The aim of this article is to analyse to what extent the nine most implemented measures of diversity management programmes that focus on "sexual orientation" positively influence the working climate for gays and lesbians. The analysis is based on the structural climate approach (Phesey et al. 1971).

The empirical basis of the analysis is data taken from an online survey conducted the beginning of 2008 in Germany. A total of 2322 gays and lesbians took part in the survey and the analysis focuses on a partial sample of 487 homosexual employees. The survey considered the existence of particular diversity measures at the workplace on the basis of the catalogue from Köllen (2007). The working climate was measured by using the 20 items containing LGBTCI (Lesbian, Gay, Bisexual and Transgender Climate Inventory) from Liddle et al. (2004). The interrelation of the concrete diversity measures and the workplace climate was analysed by a multi-stage regression model. The existence of the diversity measures were taken as independent variables and the LGBTCI was taken as dependent variable.

The significant result is that, more than 25% of the total variation of the perceived working climate can be explained by concrete diversity management measures. The equal acceptance of marriages and registered life-partnerships has by far the biggest positive impact on the perceived working climate and, therefore, is a suitable initial point for organisations that are starting to integrate "sexual orientation" into their diversity activities.

1. Introduction

In German speaking countries "sexual orientation" is still a highly taboo dimension within the economic discourse of diversity and diversity management. Analysing German speaking business research projects in the field of diversity and diversity management, Krell et al. (2006) show that between 2001 and 2006, no research projects were conducted on "sexual orientation".

According to their study, the most examined dimensions of diversity have been gender, age and culture (including ethnicity and nationality) (see Krell et al. 2006). The same situation occurs in German practice. Although one can observe a generally increasing diffusion of diversity management concepts in German practice over the last five years, "sexual orientation" is still the most denied core-dimension of diversity in companies' and organisations' diversity policies - compared to age, gender, mental and physical abilities, ethnicity, race and religion (Köllen 2007). It can be stated that the bigger a company is the more probable is the integration of the dimension "sexual orientation" into its diversity programme. Table 1 gives an overview of diversity activities of the German DAX-listed companies.

22 out of 30 Dax-listed companies follow some kind of diversity management strategy, but only seven companies estimate the dimension "sexual orientation" as a relevant field of action. In this context, the integration of the wording of the German "General Equal Treatment Act – AGG" into a corporate code of conduct and the signing of the "Charter of Diversity" do not constitute an explicit integration of the dimension "sexual orientation" because there are no concrete measures related to this, but rather mere commitments.[1]

The measures implemented by these seven companies can be subsumed under four categories. The first category is *networks* - five out of seven companies have established officially supported gay and lesbian employee networks. The second category is *corporate guidelines* that equalize registered gay and lesbian life-partnerships and heterosexual marriages in terms of corporate benefits to different extents. *Sponsorship and gay marketing* - the third category - mainly appears in public relations, through advertising in lesbian and gay media or through visible presence at gay and lesbian events like pride parades or parties. The fourth category is *sensitization and thematization*, and includes intra-company communication via intranet or employee magazines and the integration of gay and lesbian issues in management training (see Köllen 2007). Other companies that have integrated "sexual orientation" in their overall diversity program in Germany for instance are Ford (Alvarez 2007), Deutsche Bahn (Heuer / Engel 2006) and - unlike its parent company - Volkswagen Financial Services.

Analyzing the significance of "sexual orientation" as a diversity dimension in research and practice on an international level, Tonks (2006) arrives at the same findings. Questioning why so few business researchers and economists work on issues that are related to sexual orientation, Klawitter (1998) finds four different barriers as answers: "discrimination against sexual

---

1   The "Charter of Diversity" (dt.: Charta der Vielfalt) is the German adaptation of the French "charte de la diversité". It is a general commitment to recognize and appreciate diversity and to create a workplace climate that is free from prejudices. In signing this agreement companies do not have to fear any kind of sanction or penalty. Out of the DAX-listed companies only Beiersdorf, BMW, Fresenius, K+S, Linde, MAN, Merck, Münchener Rück and Salzgitter did not sign the Charter up to now (April 2010).

minorities, the lack of interest and knowledge about sexual orientation, the absence of support for this research, and the scarcity of appropriate models and data" (Klawitter 1998: 55).

Focusing on the impact concrete diversity measures have on the perceived working climate for gays and lesbians, this article and the underlying research project contribute to close this research gap. Economically, this research focus is of enormous relevance, because for employers the working climate can be seen as one of the most important parameters for attracting and retaining homosexual employees. Taking into account that between 4% and 17% of the population and, thus, also of the workforce does not live exclusively heterosexually (Lubensky et al. 2006) this is an important issue for all organisations. Theoretically this article follows the structural approach to working climate.

Table 1: The diffusion of diversity management among DAX-listed companies and the integration of the dimension "sexual orientation" in existing programs

DAX-listed Company (December 2009)	Diversity Management (in Germany)	"Sexual Orientation" as Diversity Dimension
Adidas AG	X	
Allianz AG	X	
BASF AG	X	
Bayer AG	X	
Beiersdorf AG	X	
BMW AG	X	
Commerzbank AG	X	X
Daimler AG	X	X
Deutsche Bank AG	X	X
Deutsche Börse AG		
Deutsche Lufthansa AG	X	X
Deutsche Post AG	X	X
Deutsche Telekom AG	X	X
E.ON AG	X	
Fresenius Medical Care AG & Co KGaA		
Fresenius SE		
Henkel KGaA	X	
Infineon Technologies AG		
K+S AG		
Linde AG	X	
MAN AG		
Merck KGaA	X	
Metro AG	X	
Münchener Rück AG	X	
RWE AG	X	
Salzgitter AG		
SAP AG	X	X
Siemens AG	X	
ThyssenKrupp AG	X	
Volkswagen AG		

Source: Köllen 2010: 37

2. Theoretical framework

Moran and Volkwein (1992) define a very broad approach to the phenomenon of climate:

"Organizational climate is a relatively enduring characteristic of an organization which distinguishes it from other organizations: and (1) embodies members collective perceptions about their organization with respect to such dimensions as autonomy, trust, cohesiveness, support, recognition, innovation, and fairness; (b) is produced by member interaction; (c) serves as a basis for interpreting the situation; (d) reflects the prevalent norms values and attitudes of the organization's culture; and (e) acts as a source of influence for shaping behavior" (Moran / Volkwein 1992: 20).

Their definition combines the structural, perceptual, and interactive climate approach and offers in addition a cultural approach (Moran / Volkwein 1992). In order to analyse the interrelation of diversity management measures and the perceived working climate, the structural aspects of working climate are the most important. The structural approach assumes that the organisational climate primarily results from organisational conditions and organisational characteristics. These characteristics influence the individual perception of the members of the organisation, and the climate, therefore, is derivable as a verifiable aspect of the organization (Payne / Pugh 1976). The influence of the individual's personality on the perception of the workplace climate is not denied but the emphasis of this article is put on structural determinants. Therefore, the concrete measures of diversity management that are related to sexual orientation are considered as structural aspects of the organisation in the following paper.

3. Research Method

For research projects on homosexuality in social sciences, Sullivan and Losberg (2003) identified three different research methods that follow different criteria for collecting and analysing data. They distinguish between quantitative research, qualitative research and queer studies. Most of the studies and research projects use qualitative methods or approaches of queer studies (Gamson 2000). In terms of sampling, a random sample is the most representative type of data collection, but in the area of research on homosexuality there are several difficulties. First of all, it has to be clarified when a person can be categorized as gay or lesbian. Furthermore, in a lot of areas of life, homosexuality still has a stigmatizing effect that complicates access to the field. For fear of discrimination they can refuse to self-identify as homosexual and to take part in a survey. Therefore, research projects on homosexuality, most of the time, are not based on random samples (Sullivan / Losberg 2003). Because of the scarcity of quantitative business research on homosexuality in German speaking countries, this project chose a quantitative approach. An online questionnaire was used and the working climate was measured by employing the 20 items containing LGBTCI (Lesbian, Gay, Bisexual and Transgender Climate Inventory) from Liddle et al. (2004). The LGBTCI measures formal and informal aspects of workplace climate, and it can have a value between 20 and 80 that corresponds to a perceived working climate for gays and lesbians ranging from hostile to supportive. Using the translation - back translation method (Harkness 2003) the item catalogue was transferred into German. The internal consistency (or reliability) of the German catalogue is checked by a cronbachs alpha value that is even higher than the value of the English catalogue (0.96 compared to 0.95). For measuring the prevalence of diversity management measures related to sexual orientation the study referred to a catalogue from Köllen (2007). In concrete terms, the existence of the following was asked for:

- organisational equalization policies of life-partnerships and marriages in general (life_part_gen),
- organisational equalization of life-partnerships[2] and marriages as for the company pension plan (life_part_pens),
- organisational equalization of life-partnerships and marriages as for extended benefits of the health insurance (life_part_health),
- the integration of gay and lesbian issues in management trainings (training),
- mentoring programmes for gays and lesbians (mentoring),
- lesbian and gay marketing activities (marketing),
- an official lesbian and gay (or: LGBTCI-) network in the organisation (network_of),
- a non-official lesbian and gay (or: LGBTCI-) network in the organisation (network_inof),
- activities that make homosexuality a topic within the organisation (e.g. articles in the intranet or in magazines, etc.) (thematization).

In addition, demographic data was collected. The question of categorizing the sexuality and gender of the participants was solved by a self-declaratory approach. The analysis only contains data from participants that define themselves as gay or lesbian.

---

2   In Germany the name for registered unions of same sex partners is "eingetragene Lebens-partnerschaft".

4. Data collection and data analysis

The online survey was conducted at the beginning of 2008 in Germany. For proofing and adjusting the questionnaire, a pre-test was conducted in January. Participants of a discussion meeting organised by the German lesbian and gay association (LSVD) in Frankfurt/Main were asked to fill out and to comment on the questionnaire. 34 gays and lesbians complied with the request. As a result, minor modifications regarding ambiguous wording were made. To reach a large number of gays and lesbians, and to avoid a regional bias within Germany, five experts from different regions of Germany were asked to list lesbian and gay web forums, associations and representatives of interest. Furthermore, individual-related contact data of all German regional and nationwide lesbian and gay journals, newspapers, radio shows and their websites were selected. 71 letters of inquiry containing the link to the online questionnaire and a short presentation of the study background were sent to the representatives. They were asked to broadly distribute the request, and most of them supported the study by integrating the call for participants into their newsletters, websites or printed journals. The online-questionnaire was activated in February and March, and by the end of March 2322 gays and lesbians had taken part in the survey, with 63% of the participants identified themselves as lesbians and 37% as gay.

The following analysis focuses on a partial sample of 487 homosexual employees. The partial sample contains the data from the participants that indicated valid values for all diversity measures ranging from 1 (= exists for sure) to 4 (= does not exist for sure). The 5-coded value (= I do not know) had to be defined as missing value - otherwise a metric usage of the scaling could not be ensured.

The interrelation of the concrete diversity measures and the workplace climate was analyzed by a multi-stage regression model. The existence of the diversity measures were taken as independent variables and the LGBTCI was taken as dependent variable.

5. Results and discussion

The results of the multi-stage regression are outlined in Table 2.

Statistically, the Durbin-Watson Value of 1.913 indicates that there is no autocorrelation of the residues. Four measures of diversity management have a positive impact on the perceived working climate for lesbians and gays. 26.8% of the individual variances of climate perceptions can be explained by these measures. Taking into account that, besides these concrete organisational aspects, there are more organisational, individual-psychological, biographic and cultural factors that influence the personal estimation of the working climate for gays and lesbians, 26.8 % has to be categorized as a high value.

Table 2: Model Summary of the multiple regression analysis

Model	R	R^2	Adjusted R^2	Std Error of the Estimate	R^2 Change	F Change	df1	df2	Sig. F Change	Durbin-Watson
					Change Statistics					
1	.430(a)	0.185	0.183	12.50129	0.185	109.936	1	485	0.000	
2	.488(b)	0.238	0.235	12.09992	0.053	33.710	1	484	0.000	
3	.510(c)	0.260	0.256	11.93400	0.022	14.551	1	483	0.000	
4	.518(d)	0.268	0.262	11.88404	0.008	5.070	1	482	0.025	1.913

a. Predictors: (Constant), life_part_gen
b. Predictors: (Constant), life_part_gen, thematization
c. Predictors: (Constant), life_part_gen, thematization, life_part_pens
d. Predictors: (Constant), life_part_gen, thematization, life_part_pens, marketing
e. Dependent Variable: LGBTCI

The equalization of life-partnerships and marriages has by far the biggest impact – the R^2 value of 0.185 in model 1 indicates that 18.5% of the variances in working climate perception can be explained by this measure. Furthermore, the thematization of homosexuality accompanied by an organisational de-tabooing of homosexuality contributes to an amelioration of the perceived working climate. Articles in staff magazines or in the intranet can be examples of such thematizations. A minor impact on the working climate emanates from the concrete equalization, as for example the company pension plan and the existence of gay marketing activities. The low impact of the equalization of the right to a pension can be explained by its high correlation with the item of general equalization policies, whereas gay marketing represents a totally different kind of diversity measure. The knowledge of the existence of an external gay marketing strategy by the participant's organisation, therefore, positively effects the perception of the internal climate. Apparently, a measure that primarily targets and appreciates lesbians and gays as customers, simultaneously positively effects the perceived appreciation of gay and lesbian employees.

On the other hand, both gay and lesbian networks and management trainings only have a small and not significant influence on the perceived working climate. But it has to be considered that networks very often are the starting point for companies that implement sexual orientation related diversity strategies and, therefore, these networks very often jumpstart equalization policies and marketing activities (Köllen 2010). Thus, their value for enhancing organisational climate for homosexual employees can be described as meaningful. Primarily, for the working climate, the function of the networks is not based on the social capital approach (Bourdieu 1983) but on their ability to actively initiate organisational changing processes. Networks that do not have such competences and room for manoeuvre are of no importance for the organisational climate. Just as unimportant for the climate are mentoring programmes for gays and lesbians.

6. Conclusion

Considering the importance of the working climate for gays and lesbians to recruit and to retain homosexual employees for employers, it is worthwhile implementing diversity management measures that are related to "sexual orientation". As a possible first step the organisation should equalize life-partnerships (there are other expressions for this in other countries) and marriages, or the organisation should establish a gay and lesbian network and entitle it with far-reaching responsibilities to continue the implementation process. In Germany there is a certain pressure to accelerate the implementation of equalization policies because of recent adjudication based on the "General Equal Treatment Act – AGG". There are several indicators that discrimination of life-partnerships cannot be legitimized anymore by the special protection of marriages (as part of the German constitution) in the future. It can be assumed that, an equalization policy that only follows the law will not have the same positive effect on the working climate as an equalization-policy that seems to be implemented as a result of the organisations' belief and as a "free" decision. Among the gay and lesbian employees, the latter would be much more likely to provide the perception of being appreciated. Therefore, an implementation of an extensive equalization policy in the very near future pays off for employers.

References

Alvarez, A. (2007): Praxisbeispiel Ford-Werke GmbH, Köln: Erfolgreiche Implementierung von Diversity Management. In: Krell, G. (Ed.): Chancengleichheit durch Personalpolitik. Gleichstellung von Frauen und Männern in Unternehmen und Verwaltungen. Rechtliche Regelungen - Problemanalysen – Lösungen. Wiesbaden, 81-88.
Bourdieu, P. (1983): Ökonomisches Kapital - Kulturelles Kapital - Soziales Kapital. In: Kreckel, R. (Ed.): Soziale Welt, Soziale Ungleichheiten - Sonderband 2, 183-198.

Gamson, J. (2000): Sexualities, Queer Theory and Qualitative Research. In: Denzin, N. / Lincoln, Y.: Handbook of Qualitative Research. Thousand Oaks, 347-365.

Harkness, J. (2003): Questionnaire Translation. In: Harkness, Janet A. / van de Vijver, F. / Mohler, P. (2003): Cross-cultural Survey Methods. New York, 35-56.

Heuer, K. / Engel, E. (2006): Diversity Management bei der Deutschen Bahn AG - Ein Beitrag zur Kundenzufriedenheit. In: Becker, M. / Seidel, A.: Diversity Management. Unternehmens- und Personalpolitik der Vielfalt. Stuttgart, 363-380.

Klawitter, M. M. (1998): Why aren't more economists doing research on sexual orientation? Feminist Economics 4 (2), 55-59.

Köllen, T. (2007): Part of the Whole? Homosexuality in Companies' Diversity Policies and in Business Research: Focus on Germany. The International Journal of Diversity in Organisations, Communities and Nations 7 (5), 315-322.

Köllen, T. (2009): Über den Umgang von Lesben und Schwulen mit der eigenen Homosexualität am Arbeitsplatz - der Zusammenhang von Diversity Management und arbeitsplatzbezogenen Selbstentwürfen. PhD. Vienna University of Economics and Business Administration.

Köllen, T. (2010): Bemerkenswerte Vielfalt: Homosexualität und Diversity Management - Betriebswirtschaftliche und sozialpsychologische Aspekte der Diversity-Dimension 'sexuelle Orientierung'. München / Mering.

Krell, G. / Wächter, H. / Pantelmann, H. (2006): Diversity(-Dimensionen) und deren Management als Gegenstände der Personalforschung in Deutschland, Österreich und der Schweiz. In: Krell, G. / Wächter, H. (Eds.): Diversity Management. Impulse aus der Personalforschung. München, / Mering, 25-56.

Liddle, B. J. / Luzzo, D. A. / Hauenstein, A. L. / Schuck, K. (2004): Construction and validation of the lesbian, gay, bisexual, and transgendered climate inventory. Journal Of Career Assessment 12 (1), 33-50.

Lubensky, M. / Holland, S. / Wiethoff, C. / Crosby, F. (2006): Diversity and Sexual Orientation: Including and Valuing Sexual Minorities in the Workplace. In: Stockdale, M. / Crosby F. (Eds.): The Psychology and Management of Workplace Diversity. Malden, Oxford, Carlton, 206-223.

Moran, E. T. / Volkwein, J. F. (1992): The Cultural Approach To The Formation Of Organizational-Climate. Human Relations 45 (1), 19-47.

Payne, P. / Pugh, D. S. (1976): Organizational structure and climate. In: Dunnette, M. D. (Ed.): Handbook of industrial and organizational psychology. Chicago, 1125-1173.

Pheysey, D. C. / Payne, R. L. / Pugh, D. S. (1971): Influence Of Structure At Organizational And Group Levels. Administrative Science Quarterly 16 (1), 61-73.

Sullivan, G. / Losberg, W. (2003): A Study of Sampling in Research in the
Field of Lesbian and Gay Studies. In: Journal of Gay & Lesbian Social
Services, 2003, 15(1/2), 147-162.
Tonks, G. (2006): Sexual Identity: HRM's Invisible Dimension of Workplace
Diversity. The International Journal of Diversity in Organisations, Com-
munities & Nations 6 (1), 35-48.

Women's and men's implicit career theories: Prospects and barriers in women's professional development

Ann-Kathrin Vaske, Martin K.W. Schweer

The empirical study presented here focuses on the psychological construction of implicit career theories. From a dynamic-transactional perspective, these theories deal with normative expectations regarding successful professional interactions. This cognition is the result of previous (job-related) socialisation and, therefore, involves gender-typical experiences. Implicit theories are used to reduce social complexity as they structure social perception and provide orientation. Substantiated knowledge of employees' implicit career theories is necessary to establish instruments promoting women and men's careers in the context of human resource development (e.g. mentoring programmes). Initial empirical results, gathered during an ongoing dissertation project (qualitative guided interviews) on the implicit career theories of male and female employees at different hierarchical levels, underline important aspects when optimising the construction of gender-mainstreaming instruments in human resource development.

1. Barriers for women climbing the career ladder to management positions

Throughout Europe, women are less commonly found in management positions than men, both in the private and public sectors - the proportion of female managers in the European Union averaged around 32% in the year 2007, the number of female company board members was even lower (11% compared to 89% male members) in the year 2008 (European Commission 2009). This is in spite of women's relevant qualifications, which are equal to or better than their male colleagues (EACEA P9 Eurydice 2009). Possible reasons for this under-representation of women can be found in structural and situational conditions, as well as in the gender-typical characteristics of human resources.

The construction of 'career orientation'[1] describes the long-term professional efforts of certain persons, namely those with a preference for power,
promotion and high income. A facet of this is career motivation. For women,
career motivation drops during their career ladder progression; for men, it
rises somewhat (Maier et al. 2003). An important cause for this is the gender-
role-specific self-concept, in terms of assessing one's own performance. In
her study about the professional progression of female physicians, Sieverding
(1990) observed a discrepancy between the chronic self-concept and the professional self-concept at the end of the women's course of studies. Women
with a low professional self-confidence as well as low self-efficacy expectations especially showed this phenomenon. According to Sieverding's findings, a feminine self-concept, marked by low instrumentality and high ex-
pressivity parameters, is an essential career barrier for women. Similar research results suggest that, women tend to underestimate their own performance, considering it less successful than men do theirs (Ehrlinger / Dunning
2003; Sieverding 2003). This tendency is supported by corresponding attribution processes (Heider 1977), which for women are led more strongly along
lines of gender stereotypes: success is justified with reference to industriousness (thus variable); failure is regarded as proof that a task is inappropriate
for women (thus stable) (Jäckle 2008; see also Horstkemper 1992). This then
leads to further changes in the gender-role-specific self-concept.

Gender-specific prejudices are typically experienced by women as obstacles in their career ladder progression. Bischoff (2005) reports that 24% of
female managers questioned have experienced sexual discrimination. A further structural antecedent receiving research attention is the question of combining family and professional life. Habermann-Horstmeier (2007) identifies
two important impediments for women in their promotion from middle to
higher management: the lack of compatibility of family and workplace, and a
preference for male applicants. Therefore, women with children are correspondingly less likely to be found in management positions, where, in contrast, having children is an asset to men in their career paths (Kleinert et al.
2007). Only 32% of female mangers live in families with children, compared
to 53% of male managers (Kleinert 2006).

From a dynamic-transactional view (Mischel 2004) the complex interplay of personal and situational - structural antecedents has to be considered
when analysing the professional development of women and men. Only a few
present approaches like the social cognition concept BELA-M (Abele 2003)
take such an integrative concept into account.

---

1   The German term 'Karriere' is usually used in the sense of climbing up the career ladder,
     and not in the English sense of general professional development.

2. The psychological construction of implicit career theories

BELA-M shows how personal and situational conditions affect individual interactions and in the end influence action patterns (Abele 2003). In turn these action results - such as professional success or life satisfaction - have an impact on the personal and situational-structural conditions. Consequently, behavioural patterns always reflect the interpretation results regarding previous behaviour manners of interaction partners. In other words, our own behaviour is formed by the anticipated actions of our social environment (Blumer 1973).

BELA-M offers a model for the double influence of gender (Abele 2002a, b). This model demonstrates how gender shapes processes in work life from both the internal and external perspective. In the internal perspective, gender impacts as a psychological variable in terms of the gender-role specific self-concept: gender-typical professional and private goals, expectations and behaviour results. In the external perspective, gender impacts as a social category: by categorising an interaction partner as 'male' or 'female', professional interaction is structured. Existing role expectations are picked up on, this affects the self-definition, which influences action correspondingly, and thus confirms the external attribution (Abele 2003). Finally, certain ideas about professional success and career progression develop in this circular framework for action, and these structure both self and external perception. With reference to the constructions of 'implicit personality theories' (Bruner / Tagiuri 1954) or 'implicit leadership theories' (Eden / Leviatan 2005; Neubauer 1986), these ideas are termed implicit career theories (Schweer 2009). Implicit personality theories encompass individual assumptions about character traits and attitudes of interaction partners. Individuals develop prototypical associations of how an interaction partner is going to act in specific situations. Therefore, these expectations structure our perception as well as our actions. According to this, implicit leadership theories implicate cognitive representations about the prototype of a successful manager. According to Luhmann's understanding (1989), implicit personality and leadership theories can be viewed as elements of human information processing, providing orientation in a complex social environment.

Related to these psychological concepts, implicit career theories can be construed as a collection of subjective ideas about professional careers - what constitutes a satisfying and successful career? Women's and men's implicit career theories take form in the course of socialisation, primarily through socialisation in education and at the workplace and they determine professional aims and actions. We assume that these implicit career theories arise in the course of professional development due to the interplay of personal and situational conditions, which are strongly formed by gender-stereotyped internal and external attributions regarding the (management) abilities of women and men. The personal and situational antecedents, mentioned in the introduction, can be considered as action results which originate from the implicit career theories but as well reform or respectively reinforce them. What does professional success and career progression mean for the individual, and how does this influence its ability and willingness to initiate corresponding action strategies in career relevant situations? With reference to possible career barriers for women, this can be formulated as follows: Are women's personal implicit career theories experienced as being compatible with externally assigned female attributes, or indeed, compatible with women's own individually experienced attributes, and how does this affect their professional actions? From this innovative perspective we hypothesise that women and men differ in their implicit career theories.

These considerations thus form the backdrop for the following examination of the implicit career theories of women and of men in the context of a current PhD research project. In doing so, we intend to contribute a possible explanation concerning the unequal gender distribution in management positions. Since implicit career theories and their correlates have not yet been the specific focus of empirical studies, the purpose of the qualitative pilot study, introduced below, was to collect general data about this construct and its possible correlates in order to arrange a large-scale quantitative research afterwards. The following questions were primarily of interest:

- Which associations do women and men make regarding the terms '(professional) success' and '(professional) career progression'?
- How important are these constructs for them?
- Do they estimate themselves as successful?
- How do women and men explain and rate their professional development retrospectively?
- What are possible correlates of women's and men's implicit career theories?
- Is there evidence for the theory that women and men differ in their implicit career theories?

3. The Method

Data were gathered using qualitative guided interviews. The guide contains six relevant thematic areas, which are derived from the questioning; in addition, demographic data were collected. The interviews were recorded using a dictating machine and transcribed. The average length was 60 minutes. This methodical approach was explained to the interviewees at the start of the interview. No further persons were present during the interviews.

The sample
The age of the eight interviewees ranged from 30 to 48 years. With the exception of one person, all interviewees were in lower, middle or higher management. The interviewees came from various industries: personnel services, food production, automobile and aircraft production, auditing, consumer goods, health services and public administration. The organisation size ranged from between 250 to 120,000 employees. Three quarters of the participants were female. All except one were in relationships; exactly half had at least two children.

The data analysis
Qualitative content analysis (Mayring 2003) provided a basis for the data analysis. This is a systematic text analysis, enabling a content evaluation without reducing the material to quantified statements. The statements were paraphrased and classified in one of the thematic areas. The interviews were thus restricted to certain thematic areas, and for this reason irrelevant data was excluded from the analysis. Finally, the paraphrased sentences were generalised to a high level of abstraction, so that they could be classified with reference to a category or variable with the same or similar content.

4. Essential findings

Participants[2] were questioned on the phenomenon '(professional) success'. Related to this, five variables with various parameters were generated (see table 1). It is noted here that this paper does not explicitly deal with all of these five variables.

The idealistically characterised cognitions of (professional) success are broad and encompass both professional and private aspects: *Success means for me job satisfaction. But success also means life satisfaction* (Interview Nr. 1; ♀). Optimising (work) structures and conditions is similarly considered success: *Being creative, leaving something behind, demonstrating your own way of doing things* (Interview Nr. 6; ♂). The view that success is not simply reaching or carrying out management positions is also interesting:

---

2   The original language of the interviews was German. The quotations, presented below, were translated into English for this publication. A third person counterchecked the citations by translating them back into German. The re-translated statements were compared to the original citations to assure that a possible falsification of the meaning is minimised.

So in my opinion this has little relation to hierarchies. Accordingly I can be successful in my job although I deliberately decide against taking over a management position (Interview Nr. 1; ♀). In contrast or in addition to these statements a few other interviewees link professional success simply with economic independency.

To what extent do the interviewees perceive themselves as successful? Here, ambivalent answers are in evidence: approximately one third of the interviewees clearly stated that they see themselves as professionally success- ful: *Yes, I think that I have achieved a lot and that I have been professionally successful so far* (Interview Nr. 8;♀). Similarly, approximately a further third of the sample expressed more cautious self perceptions. The majo- rity of the interviewees also have the impression of being perceived as suc- cessful by their social environment: *...I am one of the few women who reached such a position in the research and development department and many would say '[name of the interviewee] is successful'* (Interview Nr. 5; ♀).

Interviewees were invited to give possible causes for their success. A broad and varied spectrum of personal aspects was named, comprising cha- racteristics, skills, knowledge and personal principles: authenticity, assertive- ness, social skills, self-discipline, industriousness, abilities, courage, and con- flict management. Situational factors in the form of positive workplace con- ditions, as well as support from line managers also contributed to (profes- sional) success.

The importance of (professional) success was seen very differently by the interviewees. One female interviewee expressed clearly how much it meant to her: *Very much. Because I define myself by my work ...* (Interview Nr. 8; ♀). In contrast, for others, *work and success is not everything* (Inter- view Nr. 5;♀). Even negative attitudes to success are visible: *I believe I don't really want to be successful at all. I want to be happy and satisfied ...* (Interview Nr. 3;♀). The importance of success can also vary in phases: *... it changes actually, along with other circumstances, whether I'm in a rela- tionship ...* (Interview Nr. 2; ♀).

The perception of the interviewees regarding 'successful women' was largely negative (in this regard only statements of the female interviewees are available). This was based on their previous perceptions of women wishing to be professionally successful. Here, more than half of the female interviewees criticised 'male women', who in terms of behaviour, but also appearance, resembled men: *What I really don't like is when women define their personal success or their career by becoming a man...just wearing pantsuits, being boyish and lacking any kind of feminine charm... such women will fail, sooner or later, I promise you. To this day I've been a foreign body in a men's world. And I managed it because I have remained a woman* (Interview Nr. 7;♀). According to the experiences of the female interviewees, this form of adaptation is a factor reducing rather than supporting promotion chances. Their ideal picture of a successful woman is portrayed by traits such as independency, natural authority, authenticity, experience, organisational and communicative skills and the ability to integrate work and private life aspects.

Table 1: Variables in the thematic area '(professional) success'

Thematic area: (professional) success	
Variables	**Parameter**
Cognitions of (professional) success	- idealistically characterized cognitions - pragmatically characterized cognitions
Importance of (professional) success	- high importance - low importance - variable importance
Self and external perception of (professional) success	- clear self-perception of being successful - ambivalent self-perception of being successful - external perception of being successful
Explanation for one's own (professional) success	- supportive factors (situational and structural)
Perception of successful women	- ideal perception - negative perception

Alongside '(professional) success' the topic 'climbing up the career ladder' was also an explicit focus of the interview study. Five variables were developed in this topic, with corresponding parameters (see table 2).

A somewhat idealistic cognition of climbing up the career ladder becomes clear in the following interviewee statement: *You do something that you hadn't foreseen at the start of your career ... in other words you exceed your own expectations* (Interview Nr. 7; ♀). An important element of climbing up the career ladder comes up again here with other interviewees: climbing up the career ladder wasn't consciously a goal, but rather arose by itself as a consequence of interest and enjoyment at the workplace or in the subject. In spite of these interpretations of individual professional development, a large proportion of the interviewees was characterised by a certain drive regarding personal and professional development. Many of them could cite a point in time where they had the feeling of having exhausted the possibilities of a position: *What does the capacity for action look like here, do I still have capacity for action or is it all gone? If there is not more capacity... then you have to have the courage to say, okay, I'll move on to something new* (Interview Nr. 6; ♂). Further responses mentioned supportive aspects regarding the career development are (already in childhood assumed) responsibility, self-confidence, a certain drive for independency, but also situational conditions such as the influence of role models. Significant obstacles were touched upon only by the female interviewees. Professional discrimination on account of being a woman, problems combining work and family life, as well as work related health issues was cited. Difficulties combining family and work were a topic important to the majority of interviewees. Correspondingly, this topic in part dominated interview time. Interviewees with children stress the perceived double-strain: *Your child is ill, and doesn't sleep, you spend the night awake... and then you have to prepare that tough meeting with your boss the next day. And no-one has consideration for you, that you have spent a sleepless night. That's the double strain, and those years were hard ...* (Interview Nr. 5; ♀).

It is notable that none of the interviewees gave the notion of climbing up the career ladder positive attributes. The majority of the sample experience career progression as not particularly important. They stress that climbing up the career ladder is generally unimportant, should not have priority over private life, and is to be regarded critically: *...and I find that a pity, a pity because of the time lost. You really only live once. So I'm somewhat sceptical there... yeah, I do regard that very critically... this career ladder climbing in itself, getting right to the top* (Interview Nr. 3; ♀). Several interviewees report that performance has also been a natural part of the family culture: *... in our family it has been self-evident to show a willingness to perform...I always had to contribute, for example I have already been driving the harvester as a sixteen year old girl* (Interview Nr. 7; ♀).

Table 2: Variables in the thematic area 'climbing up the career ladder'

Thematic area: climbing up the career ladder	
Variable	Parameter
Cognitions of climbing up the career ladder	- climbing up the career ladder as professional development - idealistic cognitions
The importance of climbing up the career ladder	- neutral importance - low (negative) importance
Self and external perception of climbing up the career ladder	- self perception of having climbed up the career ladder - external perception of having climbed up the career ladder
Explanation for one's own climbing up the career ladder	- supportive factors (situational and human resources) - impedimental factors (situational)
Future perspectives	- future plans consciously kept open - end of career progression / no further promotion intended - professional change intended

Performance is the third thematic area dealt with in the interview study, and in the context of implicit career theories, closely linked with (professional) success and career progression (see table 3).

Patterns of explanation for careers and for professional success are to be found in the parameters generated for the variables 'performance orientation' and 'performance motivation'. Performance orientation seems to be easily identifiable for the interviewees and was established as early as childhood. Further to this, one third of interviewees are active in performance sport.

Enjoying competition and also enjoying a constantly increasing performance level with corresponding feelings of contentedness are mentioned as motivational elements: ...*it is simply a contentedness hormone kick. You simply notice that you have tested your limits, you are happy, you are exhausted (Interview Nr. 4; ♂)*. In the context of performance motivation the interviewees mention intrinsic factors such as curiosity, the fulfilment of reaching goals and the desire to give something back to society. But also proving oneself and competing with others are motivational aspects for performance: *I always had to compete with men...it has never been a gratification to compete with women; I always wanted to defeat men* (Interview Nr. 5; ♀). Making money is an extrinsic factor for performance motivation: ...*by now I admit, I am earning so much money, I am not free anymore to decide 'I am packing up'. Because ... I got used to the money* (Interview Nr. 7; ♀).

Table 3: Variables in the thematic area 'performance'

Thematic area: performance	
Variable	Parameter
Performance orientation	- performance motivation going back to childhood - interest in performance sport
Performance motivation	- intrinsic factors - extrinsic factors

5. Discussion of results

The findings of this work-in-progress indicate that the construction 'climbing up the career ladder' has negative rather than positive associations for most interviewees - career progression interferes with (and thus damages) private life substantially. Correspondingly, implicit theories might be expected to display a relatively narrow understanding of career ladder climbing, with high workloads. This image is, however, not to be found among most interviewees; rather, their cognitions of career progression are broad and idealistic. This may be due to a kind of demarcation, separating one's own idealised self-perception from 'the career ladder climbing of others'; and if one's own career ideas could not always be fully successfully realised, this is because certain human resources and situational conditions in the professional everyday limited their implementation. Likewise the phenomenon known as Social-Desirability-Response-Set (Schnell et al. 2005) can be considered as a possible explanation. Idealistically coloured cognitions also predominate with reference to (professional) success: success implies the integration of professional activity into a holistic concept of living one's life. Hohner et al. (2003) demonstrate in this context that, women have a stronger interest than men in the meaning of career progression, and that woman often develop a different concept of professional success than men do. These gender-typical differences did not, however, reveal themselves in the study presented here. Gender as a kind of hidden category only showed up at the topics "perception of successful women" and "impedimental factors". Possible significant gender differences between women's and men's implicit career theories can be examined in further quantitative research design studies. Therefore, the next step of the PhD research project presented here implies an empirical examination of implicit career theories in the context of a quantitative study with special focus on the correlates and on possible gender differences.

Assumed correlates of implicit career theories are the cited supportive and impedimental factors that shape careers. For women, situational-structural conditions play an important role. Experience of discrimination as well as of the energy-draining efforts to combine family and profession are central aspects strongly shaping career theories. Consequently, structural changes in organisations, for example in the context of diversity management (see Haselier / Thiel 2005), are essential, but probably not sufficient enough to develop a positive attitude towards the compatibility of family and profession. The presented findings suggest that career ladder progression and professional success are highly complex constructions. The significance of these constructions is to be found in the sensitive interplay of their mutual dependency with personal and situational conditions in professional and private life. The research results demonstrate that implicit career theories make a contribution to the variance explanation of professional success - to what extent, however, has to be analysed in the upcoming quantitative study.

When distinguishing practical implications for organisations, it is important to clarify terminology: a 'career progression support programme' could be met with resistance due to negative associations. Therefore, educative measures for human resources staff, as well as for the target group of the career development supportive measures, which take into account the complexity of the construction 'career' are essential. A holistic view of career ladder climbing reflecting the various facets of the term could thus be integrated into, for instance, company guidelines, because implicit career theories are assumedly assigned by organisational ideas and structures. The feeling of being successful is largely evoked through satisfaction, but also through experiencing membership of a space with creative and action possibilities. In this context, the work/life balance so often cited in the business and academic world, is highly relevant. Existing studies (see, for example, BMFSFJ 2005) demonstrate that realising company measures in the flexibilisation of time and location (flexi-time, using partly autonomous teams with a holistic task view and high level of independence) increases employee satisfaction and thus production; staff turnover and sick-leave can be reduced. In accordance with the findings of the study presented here, specialist and management staff's self-perception of success can be positively influenced by gender-mainstreaming instruments in human resource development.

The presented findings also point to implications far beyond the organisational context. To accomplish lasting and profound changes regarding vertical and horizontal segregation in the employment market, the isolated glance at occupational environments is not sufficient. If we look at the circumstances and conditions, which interact with the implicit career theories of women and men, it is obvious that concepts of intervention should already be realised in early childhood. Gender stereotypes, adapted in the course of socialisation, indeed provide orientation, but also affect professional development negatively, looking for instance at the gender-specific self-concepts of female and male students in the fields of science and mathematics (see Prenzel et al. 2007). In this respect, alongside business management, educational staff and parents have to be sensitised to the negative effects of gender-stereotyped attribution processes concerning female and male potentials. This conclusion involves a challenge for various areas of practice.

References

Abele, A. E. (2002a): Ein Modell und empirische Befunde zur beruflichen Laufbahnentwicklung unter besonderer Berücksichtigung des Geschlechtsvergleichs. In: Psychologische Rundschau, 53 (3), 109-118.

Abele, A. E. (2002b): Geschlechterdifferenz in der beruflichen Karriereentwicklung. Warum sind Frauen weniger erfolgreich als Männer? In: Keller, B. / Mischau, A. (Eds.): Frauen machen Karriere in Wissenschaft, Wirtschaft und Politik. Baden-Baden, 49-63.

Abele, A. E. (2003): Beruf - kein Problem, Karriere - schon schwieriger: Berufslaufbahnen von Akademikerinnen und Akademikern im Vergleich. In: Abele, A.E. / Hoff, E.-H. / Hohner, H.-U. (Eds.): Frauen und Männer in akademischen Professionen. Heidelberg, 157-182.

Bischoff, S. (2005): Wer führt in (die) Zukunft? Männer und Frauen in Führungspositionen der Wirtschaft in Deutschland – die 4. Studie. Bielefeld.

Blumer, H. (1973): Der methodologische Standort des symbolischen Interaktionismus. In: Arbeitsgruppe Bielefelder Soziologen (Eds.): Alltagswissen und gesellschaftliche Wirklichkeit, Band 1. Reinbek, 80-101.

Bruner, J.S. / Tagiuri, R. (1954): The perception of people. In: Lindzey, G. (Ed.): Handbook of social psychology, 2, 634-654.

Bundesministerium für Familie, Senioren, Frauen und Jugend (BMFSFJ) (2005): Work-Life-Balance als Motor für wirtschaftliches Wachstum und gesellschaftliche Stabilität [online]. Available from: http://www.bmfsfj.de/bmfsfj/generator/RedaktionBMFSFJ/Broschuerens

telle/Pdf-Anlagen/Work-Life-Balance,property=pdf,bereich=bmfsfj, sprache=de,rwb=true.pdf.

Eden, D. / Leviatan, U. (2005): From Implicit Personality Theory to Implicit Leadership Theory. In: Schyns, B. / Meindl, J. R. (Eds.): Implicit Leadership Theories – Essays and Explorations. Greenwich, 3-14.

Education, Audiovisual and Culture Executive Agency (EACEA P9 Eurydice) (2009): Key Data on Education in Europe 2009 [online]. Available from: http://eacea.ec.europa.eu/education/eurydice/documents/key_data_series/105EN.pdf.

Ehrlinger, J. / Dunning, D. (2003): How Chronic Self-Views Influence (and Potentially Mislead) Estimates of Performance. In: Journal of Personality and Social Psychology, 84, (1), 5-17.

European Commission (2009): Report on equality between women and men – 2009 [online]. Available from: http://bookshop.europa.eu/eubookshop/download.action?fileName=KEAU09001ENC_002.pdf&eubphfUid=101 92125&catalogNbr=KE-AU-09-001-EN-C.

Habermann-Horstmeier, L. (2007): Karrierehindernisse für Frauen in Führungspositionen. Ergebnisse einer empirischen Studie an 300 Frauen aus dem deutschen Mittel- und Topmanagement. Saarbrücken.

Haselier, J. / Thiel, M. (2005): Diversity Management. Unternehmerische Stärke durch Vielfalt. Frankfurt a. M.

Heider, F. (1977): Psychologie der interpersonalen Beziehung. Stuttgart.

Hohner, H.-U. / Grote, S. / Hoff, E.-H. (2003): Geschlechtsspezifische Berufsverläufe: Unterschiede auf dem Weg nach oben. In: Informationen für die Beratungs- und Vermittlungsdienste der Bundesanstalt für Arbeit, 5, 587-590.

Horstkemper, M. (1992): Koedukation in mathematisch-naturwissenschaftlichen Fächern – zweifelhafter Gewinn für die Mädchen oder Entwicklungschance für alle? In: Grabosch, A. / Zwölfer, A. (Eds.): Frauen und Mathematik. Die allmähliche Rückeroberung der Normalität? Tübingen, 91-111.

Jäckle, M. (2008): Schule M(m)acht Geschlechter. Eine Auseinandersetzung mit Schule und Geschlecht unter diskurstheoretischer Perspektive. Wiesbaden.

Kleinert, C. (2006): Frauen in Führungspositionen. Karriere mit Hindernissen. IAB Kurzbericht [online]. Available from: http://doku.iab.de/kurzber/2006/kb0906.pdf.

Kleinert, C. / Kohaut, S. / Brader, D. / Lewerenz, J. (2007): Frauen an der Spitze. Arbeitsbedingungen und Lebenslagen weiblicher Führungskräfte. Frankfurt a. M.

Luhmann, N. (1989): Vertrauen. Ein Mechanismus der Reduktion sozialer Komplexität. Stuttgart.

Maier, G. W. / von Rosenstiel, L. / Wastian, M. (2003): Berufseinstieg und erste Berufserfahrungen wirtschaftswissenschaftlicher Absolventinnen und Absolventen – ein geschlechtsbezogener Vergleich. In: Abele, A.E. / Hoff, E.-H. / Hohner, H.-U. (Eds.): Frauen und Männer in akademischen Professionen. Heidelberg, 17-29.

Mayring, P. (2003): Qualitative Inhaltsanalyse. Weinheim, Basel.

Mischel, W. (2004): Toward an integrative science of the person. In: Annual Review of Psychology 55, 1-22.

Neubauer, W. (1986): Implizite Führungstheorie und Führungserfahrung bei Vorgesetzten. In: Daumenlang, K. / Sauer, J. (Eds.): Aspekte psychologischer Forschung. Göttingen, 75-90.

Prenzel, M. / Arlert, C. / Baumert, J. / Blum, W. / Hamman, M. / Klieme, E. / Pekrun, R. (2007): PISA 2006. Die Ergebnisse der dritten internationalen Vergleichsstudie. Münster.

Schnell, R. / Hill, P. / Esser, E. (2005): Methoden der empirischen Sozialforschung,7. Auflage. München.

Schweer, M. (2009): Frauen auf dem beruflichen Vormarsch? Zu selektiven Wahrnehmungs- und Bewertungsprozessen im Zuge geschlechtstypischer Karrierewege. In: Schweer, M. (Ed.): Sex and Gender. Interdisziplinäre Beiträge zu einer gesellschaftlichen Konstruktion. Frankfurt a. M., 153-170.

Sieverding, M. (1990): Psychologische Barrieren in der beruflichen Entwicklung von Frauen. Das Beispiel der Medizinerinnen. Stuttgart.

Sieverding, M. (2003): Frauen unterschätzen sich: Selbstbeurteilungs-Biases in einer simulierten Bewerbungssituation. In: Zeitschrift für Sozialpsychologie, 34 (3), 147-160.

She gets less: gender differences in resource allocation to new professors at RWTH Aachen University

Heather Hofmeister, Julia Hahmann

The paper examines gender differences in resource allocation to newly hired women and men professors at RWTH Aachen University. Negotiation records of 40 cases of newly hired professors from 2005 to 2008 were ano-nymously coded and analyzed to examine the negotiation between the new professor and university for start-up funding, number of scientific positions, and number of support staff positions. Due to low case numbers especially for women on the full professorship-level, we compare men and women's resource allocation at the associate-professor level. We hypothesize that gender differences in the received amount of resources may exist because prior research suggests that (1) women tend to ask for less and (2) negotiators tend to grant women fewer resources than they grant to men, all else being equal. Our data show that new professors, male and female, request the same amount of start-up funding and number of scientific positions (no gender difference in requests). But the resources finally granted show large diffe-rences, whereby women receive significantly less than their male colleagues.

1. Introduction

"Each generation of young women, including those who are currently senior faculty, began by believing that gender discrimination was "solved" in the previous generation and would not touch them. Gradually, however, their eyes were opened to the realization that the playing field is not level after all, and that they had paid a high price both personally and professionally as a result." (Pardue / Hopkins / Potter / Ceyer 1999)

Gender inequality in the educational system is well-documented. Men are significantly overrepresented among the ranks of professors and university presidents in Europe and North America, and studies like the one cited above from MIT in the mid-1990s document the processes by which this imbalance occurs (Pardue / Hopkins / Potter / Ceyer 1999). One aspect of gender inequality in education that has been rarely measured is the difference in men and women's willingness to ask for resources as they start new positions. To what degree are these differences, if any exist, exacerbated or reduced by the institution in actually awarding resources at the start of a professorship? This paper compares gender differences in the requests for and final award of resources for all new professors hired at one German academic institution, the RWTH Aachen University, between 2005 and 2008 (approximately 40 cases). Resources measured in this paper are start-up funds, scientific assistant positions, and support staff.

2. Gender Inequality in Academia

Gender inequality is pervasive in organizations, not least within the education system. Though the school system is "feminized" at the elementary school level, where the majority of teachers are women, at the university level - and particularly at doctoral-degree-granting institutions - men dominate the top positions of professor, chancellor, and president in Europe (Bundesministerium für Bildung und Forschung 2002; ETAN 2000; Niemeier / González 2004) and, although to a lesser degree, the US and Canada (AUCC 2007; Walker 2007).

Among the student population at universities, gender differences have declined in recent years, even in Continental Europe. Women represent 54% of undergraduate students in the EU-15 and EU-25 in 2004 (Europäische Gemeinschaften 2005), up from 52% in 1998. In the US, 60% of the undergraduates are women in 2004 (56% in 1998) (National Center for Education Statistics 2006). But the ETAN-Report of the European Commission (2000) points out that the rate of female scientists declines the further the scientific career progresses. While the level of women and men students is nearly equal, the percent of female professors at the full professor level (called W3/C4 in Germany) lies clearly below parity (ETAN 2000). On Continental Europe, women hold only 15% of senior academic positions (EPWS 2006). Under 10% of German university presidents are female (CEWS 2006). To illustrate the contrast, women already hold 25% of university presidencies in the United States, including the presidencies of ivy-league institutions such as Princeton (Shirley M. Tilghman), Harvard (Drew Gilpin Faust), and Brown (Ruth J. Simmons) (Ireland 2007; Walker 2007).

The lack of male role models in elementary-level schools may pose a particular problem for the development and socialization of boys (Jordan / Cowan 1998; Thorne 1998). But the overabundance of men and lack of women within the upper teaching and research positions in universities poses other problems (Stewart / LaVaque-Manty / Malley 2004). The future leaders of most organizations, from government to industry to education to non-profit, receive their final education within universities. The role modeling of male authority within universities has effects in a much broader range of organizations. When societies offer young men and women only, or primarily, images of male leadership and professional competence within the universities, young men and women are left few options but to identify only, or primarily, men as competent, capable, and deserving of upper level positions within *all* organizations (Rahm / Charbonneau 1997; Wetterer 2002). The importance of correcting the gender inequalities within universities is high, as the ripple effects should be felt within other organizations over the coming decades (von Alemann 2005).

2.1 Do women ask for less?

Are there gender differences in negotiation? Do women ask for less, and, therefore, receive less, than comparably placed men? A book on the topic by Babcock et al. (Babcock / Laschever / Gelfand / Small 2003) suggests that exactly that is taking place, that women do not ask as much, or at all, and so their starting point is lower than men's. Reasons are many.

An implicit link between gender stereotypes and negotiation procedures exists in the minds of many negotiators (Kray / Thompson 2005). Negotiators don't have to believe in the link, but just knowing about this possible connection might change the behavior in the situation of negotiation. The gender stereotypes describe the man as strong, dominant and rational, the woman as weak, submissive and emotional (Tannen 1990). For a woman to act in a way according to male attributes (assertive and tough) detracts from the woman's standing in the negotiation, rather than adding to it, however, because it goes against the expectation for women's behavior; the same seems to be true for men following female-attributed behavior in negotiation (Curhan / Overbeck 2008).

In a study of negotiations using role playing, Nadler and Nadler found that the worst negotiation outcome was when women playing "subordinates" negotiated with men playing "supervisors" (the case in most university negotiation situations for women) and the highest or best negotiation outcome was when men playing subordinates negotiated with men playing supervisors (the case in most university negotiation situations for men). Women "supervisors" were more likely than men "supervisors" to raise their offers for both women and men subordinates (Nadler / Nadler 1987).

It is important to point out that negotiation influences not only the salary on a monthly basis (and even a small difference accumulates to a big income difference when calculating over the long term). Differences in the numbers of scientific staff result in differences in publications, research proposals and acquired third party funds. The number of support staff has effects on the organization of work routines. One area of inequality influences many other areas of inequality. A good starting situation can set a scientist on a very successful trajectory; a situation of disadvantage relative to peers (at the same or other universities) sets a scientist on the opposite path.

Persistent gender inequalities within organizations are caused in part by divergent starting positions (England 1997; Grusky 2001). Men are more likely to earn more, have higher positions of power, have more of other kinds of resources (rooms, staff, secretarial support), and enjoy more job security (England 1997; Kilbourne / Farkas / Beron / Weir / England 1994; Reskin 1997; Reskin / McBrier 2000). The same processes that produce gender inequalities also produce race, ethnicity, social background, and age inequalities (Grusky 2001). Inequality-generating processes can be organized along a few main dimensions; here we describe gender segregation and gender discrimination.

2.2 Gender Segregation

Gender segregation depicts the concentration of men and women in different areas of the labor market: in various fields of work, industries and levels of hierarchy (Reskin 1997). This separation causes gender inequalities concerning salary, benefits, and pension payments. Segregation not only influences the professional life; it also has an impact on the private life. Men, with higher positions and average earnings than women, are more likely financially to be able to support an unpaid spouse who can manage the home sphere, leaving more time and energy for the male earner to invest further in the career. We elaborate the two types of segregation, horizontal and vertical, with examples from universities.

2.2.1 Horizontal segregation

Horizontal segregation describes the concentration of women and men in specific and separate fields of work, as for example women's concentration in humanities, social sciences, biology, and medicine, and men in other fields of work, such as engineering, physics, and computer science (ETAN 2000; Krimmer / Stallmann / Behr / Zimmer 2003b) . Difference does not have to mean disadvantage, and at first glance, this form of segregation does not seem to be the source of social inequality. However, jobs in branches dominated by female workers are paid less and have lower levels of social prestige (England 1997). Horizontal segregation creates income and status inequality (Bielby 2000; Committee on Maximizing the Potential of Women in Academic Science and Enginieering / National Academy of Sciences / National Academy of Engineering / Institute of Medicine 2006). We hypothesize that one of the reasons for differences in resource allocation is the higher probability of women being concentrated in disciplines that get fewer resources and the higher probability of men being in disciplines with a greater allotment of resources.

2.2.2 Vertical segregation

Vertical gender segregation is a more obvious form of social inequality than horizontal segregation and describes the situation where women and men work in the same field, but women are in lower positions. This inequality, however, is often not based on actual performance differences, as women tend to invest more effort into their work than their male colleagues do (England 1997). Rather, it reflects a tendency in the minds of women and men in gatekeeping functions (such as search committees) to assume that it is more appropriate or easier to justify a man holding the higher position. Men, therefore, often hold the higher respected and better paid positions, even if women are the majority of workers in the field (Williams 1998).

At the university, we hypothesize that women who are hired more often hold the lower-level W2/C3 (associate) professorships than the full professorships, while men are more likely than women to obtain W3/C4 (full) professorships (ETAN 2000; Krimmer / Stallmann / Behr / Zimmer 2003a). These differences will create differences in resource allocation; therefore, we control for type of professorship in our analyses.

2.3 Discrimination

Discrimination is defined as different treatment based on certain significant distinguishing marks (e.g. religious affiliation, bodily characteristics like skin color or disabilities, sex, age, social origin, race, ethnicity, or nationality) (Grusky 2001). Discrimination affects a person's access to resources and social participation. Positive discrimination leads to advantages for certain social groups, and negative discrimination leads to disadvantages for certain social groups (Markefka 1995). Discrimination of social groups can take two forms, overt and covert. Differences in resource allocation may stem from discrimination against women (or men), or discrimination against the kinds of scientific fields where women (or men) are concentrated.

3. Data and Methods

The RWTH Aachen University is actively examining its practices and policies related to its low percent of women professors (at around 8% in 2008,
the lowest in Germany where the average is 15% and among the lowest in
Europe) (RWTH 2009). For this reason, the university has made its data
available for scientific analysis in order to better understand myriad sources
of gender inequalities so as to counteract them.

Data are from the *ARCE Study 2008-01: Search Committee Results
Study,* collected and analyzed within the Aachen Research Commission for
Equity (ARCE) led by Heather Hofmeister, Professor of Sociology with a
specialty in Gender and Life Course Research. We evaluate gender differences among professors and professorships by comparing negotiation data between the candidate and the university between January 2005 and March
2008 (40 cases) at RWTH Aachen University. This time window was chosen
because in January 2005 a new national professorship pay scale and negotiation system started, based on service-related rather than age-related rewards.

Each search committee folder was immediately given a numeric identity
in the personnel office to make it anonymous, as these are highly confidential
data. Data were coded for a variety of aspects, including the resources that
the final candidate requested, and the resources that the university granted.
These resources include scientific staff, support staff (secretaries and laboratory personnel), rooms, and start-up funds for equipment, as well as a yearly
household expense account.

During the negotiation process, the candidate is asked to specify his or
her wishes concerning the number of rooms, the number of scientific and
support staff, and additional money for office furniture and equipment. This
information is used by the department, the "faculty" or school, and the main
university administration to determine who can offer which resources. Negotiations within the university (department, school, and main administration)
result in an offer for the candidate that is negotiated between the candidate
and the chancellor in a final meeting. The initial request letter and the results
of the final negotiation are saved in the personnel file, providing starting and
ending data for the negotiation process. Out of the 40 cases in our database,
some data are missing for some of the stages or aspects of analysis. Therefore
our final sample size for some analyzes are as low as 5 cases. Other dimensions of social inequality such as age, nationality, family background are also
important to analyze, but the limited sample unfortunately does not allow us
to explore these potential sources of inequality in this paper. These data
reveal only trends and do not describe every case of new hires at RWTH
Aachen.

4. Hypotheses

We hypothesize that one of several reasons for the low percent of women faculty is gender inequality in the distribution of resources, which can lead to frustration for the women faculty and increase their willingness to search for alternative positions at other universities. We have already found evidence for gender segregation in the different stages of the hiring process at RWTH Aachen University: some search committees invite women to interview at rates lower than their application proportion and others place women at disproportionately lower rank on the final list of top candidates (Färber / Spangenberg 2008; Hofmeister / Hahmann 2009).

The gender inequality in resource distribution can have two causes: 1) women do not ask for the same quantity of resources than men ask for, or 2) the organization grants resources to women at lower levels than it grants to men. If there is gender inequality in the allocation of resources independent of the request levels, the difference may reveal a value bias against women or a value bias against subjects where women are more often concentrated. We will control for these effects in the next stage of research by examining resource requests and allocation for men and women faculty members within the same subject area and same rank (for example, one male and one female mechanical engineer, one male and one female historian).

5. Results

The RWTH Aachen University, like most universities, already has more male than female professors and proportionately more women professors in the associate-professor level (W2/C3) than in the full-professor level (W3/C4). In other words, if a woman is a professor, she is likely a lower-ranking professor. Our study of the search-and-hire process for our institution suggests that this pattern is not on a path of rapid change (see Hofmeister / Hahmann 2009). Only two of the 22 new *full* (W3) professorships are held by women. To assure anonymity of these two female full professors and because of limitations to the generalizability with so few cases, we concentrate our comparison of their requested and attained resources on the W2/C3 (associate) professorship level.

In Figure 1 we present the one-time start-up funding the candidate requested and the university granted to each new associate professor, in euro, differentiated by gender. There is no gender difference in the level of start-up funds that associate professors request: women as well as men are requesting on average 109.000 euro and 104.000 euro respectively. However, the amount received is different. Whereas male candidates received approximately 74.000 euro from the university, or roughly 75% of their requested start-up funding, female candidates only obtained 40.000 euro on average, an amount that is under 40% of their request. New male W2 professors receive nearly double the start-up funding as their female colleagues. These finances can be used to buy technical equipment and furniture for offices, attend expensive conferences, and hire student assistants. Considerably less start-up capital is available for the new women professors to equip their working place. This unequal treatment most likely has an impact on the quality and quantity of work that the new professors are able to produce in their first years. The reasons for the inequality are most likely covert (there is no rule posted that women should receive less than half what men receive), but the consequence is overtly discriminatory.

Figure 1: One time payments divided by level of professorship and gender.

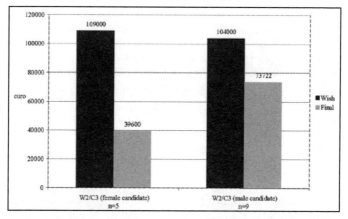

Source: ARCE 2009-01

Scientific staff positions are another important aspect of the negotiations for new professors. These are positions either for post-doctorates or doctoral students, scientists or upcoming scientists who can assist in the research program of the professor. Once again, male as well as female incoming professors request the same staff, on average 1.4 scientific employees (see Figure 2). It cannot be established from the data in figures 1 and 2 that women have less ambition or are afraid to ask for the same resources that men ask for. But whereas male candidates' wishes for staff positions are fully met by the university, female candidates receive less than half the staff they ask for, and nearly half of the staff that their male colleagues receive (0.8 scientific employees on average per female professor). The quantity of scientific staff has a large influence on the amount of publications, external funding applications, and the range of teaching offers that a professor can produce. Professors with a larger staff can produce more doctoral candidates and influence the visibility and influence of his or her research area in a scientific field.

Figure 2: Requested and received amount of scientific staff for W2/C3-professorships differentiated by gender, absolute amounts.

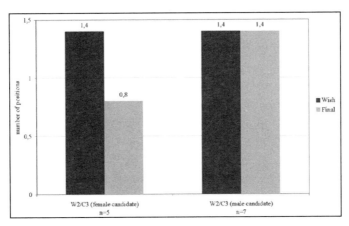

Source: ARCE 2009-01

Since the documentation of negotiation is for some processes incomplete, containing either just records of the candidate's wishes or just records of the final decision, we only have small case numbers. With these case numbers, no gender discrimination is exposed by comparing the wishes and allocations of the support staff (secretaries and lab assistants) (Figure 3). Although the male candidates ask for more support staff than women candidates do, both female and male candidates receive on average around a half-position.

To get around the problem of low case numbers, in Figure 4 we present a comparison of only the final allocation of staff, scientific and support, for which we have more cases (5 women professors and 12 men professors hired between 2005 and 2008).

The results from Figures 2 and 3 are confirmed in Figure 4 through the larger number of cases. Although female as well as male associate professors receive nearly the same quantity of support staff (though women still receive what amounts to 4 hours per week or 200 hours per year less support), there are several big differences concerning the scientific staff. On average, male associate professors receive half a position of scientific staff more than female associate professors do. This represents, for example, a doctoral position. This considerable disadvantage for the newly appointed women professors, compared to their male newly hired colleagues, will have to be compensated by the women writing more successful grant proposals to replace the missing half-position compared to their male colleagues. This disadvantage will follow their entire career at this university.

Figure 3: Requested and granted number of support staff for W2/C3 professorships divided by sex, absolute numbers.

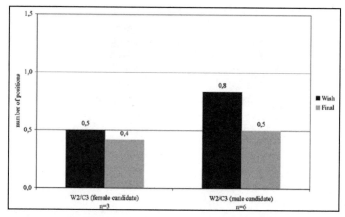

Source: ARCE 2009-01

Figure 4: Received staff of new professorships on W2/C3 level from 2005 until 2008, differentiated by gender, own calculations, absolute amounts.

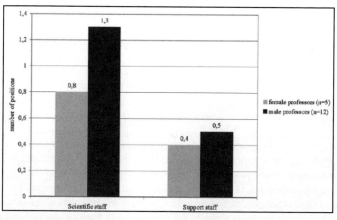

Source: ARCE 2009-01

6. Final Observations and Conclusions

We have already found and described evidence of vertical segregation in the process of professorship attainment by gender: the limitations are stronger in the chances of women to obtain full professorships compared to their chances to obtain associate professorships (Beaufays / Krais 2005; Hofmeister / Hahmann 2009).

We also find evidence of gender inequalities within the negotiation process for resources, though we recommend caution in the interpretation due to small sample size. With the sample using complete data that we do have, we find that women in our sample are not less ambitious or self-confident than men are in their requests for most resources. The difference between wishes and resources allocated by the university showed that men tend to get 75 to 100% of their requested resources, whereas women get on average half or less than half of their requested resources. The exception is for support staff, where women's requests were already less than men's requests, and the requests of women were met at nearly 100 percent (for around a half-position support staff, usually a secretarial position). In as far as gender differences in the fields of hire exist (Hofmeister / Hahmann 2009), gender differences in related resources are to be expected. However, the drastic differences between requested and allocated start-up funding cannot be a function of field alone. Additional data (in preparation) will directly compare professors within the same fields.

Comparison of international rates of women professors shows that Germany has one of the lowest numbers of full professorships held by women (ETAN 2000). The described horizontal segregation leads to a concentration of women in the fields of arts and humanities and social sciences in Germany. That this segregation is a social construction is suggested by historical research: The first dissertations and habilitations (a second dissertation) by women were written in the fields of natural sciences (Costas / Ross / Suchi 2000). Comparing women in universities in the EU, those disciplines with very few women tend to be the ones with high status, for example theoretical physics (ETAN 2000).

Individual cases of professors receiving less than requested are easy to justify because there are always special circumstances that can be described in each case. But a systematic pattern of special cases only on the side of female hires suggests that other forces besides "special circumstances" are at play. Additional data, from additional universities and a more extended time window, are necessary to determine whether these results point to a broader pattern within science. Including other aspects of diversity is also necessary in future research in order to fully understand how various social dimensions, in addition to gender, have an influence on processes of inequality in resource allocation.

References

AUCC, The Association of Universities and Colleges of Canada. 2007. "Trends in higher education. Volume 2: Faculty." Ottawa: The Association of Universities and Colleges of Canada.
Babcock, L. / Laschever, S. (2003): Women Don't Ask - Gender Negotiation and the Gender Divide. Princeton, NJ.
Beaufays, S. / Krais, B. (2005): Doing Science-Doing Gender. Feministische Studien 23, 82-99.
Bielby, W. T. (2000): Geschlecht und Karriere: Ist die Wissenschaft ein Sonderfall? In: Krais (B.) (Ed.): Wissenschaftskultur und Geschlechterordnung. Über die verborgenen Mechanismen männlicher Dominanz in der akademischen Welt, Frankfurt a. M. / New York, 55-82.
Bundesministerium für Bildung und Forschung (BMBF) (2002): Mehr Frauen an die Spitze! Gender Mainstreaming in Forschungseinrichtungen. Bonn: Bundesministerium für Bildung und Forschung (BMBF), 28.
CEWS (2006): Frauenanteile an den Hochschulleitungen, 1996-2006 [online]. Available from: http://www.cews.org/statistik/gremien-drittmittel.php?aid=61&cid=19.
Committee on Maximizing the Potential of Women in Academic Science and Enginieering / National Academy of Sciences / National Academy of Engineering /Institute of Medicine (2006): Free Executive Summary: Beyond Bias and Barriers: Fulfilling the Potential of Women in Academic Science and Engineering, Edited by N. A. o. Sciences: National Academies Press.
Costas, I. / Ross, B. / Suchi, S. (2000): Geschlechtliche Normierung von Studienfächern und Karrieren im Wandel. In: Historical Social Research (2), 23-53.
Curhan, J. R. / Overbeck, J. R. (2008): Making a positive impression in a negotiation. Gender differences in response to impression motivation. Negotiation and Conflict Management Research 1, 179-193.
England, P. (1997): The Sex Gap in Pay. In: Dunn, D. (Ed.): Workplace/Women's Place: An Anthology. Los Angeles, 74-87.
EPWS (2006): European Platform of Women Scientists Newsletter, Issue 4, Aug-Sept 2006. In: Huminic-Orzu, A. / Jochimsen, M./ Michalowitz, I. (Eds.): European Platform of Women Scientists Newsletter. Brussels: EPWS.

ETAN, Expert Working Group on Women and Science (2000): Science policies in the European Union - Promoting excellence through mainstreaming gender equality. Brussels: European Commission.

Europäische Gemeinschaften (EG) (2005): Europa in Zahlen - Eurostat Jahrbuch 2005. Luxemburg: Amt für Amtl. Veröff. der Europ. Gemeinschaften, 82.

Färber, C. / Spangenberg, U. (2008): Wie werden Professuren besetzt? Chancengleichheit in Berufungsverfahren. Frankfurt a. M. / New York.

Grusky, D. B. (2001): Social Stratification: Class, Race, & Gender in Sociological Perspective. Boulder, Colorado, 911.

Hofmeister, H. / Hahmann, J. (2009): Explaining gender inequalities in organizations: Where does the inequality creep in? Comparing resource allocation of male and female professorships, from academic position design and planning through hiring and negotiation. In: Gender and Diversity in Organizations. Paris.

Ireland, C. (2007): Women of the Ivies. Presidents Past, Present, Future Exchange Ideas. In: Harvard University Gazette Online.

Jordan, E. / Cowan, A. (1998): Warrior Narratives in the Kindergarten Classroom: Renegotiating the Social Contract? In: Kimmel, M. S. / Messner, M. A. (Eds.): Men's Lives, Fourth Edition, Boston, 127-140.

Kilbourne, B. S. / Frankas, K. B. / Weir, D. / England, P. (1994): Returns to Skill, Compensating Differentials, and Gender Bias: Effects of Occupational Characteristics on the Wages of White Women and Men. American Journal of Sociology 100 (3), 689-719.

Kray, L. J. / Thompson, L. (2005): Gender Stereotypes and Negotiation Performance: An Examination of Theory and Research. Research in Organizational Behavior 26, 103-182.

Krimmer, H. / Stallmann, F. / Behr, M. / Zimmer, A. (2003a): Karrierewege von ProfessorInnen an Hochschulen in Deutschland. Wissenschaftskarriere & Gender, Westfälische Wilhelms-Universität Münster, Münster.

Krimmer, H. / Stallmann, F. / Behr, M. / Zimmer, A. (2003b): Karrierewege von ProfessorInnen an Hochschulen in Deutschland. Projektbericht WiKa. Projekt Wissenschaftskarriere. Wissenschaftskarriere & Gender, Westfälische Wilhelms-Universität Münster, Münster.

Markefka, M. (1995): Vorurteile, Minderheiten, Diskriminierung. Neuwied.

Nadler, M. K. / Nadler, L. B. (1987): The Influence of Gender on Negotiation Success in Asymmetric Power Situations. In: Nadler, L. B / Nadler, M. K. / Todd-Mancillas, W. R. (Eds.): Advances in Gender and Communication Research. Lanham, Maryland.

National Center for Education Statistics, NCES (2006): Participation in Education: Undergraduate education [online]. Available from (http://nces.ed.gov/programs/coe/2007/section1/table.asp?tableID=672).

136 Heather Hofmeister, Julia Hahmann

Niemeier, D. A. / González C (2004): Breaking into the Guildmasters' Club: What We Know About Women Science and Engineering Department Chairs at AAU Universities. In: NWSA Journal (16), 157-171.

Pardue, M.-L. / Hopkins, N. M. / Potter, C. / Ceyer, J. (1999): Moving on from discrimination at the Massachusetts Institute of Technology [online]. Available from: http://www.nature.com/nature/debates/women/women_1.html.

Rahm, J. / Charbonneau, P. (1997): Probing stereotypes through students' drawings of scientists. In: American Journal of Physics (65), 774-778.

Reskin, B. F. (1997): Sex Segregation in the Workplace. In: Dunn, D. (Ed.): Workplace/Women's Place: An Anthology. Los Angeles, 69-73.

Reskin, B. F. / McBrier, D. B. (2000): Why not ascription? Organizations' employment of male and female managers. In: American Sociological Review (65), 210-233.

RWTH Aachen (2009): Zahlenspiegel 2008. Rheinisch-Westfälische Technische Hochschule Aachen, Aachen.

Stewart, A. J. / LaVaque-Manty D. / Malley J. E. (2004): Recruiting Female Faculty Members in Science and Engineering: Preliminary Evaluation of one Intervention Model. In: Journal of Women and Minorities in Science and Engineering (10), 361-375.

Tannen, D. (1990): You Just Don't Understand: Women and Men in Conversation. New York.

Thorne, B. (1998): Girls and Boys Together...but Mostly Apart: Gender Arrangements in Elementary School. In: Kimmel, M. S. / Messner, M. A. (Eds.): Men's Lives, Fourth Edition, Boston, 87-100.

von Alemann, A (2005): Can we break through the Glass Ceiling? The Exclusion and Inclusion of Women in Economic Leadership Positions in Europe. In: Torún, N. (Ed.): Rethinking Inequalities. Copernicus University.

Walker, C. (2007): Women Increasingly Likely to be Leaders in U.S. Higher Education: Harvard University latest of top U.S. colleges to appoint women as president [online]. Available from (http://www.america.gov/st/washfile-english/2007/February/20070216150659bcreklaw0.9029352.html).

Wetterer, A. (2002): Arbeitsteilung und Geschlechterkonstruktionen. Gender at Work in theoretischer und historischer Perspektive. Konstanz.

Williams, C. L. (1998): The Glass Escalator: Hidden Advantages for Men in the "Female" Professions. In: Kimmel, M. S. / Messner, M. A (Eds.): Men's Lives, Fourth Edition. Boston, 285-299.

Exploring Diversity in Academic Careers: On Methodological and Theoretical Challenges

Karin Schlücker

Dedicated to my father.
His death while I was finishing this paper tested
profoundly my work-life-balance in the academy.

As in women's, gender, and feminist studies, inquiry into diversity has to face the problem of 'intersections' in diversities, while the concept of intersections still presents both a theoretical and empirical challenge. Thus, in order to design a qualitative research project to explore the effects of diversity on professional trajectories in academia, the author accounts for the strategy of a theoretical sampling as it was suggested by the Grounded Theory to avoid a sample of clear-cut 'diverse' groups among interviewees.

At the same time, however, the radically 'open' proceeding of a consistent theoretical sampling provides an obstacle for more practical purposes, especially within the framework of recent German science policies for funding and conducting research. Conclusions treat such observations as 'data' in inquiry. They recall the pivotal position which the quality of 'work output' should have in research on managing diversity; and they point at difficulties in grappling with the quality of work output in academia as well as with the 'external' influence of diversity on scientific outcomes in general.

1. Introduction: 'Gender and Diversity' as a Research Area

As this anthology and its preceding conference reflect, a new research area is blossoming in Germany. Only ten years ago publications on gender and diversity were hard to find. The term for this young research area, however, can be baffling: Shouldn't gender be just one aspect of diversity as any other - as for example age, ethnicity/race, religion or sexual orientation?

The striking combination of terms thus reflects that two discourses – following Michel Foucault (e.g. 1977) a combined set of practical and symbolic arrangements – meet in such a topic:

1) The *gender* discourse emerged from the second women's movements during the 1960s to 1980s, claiming equal rights and opportunities. As by comparable movements – the gay movement or the black civil rights movement in the U.S.A. – some institutional and cultural changes could be initiated, while in feminist, women's, and gender studies, a tenuous establishment in academia was achieved. In terms of the 'identity politics' (Butler 1990) of such movements, the gender discourse focused basically on differences in sex/gender. But the voices for example of black, lesbian, and disabled women propelled the challenge to take the diversities *between* women into account. Accordingly, since the 1990s, it became a main challenge to address theoretically and in research the multiple 'axes of difference' (Knapp / Wetterer 2003) – as gender, race, class, disability, sexual orientation 'and so on' – and the multiple 'intersections' in which they crisscross in individual lives (Crenshaw 1989; Knapp 2005; Davis 2008).

2) The younger discourse on *managing diversity* was developed in the 1990s in the U.S.A. and reached Germany and the EU around the turn of the century. It might be regarded as one of the effects in institutional and cultural changes, which were mentioned before. But at the same time a profound switch in arguments was provided: When companies face unknown challenges on diversifying and globalising markets, differences within the workforce could turn into a potential *asset* for the successful performance on such markets – and morally based demands for equal opportunities could be transformed into the prospect of competitive advantages (see on EU-developments: Merx / Vassilopoulou 2007: 354-360). The diversity discourse started to sell (and to replace discourses on affirmative action or gender mainstreaming). Starting with different ethnic-cultural backgrounds, and embracing gender and gay demands, lists of further diversity attributes, which might be valuable and should be considered, soon grew. Hence, the discourse of *managing diversity* has to face a similar challenge in theoretical development and research as the gender discourse.

Considering such a background, I started to design a qualitative research project to explore the effects of diversity on professional trajectories in academia, especially in the take-off period between a master's degree and the establishment of a vocational position. Comparing career paths in the U.S.A. and Germany, it also aims at identifying policies and regulations that provide obstacles or opportunities. Thus, the collection and analysis of data was designed to combine document analysis and open interviewing in order to confront institutional regulations and policies by the viewpoints and experiences of graduate students, faculty members, and professionals who left academia.

2. On the Challenge of Intersections

The biggest challenge arose from planning a sample, which would allow for addressing *intersections* in diversities, as current diversity attributes along single axes of difference do not provide distinct, mutually exclusive categories. To explain and unfold this core problem as briefly as possible, I should recap the main methodological strategies in social research for dealing with differences in population structures:

The relevant data in quantitative research has to be collected by a system of exclusive categories for each variable (axis) and its parameter values: e.g. gender: male/female; sexual orientation: hetero-/homosexual; age (defining age cohorts); class/economic position (defining e.g. income groups) et al. A large random sample taken from the universe of relevant real cases can then be supposed to provide all kinds of data for statistically based testing or probing systematically into their combinations. Samples in qualitative inquiry, on the contrary, have to be relatively small to permit a more in-depth analysis of single cases. Thus, a comparative sampling strategy would be to plan a sample structure with combined subgroups. Its most simple form is presented by a cross tabulation, just for illustration with ten cases in each subgroup:

		sexual orientation	
		heterosexual	Homosexual
gender	male	10	10
	female	10	10

Depending on the workforce doing research and the intensity of the single case analysis, a total of 40 cases can already present a considerably big sample in a qualitative inquiry. But, by adding more variables, the number of subgroups in logically systematic combinations will grow exponentially: Adding only a third variable with just two parameter values – as e.g. a 'race/ethnicity' axes with just two parameters: white/non-white – would already double the total numbers of subgroups from four to eight, thus pushing the number of necessary participant cases from 40 up to 80 or cutting the number of single cases in each group in half:

sexual orientation		heterosexual		Homosexual	
race/ethnicity		white	non-w.	white	non-w.
gender	male	5	5	5	5
	female	5	5	5	5

Adding more variables and parameters, the number of subgroups in systematic combinations will explode further, while up to now, my argument focused only on differences that can be ascribed to individuals. Taking further social conditions into account – in academia e.g. discipline's subcultures, different study programmes, different national regulations – would add even more variables/subgroups.

Additionally, we would need to recruit members of all those subgroups which can be constructed logically. To illustrate this difficulty by example: In debates on the German education crisis during the 1960s, the 'rural catholic girl from a workers family' represented the (statistically constructed) group with the least chance for higher education. With additional diversity attributes, we might have to look for a disabled catholic lesbian descending from a rural worker's family on an academic career track to fill up a logically constructed subgroup.

This problem usually does not occur in quantitative research because in statistical analysis, it is not the intersection of such diversity attributes in the social position of a *single* person which is of interest. Nevertheless for the data analysis, the system of variables/categories and their parameter values constitute a comparable cross tabulation with a comparable exploding number of subgroups. To handle such a number, the researcher 'typically must break down intersectionality into its constituent parts to analyse the pairwise relationships between detailed groups, often with the aim of reconstructing it later' (McCall 2003b: 20). Thus, with each variable added, the size and complexity of a quantitative study will grow also quickly.

As a consequence, qualitative studies with the described type of planned sample structure, as well as quantitative studies, tend to limit the number of variables taken into account – a perfectly reasonable means to keep an inquiry manageable. Accordingly, McCall (2003b: 20) supposes the methodological challenge of intersections to be one reason for the compartimentalisation of research along the single axes of difference with "little overlap among them"; and, accordingly, in the overlapping sections, combinations of two variables are prevalent (Lutz 2004: 476; Räthzel 2004: 252-253; see also the anthology at hand).

Finally, there is a further aspect to the basic methodological problem – the axes of difference and related diversity attributes do not provide distinct, mutually exclusive categories. By way of a brief illustration, I want to recall a recent famous example: Barack Obama. Entangled by the media reporting during the 2008 campaign, one hardly could avoid knowing that besides his black Kenyan father, he had a white American mother who mostly raised him. Thus, what made him the 'first black president' of the U.S.A. with all its high symbolic value?

Critical theory, discourse analysis, and deconstructionism in feminist, women's, and gender studies call attention to the diversity attributes, which are also used in research to construct a system of categories for different subgroups. And they offer an answer: These diversity attributes originate from, and are part of, the socio-cultural discursive *construction* of differences between persons – differences with the dominant centre of the white, bourgeois, heterosexual male (as neatly presented in the gallery of former U.S. presidents) and with the tendency for mutual exclusion in the logic of identity. Obama *has to be* identified as white *or* black; children *have to be* male *or* female[1], and so on.

3. The Strategy of Theoretical Sampling

Thus, there are a number of reasons to avoid clear-cut categories defining diversity attributes and related subgroups in sampling right from the beginning – and the Grounded Theory offers a strategy of sampling in qualitative inquiry, which would allow one to do so. In the tool box of qualitative methods, it was established as theoretical sampling. This term might be misleading as it might suggest a sampling according to preconceived theoretical assumptions; but to explain it more precisely, I have to remind readers of basic leading concepts in quantitative and qualitative research.

According to the fallibilist methodology, as developed and advanced by Popper (2002), Reichenbach (1951), and Lakatos (1976; in summarizing discussion: Ritsert 2003), quantitative research follows – in terms of logic – a *deductive* research design basically organised to test hypotheses. Before a researcher can start collecting data, the instrument of data collection has to be designed: Variables, their parameters, and then indicators have to be defined *applying pre-existing* (more or less) theoretical assumptions to assign what exactly has to be measured in order to allow, finally, empirically based conclusions, decisions or statements, about the leading research questions and/or the inspected hypotheses.

In contrast, qualitative research as represented by the Grounded Theory organises a different line of concern, as it focuses on *developing and inventing* theoretical concepts based on the empirical research (Glaser / Strauss 1967; Strauss 1991). Thus, in terms of logic, it aims to proceed rather in an *inductive* mode, concluding from empirical data 'up to' more general theoretical statements and discoveries. Accordingly, a theoretical sampling, as suggested by the Grounded Theory, aims to develop - within the process of data analysis - those theoretical assumptions, which guide the next steps in sampling.

To do so, the researcher starts to analyse one first case, which can be chosen almost arbitrarily within the relevant universe of cases. After developing his or her first preliminary hypotheses during the case analysis, a next case for analysis has to be chosen to provide the opportunity for case com-

---

1   As a literary voice: See Eugenides (2004).

parison; a minimum or maximum contrast, in at least one interesting respect, is suggested for this purpose. In analysing the second case and then comparing both, first ideas and concepts can be tested, then dismissed or maintained, and other might evolve. Choosing a third and fourth case and so on, the researcher proceeds further from case to case; analysing and comparing data, developing, testing, and more and more integrating maintained concepts and hypotheses – until a 'saturation' is supposed to occur: Analysing and comparing next cases turn out to only confirm what had been developed before. The researcher can pass on to finalizing results.

So far so good. But a basic claim has been disputed: the claim that the data evaluation could proceed in a purely inductive mode with researchers ignoring or – with a notion stemming from phenomenology – 'parenthesising' their prior knowledge and presuppositions (Schlücker 2008: 56-59, comparing concepts). Strictly speaking, the Grounded Theory did not even argue for this claim. Strauss (1991: 36) considered the researchers' knowledge and experiences, rather, as a legitimate part of the accessible data pool. But to cut short methodological sophistry (Schlücker 2008: 295-300): I hold the view that it is essential *to reflect* on those assumptions and presuppositions, which – intentionally or unwittingly – find their way into empirical work. In research on diversity this includes reflecting on those diversity attributes, which we tend to apply almost naturally with the risks of reification.

Proceeding that way in the basic steps of a theoretical sampling, research on intersections in diversity can avoid the difficulties of a planned sample as outlined before: having to decide right in the beginning on two, or at most three variables/categories to investigate (Davis 2008: 25), and defining related subgroups according to current diversity attributes. This might allow theoretical considerations to be generated – as Räthzel (2004: 254) insists – which go beyond simply probing into single intersections and typing similarities or differences between the effects of two axes of difference. In this respect, the project's aims include a contribution to the debates and theoretical developments on intersections.

4. On Obstacles in the Academy

As laid out, there are good theoretical and methodological reasons to favour a thorough theoretical sampling to explore diversity in academic careers. However, more practical contexts and conditions turned out to present a serious obstacle for doing so. To illustrate this, I want to start again recalling basic differences between quantitative and qualitative research.

In quantitative research, the instrument of data collection as well as basic decisions on the sampling and the statistical instruments for data analysis are elaborated – ideally – in a strict deductive mode starting from research questions and/or theoretical hypotheses. The collecting and analysing of the data should then proceed according to plans. As we know, by experience and/or inquiries in *doing* scientific research (e.g. Knorr-Cetina 1981), plans put into practice do not always work in every respect. But in qualitative inquiry, its basic research logic sets up a more profound uncertainty:

As I mentioned before, referring to the Grounded Theory, qualitative research focuses on developing and inventing theoretical concepts based on the empirical research; in other words: its leading aim is to generate *new* ideas, concepts, insights. Accordingly – and again ideally – qualitative methods are laid out to allow and even to foster *unexpected* findings. Yet by definition, the emergence of something unexpected cannot be planned. Thus compared to quantitative research, a qualitative inquiry is basically a more uncertain, riskier enterprise (Schlücker 2007: 261).

It is even riskier when following thoroughly the concept of theoretical sampling, instead of planning ahead a sample structure as outlined before. As a kind of compromise, Flick (1995: 78-91) has suggested restricting the step-by-step procedure of theoretical sampling to the data analysis of such a planned sample structure: Its fixed number of cases and the limited number of variables serves as a means to keep the inquiry feasible; because in a pure theoretical sampling, as suggested by the Grounded Theory, the moment when a 'saturation' is supposed to occur – so that the researcher can end collecting next case data and start finalising results – cannot be planned or anticipated.[2]

In the organisational framework for scientific research, this turns out to be a tremendous handicap – and in Germany especially after its basic reorganisation since about ten years. At this point one might recall that during those same ten years or so in Germany, the research on *managing diversity* started to blossom. I already mentioned some developments that probably contributed: the women's, gay, and black civil rights movements; international companies facing unknown challenges on diversified and globalising markets; EU-regulations providing swifts in arguments. But in Germany, there might also be an additional one:

New funding and legal regulations were implemented in order to set up the mostly government-run German universities to act like companies in globalising markets. The organisational reform arranged a new competition between academic units to identify and support 'lighthouses of excellence', as the favoured metaphor puts it – with the more or less outspoken aim that those lighthouses should be able to compete with the worldwide, most pres-

---

2   In a closer look at it, we actually have to talk about points of saturation in plural. Not basically different from Poppers concept of an incremental approach towards knowledge, a saturation up to the point of conclusions ready for finalizing results might occur in some aspects, while research in other aspects still has to go on.

tigious U.S. American universities. At ambitious German universities, the discourse on *managing diversity* started to sell, as it was seen that respecting and managing diversity could turn into a potential asset for a successful performance by attracting and encouraging good researchers and students regardless of gender, race or other diversity attributes.

So the market for research projects exploring diversity within the academy grew – while the framework for a qualitative inquiry probing into the full complexity of intersections got even more restricted than before. To roughly sketch two aspects: Within the new framework conditions for research in Germany, the pressure on research projects to produce results within a tightened study period grew. As Münch (2006: 448, own translation) bluntly puts it, a "highly vital criterion in judging applications for research funding is the probability that certain results can be produced in the available time of normally two years" (while in the humanities, in the 1990s, at least a three year study period had been more 'normal' yet). Under these conditions, a qualitative inquiry meant to follow closely the basic concept of a theoretical sampling turns into a kind of worst case-scenario. Additionally, the pressure to publish in top peer-reviewed journals also grew, whilst McCall (2003b: 20) already had outlined its 'hostility' even to quantitative studies exploring the complexity of intersections.

Thus all in all, there seems to be a peculiar contraction in German developments: While the research area of *gender and diversity* grows and the interest in exploring the crisscrossing intersections of diversity should be raised, the practical research framework for to do so turned out to be even more restricted.

5. Conclusions: The Challenge of Academic/Scientific Work Output

In order to draw my conclusions, I suggest treating such observations as data, which also ought to be analysed as a part of the inquiry.

One argument to do so already came across, namely Strauss' claim (1991: 36) to consider the researchers' knowledge and experiences as part of the accessible data pool. Furthermore, in line with Critical Theory and others (Schlücker 2008: 488), I hold the view that any inquiry and "manufacturing of knowledge" (Knorr-Cetina 1981) has to reflect on its conditions and aims. Yet, in doing research on *diversity in the academy*, there is a specially striking twist: What the researchers *do* in daily work – to design and conduct research projects, to attend conferences, to add papers to the list of accomplished works in the CV – all such activities are part of the research *subject* at the same time. They – to include myself explicitly: 'we' in all our diversity – do not study some aspects of reality 'out there', but *own* reality, everyone a potential case in the universe of relevant cases.

Hence, what preliminary hypotheses and considerations could be drawn from the briefly outlined observations? Firstly, they just seem to confirm and to illustrate the presupposition that the conditions and circumstances of research as a pivotal academic task can have an influence on the kind of work output, the kind of knowledge which can be manufactured.

In different contexts, this would be no striking news at all; in research on human resources management, for example, hardly anybody would be surprised to hear that the circumstances and conditions of work can have an influence on its output. Furthermore, the concept of *managing diversity* includes the claim that "diverse teams produce more innovative solutions and perform better" (as it is taken for granted in *Call for Papers*, 2009: 1). In other words, it is presupposed that those 'conditions' of work can have an influence on its output, which come along with the individuals completing the task. Applied to scientific work, this concept is also all but new. In a term by Max Weber which gave its name to an early debate during the funding of German sociology in the beginning of the 20th century: different 'value judgements' which arise from different (sub-)cultural backgrounds and perspectives would exercise effects on the researcher's scientific performance (Ritsert 2003: 11-63). Even Popper (1971: 112-113) did not deny that the social background of a researcher inevitably has a part in his or her work output.

Yet, secondly, this leads straight onto the mine-field of long debates in the history, philosophy, and social study of science. As central speakers on dominant strands of such debates, Weber and Popper also hold firmly to the view that the outcomes of scientific endeavours *should* depend *solely* on those (internal) scientific guidelines and methods to guarantee the rationality and objectivity of research outcomes. In other words: good science *should* be free of (external) influences from whatever else conditions and circumstances.[3] Accordingly, from this point of view, diversity among researchers is irrelevant at best.

Moreover, this leads into the midst of current science policies, as the problem how to judge the quality of research output and academic performance is a central one herein. It leads into debates on the role and effects of fixing 'gold standards' for research quality by National Research Councils as in Canada and the U.S.A. And it leads into the question of criteria – as, well known, for example citation indices and the number of peer reviewed publications – to identify the excellence of 'lighthouses' as well as the performance of single researchers.

---

3 Popper (1971) entrusted the mutual criticism within the scientific community with eliminating such influences.

Thus, the kind and quality of academic work output is a hot issue in a double respect. However, in doing research on the chances and obstacles for academic careers and on diversity in the academy in general, it cannot be ignored. Based on previous work (Schlücker 2008), I suppose as a 'sensitiving concept' using a Grounded Theory term that in analysing the character and quality of academic work output, one has to take into account also its explicit or implicit aims and purposes. Again, in an entrepreneurial context with its distinction between long term and short term objectives for example, this assumption might not be at all surprising; what might be a better work output in one respect, might not be so in another. And with an attention in this respect, it might even be possible to find an explanation for the peculiar contradiction in recent German developments.

References

Butler, J. (1990): Gender Trouble: Feminism and the Subversion of Idenity. New York, London.

Call for Papers (2008): Going Diverse: Innovative Answers to Future Challenges. International Conference on Gender and Diversity in Science, Technology, and Business, 29-30 October 2009. Aachen.

Crenshaw, K. (1989): Demarginalizing the Intersection of Race and Sex: A Black Feminist Critique of Antidiscrimination Doctrine, Feminist Theory, and Antiracist Politics. In: Phillips, Anne (Eds.): Feminism & Politics. New York, 314-343.

Davis, K. (2008): Intersectionality in Transatlantic Perspective. In: Klinger, C. / Knapp, G.-A. (Eds.): ÜberKreuzungen: Fremdheit, Ungleichheit, Differenz. Münster, 19-35.

Eugenides, J. (2002): Middlesex. New York.

Flick, U. (1995): Qualitative Forschung: Theorien, Methoden, Anwendungen in Psychologie und Sozialwissenschaften. Reinbek b.H.

Foucault, M. (1977): Die Ordnung des Diskurses. Frankfurt a. M.

Glaser, B. G. / Strauss, A. L. (1967): The Discovery of Grounded Theory. Chicago.

Klinger, C. / Knapp, G.-A. (2008): ÜberKreuzungen: Fremdheit, Ungleichheit, Differenz. Münster.

Knapp, G.-A. (2005): Race, Class, Gender: Reclaiming Baggage in Fast Travelling Theories. In: European Journal of Women's Studies, 12 (3), 249-265.

Knapp, G.-A. / Wetterer, A. (Eds.) (2003): Achsen der Differenz: Gesellschaftstheorie und feministische Kritik 2. Münster.

Knorr-Cetina, K. (1981): The Manufacturing of Knowledge: An Essay on the Constructivist and Contextual Nature of Science. Oxford.

Lakatos, I. (1976): Proofs and Refutations: The Logic of Mathematical Discovery. Cambridge.

Lutz, H. (2004): Migrations- und Geschlechterforschung: Zur Genese einer komplizierten Beziehung. In:

Becker, R. / Kortendiek, B. (Eds.) (2008): Handbuch Frauen- und Geschlechterforschung: Theorie, Methoden, Empirie. Wiesbaden,476-484.

McCall, L. (2003a): Complex Inequality: Gender, Class, and Race in the New Economy. New York.

McCall, L. (2003b): Managing the Complexity of Intersectionality. New Brunswick [online]. Available from: http://www.rci.rutgers.edu/~lmccall/signs1f-ext.pdf.

Merx, A. / Vassilopoulou, J. (2007): Das arbeitsrechtliche AGG und Diversity-Perspektiven. In: Koall, I. / Bruchhagen, V. / Höher, F. (Eds.): Diversity Outlooks: Managing Gender & Diversity zwischen Business Case und Ethik, Münster, 354-385. [online]. Available from: http://www.idm-diversity.org/files/Merx-Vassilopoulou-AGG_Diversity.pdf.

Münch, R. (2006): Drittmittel und Publikationen: Forschung zwischen Normalwissenschaft und Innovation. Soziologie, 35 (4), 440-461.

Popper, K. R. (1971): Die Logik der Sozialwissenschaften. In: Adorno, T. W. et al. (Eds.): Der Positivismusstreit in der deutschen Soziologie. Neuwied, Berlin (3rd. ed.), 103-122.

Popper, K. R. (2002): The Logic of Scientific Discourse (1935/1959). London, New York.

Räthzel, N. (2004): Rassismustheorien: Geschlechterverhältnisse und Feminismus. In: Becker, R. / Kortendiek, B. (Eds.): Handbuch Frauen- und Geschlechterforschung: Theorie, Methoden, Empirie. Wiesbaden, 248-256.

Reichenbach, H. (1951): The Rise of Scientific Philosophy. Berkeley.

Ritsert, J. (2003): Einführung in die Logik der Sozialwissenschaft. Münster.

Schlücker, K. (2007): Qualitative Forschung zwischen *claims*, *tools* und Epistemologie. In: Erwägen Wissen Ethik (zuvor: Ethik und Sozialwissenschaften) 18, (2), 260-262.

Schlücker, K. (2008): Vom Text zum Wissen: Positionen und Probleme qualitativer Forschung. Konstanz.

Strauss, A. L. (1991): Qualitative Sozialforschung: Datenanalyse und Theoriebildung in der empirischen und soziologischen Forschung. München.

Highly skilled female Migration in an enlarged Europe: the case of women scientists at German Universities

Andrea Wolffram

Modern knowledge societies can't afford to ignore available qualification, knowledge and skills among its members against the background of globalisation, increasing mobility and demographic changes in these societies. In the course of EU enlargement, increasing transnational mobility of highly skilled women with science and engineering education leads to the question of their integration into the German academic labour market. In this article the carrier barriers and promotive factors of career progression for these women shall be discussed with particular focus on universities. At first, the intertwinement of the mobility of scientists and the migration of the highly skilled in the context of EU enlargement shall be discussed. Then the perspective is narrowed to women scientists at German universities. Here an intersectional perspective shall be introduced in order to uncover discriminatory practices towards female scientist at universities regarding their worse career progression compared to their counterparts derived from their status as women and/or due to their status as migrant. Tentative answers will be given to the question regarding the mechanisms of integration and allocation of female scientists with migration background at German universities on the basis of initial findings from an empirical study.

1. Introduction

Modern knowledge societies are dependent upon the broad development of qualification, knowledge and skills among its members. Against the background of EU enlargement, globalisation and internationalisation processes, as well as increasing mobility and demographic change, these societies cannot afford to ignore available potential. Nevertheless, there is a disparity between the demand of highly skilled specialists in science and technology and the occupational integration of women who are highly qualified in these fields. In Germany, the participation of women in science and technology is still low and their career prospects compare negatively to their male colleagues. Since the 1990s a relevant group of highly skilled women with an education in technology and natural sciences has migrated from the post-socialist Eastern European countries to Germany. Given this increasing transnational mobility of highly skilled women, the question of their integration into the German academic labour market arises. With regard to the academic sector, the main focus of this article is on the integration of the migrant female scientists and engineers at German universities and possibility of their perusing a scientific career. By analysing the specific situation of highly skilled female scientists with a migration background at German universities, the relevance of mechanisms of upgrading as well as of downgrading and exclusion from university careers on the basis of gender is being contextualised by taking the cultural background and nationality of female scientists into consideration. To date, highly skilled female academics in technology and natural sciences have been sparsely considered within research about gender equality at universities and migration studies.

2. Mobility of women scientists within the context of the EU enlargement

For several years now, the European Commission has been concerned with the labour force within Europe which has not adequately responded to the new demands of an internationalised and globalised labour market. The particular focus of the Commission's "Action plan for skills and mobility"[1] is occupational mobility. Occupational mobility is also central to the European Employment Strategy (EES) in promoting excellence and competitiveness, and in solving skills shortages and bottlenecks in key areas of employment such as engineering and science (European Commission 2006). Scientists certainly have an understanding of the importance of mobility to science as a whole, but their own mobility is much more likely to be shaped by considerations related to their ability to work effectively and successfully in their chosen field, as well as by their familial and personal contexts. Nevertheless, the "expectation of mobility" in science plays an important role in shaping the European Research Area (ERA). Research argues that improved economic opportunities and advanced migration policy in destination countries promote highly skilled mobility (Morano-Foadi 2005: 133).

    In the new member countries, and the Eastern European countries as a whole, the need for occupational mobility is much higher than in the old member countries. The collapse of the socialist regimes in the aftermath of the events of 1989 heralded a new phase in European migration. Slany (2008)

---

1   COM (2002) 72 final in: http://eur-lex.europa.eu/smartapi/cgi/sga_doc?smartapi! celexplus!prod!DocNumber&lg=en&type_doc=COMfinal&an_doc=2002&nu_doc=72 (28.02.2010)

points out that this new phase of migration is witnessing a shift in the gradation of reasons for emigration. Economic reasons are among the most important ones for emigration to Western European countries, because political and economical transformation processes in most countries of Eastern and Central Europe were accompanied by increasing rates of unemployment. But these processes also opened up new opportunities as departure from the home country no longer implied leaving for ever (Morokvasic / Münst / Metz-Göckel 2008: 10). Completely new emigratory motivations also emerged in educational terms, including student and scholar exchanges within the EU in particular (Slany 2008). Moreover, the feminisation of academic and skilled migration has been a new emerging phenomenon within this context (Krieger 2004).

In the public discourse, the fear of a low skilled labour force from the Eastern European countries invading the labour markets of neighbouring old member countries has demanded legal regulation. In this debate, however, a focus on highly skilled migrants has been neglected for a long time. With regard to this group, it is especially important to ask if migration within this group still refers to a permanent migration (exodus) or rather a commuting movement. For the new member countries the 'brain drain' has become an increasing problem and weakened the possibilities for developing their economies. Substantial public capital had been invested in their training with supposed benefits for research to be brought back to society. However, new possibilities of emigration were facilitated by liberalised exit legislation of the new EU member. Freedom of circulation within the EU has made the borders inside the EU space less important for those who have citizenship or a legal status that allow them to travel freely. However, Germany did not pass its new immigration law, which facilitates the procurement of a resident and labour permit in Germany, especially for highly skilled researchers from Eastern Europe, until 2005.

While it can be argued that the ERA is designed to encourage interchange of researchers, skills balance is essential to competitiveness in the EU. The EU's research strategy actively encourages both scientific mobility and seeks to reduce regional inequality and promote balanced growth. However, despite the actions taken in the context of the European Commission Mobility Strategy, unbalanced flows are still a weakness of the ERA. There is the need in Europe to coordinate research and migration policies at European and Member Country level in order to enhance the attractiveness of all European countries and facilitate the return of researchers to their sending countries (van de Sande et al. 2005).

Against this background an urgent question is: under which conditions does EU enlargement promote either 'brain drain' or encourage a healthy degree of circulation and 'brain return'? It is evident from empirical data (Morokvasic / Münst / Metz-Göckel 2008) that permanent migration is not the foremost desired aim for many labour migrants from Eastern European countries. Commuting migration is used by low skilled labour migrants as a resource to maintain one's home base in the country of origin. However, what are the perspectives of highly skilled migrants, such as researchers? Here, empirical findings show that researchers consider important determinants in the migration decision and destination to be the research environment and conditions like research support, infrastructures and demand for natural sciences and engineering researchers (Sretenova 2003).

The female migrant situation can be summarised thus: highly skilled East-West migration flows and their causes are in a state of change with the increasing relevance of its feminisation. Given the increasing transnational mobility of highly skilled women, the question of their integration into the German labour market thus arises. In the case of the scientists among this group, the question is narrowed to their integration in the academic labour market. One decisive question is whether women scientists and engineers who have achieved a career in academia can contribute to a change of the stereotypical gendered image of science and technology, or whether migrant women will drop out in the long run through a lack of knowledge exchange, values and norms in the host country.

The periods of transition – to a knowledge society and to an Enlarged Europe – offer favourable opportunities for addressing gender equality through organisational change and the potential for established practices and patterns of segregation to be replaced with new, more equitable, social forms (Webster 2001). In this process, the new member states offer valuable knowledge and cultural diversity, due to the legacy of former gender policy combined with national cultural traditions of full employment of women. Both factors make it unlikely that East European women would leave a professional career because of of their families or due to experiences of the revival of occupational gender stereotypes in science and technology disciplines faced in Western European countries (Sretenova 2005).

3. Women scientists at German universities in the context of an intersectional perspective

In 2008 roughly one million women from Eastern European countries were living in Germany.[2] Concerning their education, around 8% of the total rate of female migrants in Germany had a university degree (Heß / Sauer 2007). The percentage of migrants with a university degree, especially from Eastern

---

2   Data were delivered on request by EUROSTAT in 2009.

European countries, is often much higher than 8%. But even considering that 8% of them had a university degree, it means that there were 80,000 highly skilled migrant women living in Germany in 2008. Around 12% of all women with a university degree in Germany are scientists and engineers. Consequently, almost 10,000 of the highly skilled migrant women with university degrees are natural scientists or engineers, and probably more, as in Eastern Europe these subjects are not as segregated as in Germany. Regarding the employment rate in these subjects, it is remarkable that in 2005 only 6,668 women with foreign nationalities were working in engineering and science with social insurance contributions. However, these were not only women from Eastern Europe but from all foreign countries.[3]

From this it follows that there has to be a huge 'brain waste' among highly skilled migrant women with Eastern European origins. Studies on migrant women in personnel services indicate that many highly skilled women, coming from Eastern European countries, work as cleaners, babysitters and caretakers, for middle class career-oriented women in the host country (Lutz 2007). This was the starting point of the study "Highly skilled migrant women in technological cutting-edge research at universities"[4] where our aim is to determine under which condition these women can pursue their academic careers or have to suffer 'de-skilling'?

A transnational perspective is most often adopted when analysing women's spatial mobility from Eastern Europe to the old member countries, which has become a strategy for maintaining migrant women's social status at home and their coping with de-skilling (Metz-Göckel / Morokvasic / Münst 2008). Another approach that is increasing in importance within migration studies is an intersectional perspective (Lenz 2007). This approach could be useful in order to understand interferences between the categories of gender and ethnicity in the context of highly skilled migration from Eastern to Western European countries.

Coming from a feminist theory perspective, I argue that gender and ethnicity are socially constructed. These categories influence not only individual identities but also provide principles of organisation in the social system.

---

3   In Germany, there exists a statistical lack of data concerning the representation of highly skilled migrant women who came from Eastern Europe. That is the reason for the approximation in order to determine a approximately number of highly skilled migrant women with science and engineering occupation. The base of data is delivered from EUROSTAT and from a working paper of the Federal Office for Migration and Refugees from Heß & Sauer (2007).

4   The study "Highly skilled migrant women in technological cutting-edge research at universities" is part of the network research project "The integration of highly qualified migrant women into the German labour market" conducted at HU Berlin, TU Hamburg-Harburg and RWTH Aachen. The network project is supported in the framework of the announcement "Women to the top" of the German Federal Ministry of Education and Research (BMBF) and the European Social Fund (ERS). (Duration: 01.05.2009 – 30.04.2011) I would like to thank Miriam Lämmerhirt and Anna Bouffier who have compiled the statistical data and carried out interviews with experts, the women scientists and engineers.

154   Andrea Wolffram

They are mutually constituted to produce and maintain social hierarchy with power differences. These power differences are infused into every aspect of social life. They shape identities, interpersonal interactions, the operation of firms and academia, as well as the organisation of economic and legal systems (Browne / Misra 2003: 489f.). As socially constructed categories gender and ethnicity are seen as a fluid, historical and situational contingent. They are constantly reproduced through social interactions (Fenstermaker / West 2002). Intersectional approaches suggest that gender and ethnicity are not independent analytic categories that can simply be added together. Rather, they fuse to create unique experiences and opportunities for an individual. Ethnicity is constructed within gendered meanings and vice versa. Within the dominant culture, these meanings provide legitimising ideologies to subordinate men and women of a specific ethnicity. The above mentioned research finding of the de-skilling of highly skilled migrant women is an impressive example: highly skilled German women are more likely to be viewed as being more qualified than highly skilled women from Eastern Europe. German women benefit from this privilege. Following from this, many German families in high-paying professional jobs have the opportunity to rely on women from Eastern Europe who relieve them of their care-giving duties by taking low-paying jobs doing housekeeping and caring for children and elderly in times of a saturated academic job market. German women then doubly benefit from the social constructions that define Eastern European women within the labour market as less qualified. This example carries the assumption that the social constructions of gender and ethnicity are systematically related to labour market dynamics to generate inequality.

Against this background is an urgent question regarding finding out what the essential conditions that determine continuity and success in the career progression of highly skilled women migrants at universities are, and vice versa; what are the factors that cause career setbacks and de-skilling? How do mobility experiences influence the academic careers of these women, and under which conditions can these experiences be made productive for career progression?

In the following, empirical findings of the study will be presented. From an intersectional perspective, tentative answers will be given to the mechanisms of integration and allocation of academic migrant women into German universities. In this context, factors that contribute to the reproduction of gender and ethnicity (in)equality, as well as conditions that lead to successful academic career progressions, will be concluded.

4. Carrier barriers and promotive factors of career progression for highly skilled women migrants in academia

The design of the study contains three expert interviews, ten biographical interviews with migrant female scientists working at German universities, and five biographical interviews with German female scientists, also working at German universities. Thus far, the three expert interviews and three interviews with migrant female scientists have been conducted. The expert interviews, which were conducted in summer 2009, were analysed through a content analysis. The biographical interviews will be analysed using a hermeneutical approach and are still a work in progress.

Initial findings of the study discussed in the following are derived from the three expert interviews and the three biographical interviews. The experts come from a university background (a gender researcher and an expert from the international office) and from politics. The female scientists who came from Eastern Europe in the course of their scientific careers work as (junior) professors at German universities.

Highly skilled women in academia: the view from experts working in the context of highly skilled mobility
Highly skilled women who have migrated from Eastern Europe to Germany face many barriers that constrain their carrier progression. These barriers are caused by law, the academic job market, politics and administration, the reconciliation of family and work, and the motive of migration. One of the most important reasons why highly skilled migrant women have difficulties in continuing their career after leaving their home country is of a legal nature. Especially for Non-EU-members, there are only a few possibilities to get a permanent permit to stay. According to the new German immigration law from 2005, scientists with specific professional acknowledgment are defined as "highly qualified" and can get a "permanent permit of stay", providing they have employment which ensures their livelihood. Only in the case of highly qualified non-EU citizens does the German Federal Employment Office have to prove that there is no German or EU citizen who can equally do the job. This was the general practice prior to 2005. But in the case of the new member countries another discriminatory practice comes into place. Professionals from Eastern European countries further encounter a non-acknowledgement of their professional certification. For most of these professions there is no official acceptance needed, so it depends on their employer if the applicant's foreign certification is accepted or not.

Another discriminatory practice lies in the German system of administering unemployment. Foreign persons who received a university degree in their native countries and who become unemployed in Germany are automatically classified as "unskilled" at the German Federal Employment Office. As a result, low-threshold employment provisions are offered to the highly skilled migrants. This practice was already identified by Gruber / Rüßler (2002) who have analysed the integration of highly skilled Jewish migrants from the former Soviet Union in the regional job market of North Rhine-Westphalia.

In general it has to be concluded that a deficient immigration policy in Germany is the main barrier for highly skilled migrants. In other countries like Great Britain, Sweden or the Netherlands, there are sophisticated programmes implemented to recruit scientists, engineers and physicians. In Germany, apart from a few exceptions, such as the qualification and integration programme for academics of the Otto Bennecke Foundation, few opportunities and official programmes are offered for these groups.

Focus on the women among the highly skilled migrants statistical data indicates a specific barrier that is noted in the intersection of the categories gender and ethnicity. In Germany, public attitude toward migrants regards them more as an inevitability than as a potential. This statement will be confirmed in a study of Engelmann und Müller (2007) where only 30% of the interviewed persons said that migrants contribute to Germany, whereas in Sweden it was 79%. Besides this ethical discrimination there is, furthermore, a discrimination based on their gender. Women face discrimination in general in the German labour market, especially in science and engineering. In the year 2004, 10% of German women worked in under qualified positions. However, concerning migrant women the number was 24%, with even 32% of migrant women from Non-OECD-countries worked in under qualified positions (ibid.).

A barrier, however, especially for migrant women in the academic culture, is a strong dependency by non-professorial academic staff on their professors and an absent monitoring system to support professors who may be concerned with a gender sensitive career development. Many professors do not highly regard the importance of a diverse research team and the demand to foster female scientists. Migrant women, in particular, who have to cope with the scientific and work culture that is characterised through an offensive presentation of their own achievements, often change their initial plans concerning their careers and have to adapt to unfortunate circumstances. According to the gender expert she didn't meet one single migrant woman, who evaluated her career in Germany positively without any restriction. She sees a need in more practical assistance for migrants by the universities and professional networks. Furthermore, monitoring, and especially more assistance from the responsible professors, are needed to improve the situation for migrant scientists in Germany.

Highly skilled women in academia: the view from the highly skilled women scientists with migration background

Scientists who came to Germany during or after their studies with the aim to do their doctoral thesis at a German university, and scientists who came with the support of special foundations like Erasmus, EU intra-European fellow-ships etc., have much better chances of acquiring an adequate job at universities following the academic education or the PhD. All three women scientists who have applied successfully for a professorship offered at German universities came to Germany in the course of their scientific careers, as a student, a PhD-student, or Postdoc. Here, it becomes already clear that the migration motive is very important in order to explain who will pursue an academic career in Germany and who will have difficulties in making career progression at German universities.

The female scientists from Eastern Europe who have acquired a professorship at a German university nevertheless face different barriers and discrimination – as women and as migrants. Two barriers shall be discussed in the following.

For female scientists with long working hours at university, the poor childcare situation in Germany is, in particular, a huge problem that female scientists from Eastern European countries are not familiar with from their home country experience. There, childcare is also the responsibility of women. However, for every child at any age there are enough childcare places available and childcare is cheap. Because institutional childcare in Germany is generally not available in the afternoon, individual solutions have to be found by the female scientists. However, migrant scientists are often-times on their own because parents and friends aren't there to provide childcare. They solve this problem through hiring a nanny which is very expensive. At universities it is not generally accepted that women leave the workplace in the afternoon in order to care for their children and then again work in the evening on their research. It is a common experience that meetings often take place in the late afternoon.

However, female scientists from Eastern Europe also face discrimination at German universities which they put in the context of double discrimination as women and as migrant. For example, migrant female professors are not familiar with the German science system, especially with the distribution of finance within the university system. In this context they know that they cannot ask their male colleagues to get this strategic important information. At university, especially in science and engineering, they have experienced that networks are strong male dominated networks. That is also the reason why one of the professors thought that she did not get the position of institutional director. The reason given being that only a strong man can fill such a position.

5. Concluding remarks

A first conclusion that can be drawn from the initial empirical findings is that poor conditions for highly skilled migrants in Germany most often cause a career break for the migrants and especially for female migrants. The workforce potential that comes to, or already lives in, Germany is not valued and not used, resulting in considerable loss of potential for the German economy.

Presently it is not possible to give a precise quantitative assessment of highly skilled women migrants in Germany. Neither German nor European institutions include this group in their statistics adequately. This can be interpreted as an indicator for the lack of awareness concerning this problematic topic, although Germany is still facing skill shortages. In general, regardless of a focus on academia or economy and industry, the huge potential of highly skilled migrant women already living in Germany is wasted. Furthermore, twenty years after the collapse of the socialist regimes, the immigration of professionals from foreign countries is still hindered by resentments and an absence of adequate immigration and integration policy. Consequently, not only the economy but also affected migrant women do suffer in the light of neglected immigration and integration policies in Germany. Highly skilled migrant women are disadvantaged twice and cannot translate their career intentions into reality, on the one hand because of gender discrimination but on the other hand, and to an even greater extent, because of their status as foreigners. Nevertheless, the initial findings of the project indicate that the categories gender and ethnicity interact with each other and intensify each other. The fact that Eastern Europe scientists who already are in Germany but who had migration motives other than continuing, in the first instance, a scientific career, have to experience a process of de-skilling with higher probability. In this regard, German universities are neglectful of the qualifications of international highly skilled academics. Even if certifications are accepted there is oftentimes no recognition of the skills. Highly skilled migrant women who successfully pursue a university career in Germany have fulfilled the demand of mobility which is an important part of the scientific culture in Germany. Either they came to Germany as student or PhD-student or mentors at university in their home countries with an international network supported the female scientists from Eastern Europe to continue their scientific career in Germany.

References

Browne, I. / Misra, J. (2003): The intersection of gender and race in the labor market. In: Annu. Rev. Sociol. 2003. (29), 487-513.

Engelmann, B. / Müller, M. (2007): Brain Waste. Die Anerkennung von ausländischen Qualifikationen in Deutschland, Augsburg.

European Commission (2006): Employment in Europe 2006. Luxembourg.

Fenstermaker, S. / West, C. (Eds.) (2002): Doing Gender, Doing Difference: Inequality, Power and Institutional Change. New York.

Gruber, S. / Rüßler, H. (2002): Hochqualifiziert und arbeitslos. Jüdische Kontingentflüchtlinge in Nordrhein-Westfalen. Opladen.

Heß, B. / Sauer, L. (2007): Migration von hochqualifizierten und hochrangig Beschäftigten aus Drittstaaten nach Deutschland. Working Paper 9 published by Bundesamt für Migration und Flüchtlinge, Nürnberg.

Krieger, H. (2004): Migration Trends in an Enlarged Europe. Dublin.

Lenz, I. (2007): Power People, Working People, Shadow People ... Gender, Migration, Class and Practices of (In)Equality. In: Lenz, I. / Ullrich, C. / Fersch, B. (Eds.): Gender Orders Unbound. Globalisation, Restructuring and Reciprocity. Opladen, 99-119.

Lutz, H. (2007): Vom Weltmarkt in den Privathaushalt. Die neue Dienstmädchenfrage im Zeitalter der Globalisierung. Opladen.

Morano-Foadi, S. (2005): Scientific Mobility, Career Progression, and Excellence in the European Research Area. International Migration, 43(5), 133-162.

Morokvasic, M. / Münst, A. S. / Metz-Göckel, S. (2008): Gendered mobilities in an enlarged Europe. In: Metz-Göckel, S. / Morokvasic, M. / Münst, A. S. (Eds.): Migration and mobility in an enlarged Europe. A gender perspective. Opladen, 9-23.

Slany, K. (2008): Female migration from Central-Eastern Europe. In: Metz-Göckel, S. / Morokvasic, M. / Münst, A. S. (Eds.): Migration and mobility in an enlarged Europe. A gender perspective. Opladen, 27-51.

Sretenova, N. (2003): Scientific Mobility and 'Brain Drain' Issues in the Higher Education Sector in Bulgaria. Research Project No 2, CSLPE, University of Leeds., Symposium on Science Policy, Mobility and Brain-Drain. Leeds.

Sretenova, N. (2005): Catching up Societies in Transition: Highly-Skilled Female Migration and Youth Drain from South East Europe to Austria in the Context of EU Enlargement. Unpublished National Report, Austrian Science and Research Office, Sofia.

van de Sande, D. / Ackers, H. L. / Gill, B. (2005): Impact assessment of the Marie Curie fellowships under the 4th and 5th Framework Programme of Research and Technological Development of the EU (1994-2002).

Webster, J. (2001): Reconciling Adaptability and Equal Opportunities in European Workplaces. Final Report for DG-Employment of the European Commission, London.

Dual Career Academic Couples: University Strategies, Opportunities, Policies

Londa Schiebinger

This article has previously been published in: Gramespacher, Elke/Funk, Julika / Rothäusler, Iris (Eds.) (2010): Dual Career Couples an Hochschulen. Zwischen Theorie, Praxis, Politik. Opladen [forthcoming].

Meeting the requirements and expectations of dual-career academic couples – while ensuring the high quality of university faculty – is one of the great challenges facing universities today. Academic couples comprise 36% of the American professoriate – representing a deep talent pool that universities cannot afford to overlook. U.S. universities are in the midst of a major transition in hiring practices. Couple hiring, when done properly, can support important institutional objectives of excellence and diversity. Our number one recommendation in this study is that universities establish protocols or guidelines for dual-career hiring. Universities have much to gain by developing agreed-upon, written protocols or guidelines for the processes whereby requests for partner hires flow efficiently through the institution.

Figure 1: Professors Jennifer Eberhardt and R. Richard Banks, Stanford University

R. Richard Banks, Jackson Eli Reynolds Professor of Law, and Jennifer Eberhardt, Associate Professor of Psychology, live dual-career lives at Stanford University (Figure 1). "Working at the same institution is critical," says Banks, "or more precisely, being able to live in the same place is critical." But achieving this wasn't easy.

Like many academics, Banks and Eberhardt met at graduate school. Their commitment to supporting both careers – while maintaining a single household – was tested as job opportunities brought cross-country moves. At one point Eberhardt held a faculty position at Yale University while Banks "made a habit of commuting to other states" for work, holding a fellowship at Harvard and a federal clerkship in New York. After several stress-filled years, Banks entered the academic job market and received several offers. When Stanford offered Eberhardt a faculty position as well, they decided to head to the West Coast. Today they are both happily tenured at Stanford, leading productive lives and raising three children.

Meeting the requirements and expectations of dual-career academic couples – while ensuring the high quality of university faculty – is one of the great challenges facing universities today. Academic couples (couples in which both partners define themselves as academics) comprise 36% of the American professoriate – representing a deep talent pool that universities cannot afford to overlook. This is an issue not only for U.S. universities but for German universities and industry as well. A recent study found that 72% of German scientists abroad cited "career opportunities for the partner" as a decisive factor for scientists contemplating a return home.[1]

In August 2008, the Clayman Institute for Gender Research[2] at Stanford University published the results of a national study, *"Dual-Career Academic Couples: What Universities Need to Know"* (Schiebinger / Davies Henderson / Gilmartin 2008). This study surveyed 30,000 faculty and reviewed dual-career hiring practices at thirteen leading public and private research universities across the U.S. The study asked the following questions:

- How many dual-career academics are there – we now have the best data nationally on the numbers.
- How can universities attract and retain the best talent?
- Does couple hiring help build a more diverse, equitable, and competitive workforce?
- How can couples best negotiate a dual-career path?
- What policies or practices have universities put in place to facilitate partner hires?

One purpose of the Stanford report is to help institutions do a better job of partner hiring. (Please note our language here: We use the terms "partner"

---

1   Figures from Heide Radlanski of the Stifterverband reported in Eick von Ruschkowski, "Raising Awareness," Science (March 7, 2003). http://sciencecareers.sciencemag.org/career_development/previous_issues/articles/2240/raising_awareness/.

2   Founded in 1974, the Clayman Institute for Gender Research at Stanford University is one of the nation's most distinguished research organizations devoted to the study of gender. The Clayman Institute creates knowledge and seeks to implement change that promotes gender equality nationally and internationally. Our current focus is on gendered innovations in science, medicine, and engineering. For more information, visit: http://www.stanford.edu/group/gender/GenderedInnovations/index.html.

and "partner hiring" rather than "spouse" or "spousal hiring" because our survey included married and unmarried partners along with same-sex and hetero-sexual couples). The number-one recommendation in this report is that universities develop agreed-upon and written policies or guidelines for vetting requests for partner hiring and seeing that process through the university (see below). The ultimate goal is not necessarily to hire more couples but rather to improve the processes by which partner hiring decisions are made.

1. Dual Careers: Competing for the Best and Brightest

To set the stage for discussions about successful recruitment and retention in today's academic market, this study begins by exploring vital interrelationships between professional status and personal life. A market economy assumes that professionals are meritorious individuals free to move to maximize their potential, and for many decades employers built recruitment programs around these assumptions. Historically, however, "free-standing individuals" have, in fact, been male heads of households with relatively mobile family units.[3] Now that women are joining the professional world in ever-greater numbers, these assumptions, and the practices and cultures built around them, require rethinking. Moreover, the majority of all professionals today are partnered with other professionals such that male *and* female professors both find themselves part of dual-career households – with all the stresses and strains that can entail. Dual-career couples need to maximize not one but two careers. Employers in industry, government, and universities are finding that old hiring practices do not always succeed in this new marketplace and are crafting new ways to anchor top talent to their institutions. And, indeed, universities are in the process of restructuring hiring practices to accommodate couples. In the same way that universities restructured hiring practices in the 1960s and 1970s in response to increased access to higher education and the advent of equal opportunity legislation, institutions are again today undergoing major transitions in hiring practices with respect to couple hiring. In the U.S., academic couple hiring has increased from 3% in the 1970s to 13% since 2000.

There are three key reasons for universities to take a new look at couple hiring:

Excellence. Our study suggests that couples more and more vote with their feet, leaving or not considering universities that do not support them.

---

3   See Committee on Maximizing the Potential of Women in Academic Science and Engineering / National Academy of Sciences / National Academy of Engineering / Institute of Medicine (2006): Beyond Bias and Barriers: Fulfilling the Potential of Women in Academic Science and Engineering, Washington, DC: National Academies Press, 5-5–5-6.

Among couple hires in our study, 88% reported that they would have refused an offer had her or his partner not found an appropriate position. Support for dual careers opens another avenue by which universities can compete for the best and brightest. A professor of medicine in our survey commented that talented academics are often partnered, and "if you want the most talented, you find innovative ways of going after them."

Diversity. The new generation of academics is more diverse in terms of gender and ethnicity than ever before. With greater diversity comes the need for new hiring practices. Institutions should not expect new participants to assimilate into current practices built around old academic models and demographics. This undermines innovation, opportunity, and equity. New hiring practices are needed to support a diverse professoriate – and one of these practices is couple hiring.

Quality of Life. Faculty today are a new breed determined more than ever to strike a sustainable balance between working and private lives. To enhance competitive excellence, universities are increasingly attending to quality-of-life issues that include partner hiring. While often costly up front, addressing the challenges of faculty members' personal lives may help universities secure their investments in the long run.

2. Academic Workforce Demographics

New hiring policies require a clear understanding of workforce demographics as well as the cultural practices and values of faculty in the 21st century. This section identifies three ways that couples enter universities (Figure 2). Developing new definitions and terminology is important as universities refine dual-hiring policies and practices.

1. Dual Hires
"Dual hires" are couples where both partners are hired as part of a negotiation. The majority of dual hires are appointed "sequentially." Typically, one partner, the "first hire," receives an initial offer and then negotiates for his or her partner. This second partner – who enters the deal through a series of negotiations that generally include a full-blown campus visit and interview – we call the "second hire" in order to overcome the negative terms often applied to this partner, such as "trailing spouse."[4]

---

4   Lisa Wolf-Wendel et al. (2003: 14) have suggested the term "accompanying hire" for the second hire. We find "second hire" or "partner hire" easier to say. Some administrators currently use "primary" and "secondary" hire, but, again, the terms "first hire" and "second hire" carry fewer value judgments.

Dual hires also include "joint hires", that small but growing number of couples who are a known couple and are recruited together by a university – there is no first or second hire. These couples often market themselves and are approached by universities as a package. Both partners may be stars, in which case everyone wants them and hiring decisions are easy. If each partner is not happily settled at his or her current institution, universities can recruit the couple strategically by offering both attractive positions. Most dual hires work at the same institution (93%), meaning that universities need clear policies for these types of hires.

Figure 2: Academic couples, by hire type

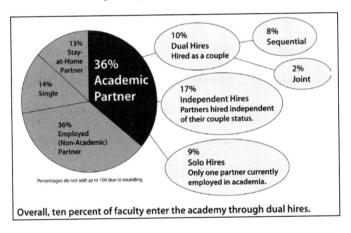

2. Independent Hires
17% of all respondents to our survey are in an academic partnership but secured employment independent of their couple status, at the same or neighboring institution(s). These respondents comprise our group of "independent hires." In these cases, either each partner replied to separate advertisements for positions and was hired without mention of a partner, or each already held a faculty position at their current institution before they met and fell in love. Only 20% of respondents fall into this latter group; the vast majority of independent hires formed a partnership before each was hired and faced the problem of finding jobs together. Coordinating jobs in this fashion (without specifically negotiating for a second partner) is not easy, and only 61% find work at the same university.

3. Solo Hires
"Solo hires" are those respondents to our survey who identify their partner as an academic, but one who is not currently employed in an academic position.

For lack of better nomenclature, we call this group "solo hires", meaning that only one partner has secured academic employment (partners, of course, may have found work outside academia). Solo hires comprise 9% of the respondents in our survey. Approximately half (48%) of the partners of solo hires do not hold a Ph.D. or professional degree and are not necessarily qualified to be employed in tenure or tenure-track positions at the universities we surveyed. But of the 52% who do hold advanced degrees, approximately one-third (31%) continue to search for faculty positions. Solo hires whose partners continue to look for academic jobs are likely to be easily recruited away if another institution can offer a partner an appropriate academic position.

3. Recruiting Women: Partners Matter

Couple hiring is particularly important for recruiting and retaining female faculty. Women faculty are more likely than men to be in an academic partnership (40% versus 34%, respectively – Figure 3). In fact, rates of dual hiring are higher among women respondents than among men respondents (13% versus 7%).

Figure 3: Partnering Patterns

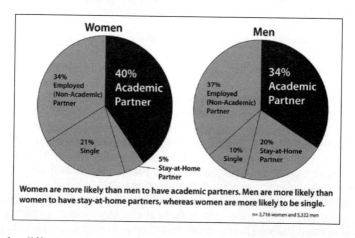

But the differences between men and women go beyond the numbers to encompass the relative value men and women attach to their partners' careers. In our survey, we asked a question: Whose career comes first in your relationship? Who follows whom? A healthy half of men in academic couples responded "mine," compared to only 20% of academic women. Academic women overwhelming (59% vs. 45% academic men) answered "we value each career equally" (Figure 4).

Figure 4: Whose career is primary?

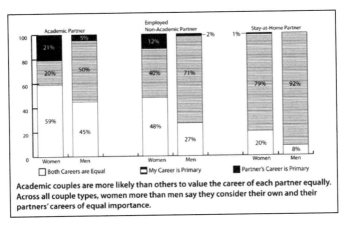

There is a problem in this asymmetry between men and women's values that leads to one of our most important findings in this study: a good number of women simply will not accept a job unless partners are accommodated. Not only do women more often than men perceive a loss in professional mobility as a result of their academic partnerships (54% for women versus 41% for men), but they actively refuse job offers if their partner cannot find a satisfactory position. In our study, the number-one reason women refused an outside offer was because their academic partners were not offered appropriate employment at the new location. These findings have significant implications: In order to recruit top women – especially in science and medicine where they partner at a very high rate with other scientists and medical professional – institutions need to have a clear process in place to vet partners for hire.

Couple hiring is important to attract more female faculty especially to fields where women are underrepresented, such as the natural sciences and engineering. Academics practice "disciplinary endogamy"; that is to say, they tend to couple in similar fields of study and are often found in the very same department. Endogamy rates are high in the natural sciences, particularly among women. Fully 83% of women scientists in academic couples are partnered with another scientist, compared with 54% of men scientists. Understanding where women (as well as underrepresented minorities) cluster can help administrator boost diversity.

Historically, men more than women have used their market power to bargain for positions for their partners. Men comprise the majority (58%) of "first hires" (or the first partner hired in a couple recruitment) who responded to our survey. They make up only 26% of second hires (meaning that women are 74% of second hires). This is shocking. An important finding in our study is that recruiting women *first* breaks the stereotype of senior academics seeking to negotiate jobs for junior partners. Remarkably, more than half (53%) of female first hires who are full professors are partnered with males of equal rank. By contrast, only 19% of male first hires who are full professors seek positions for women who are their equals in academic rank.

One university in our study is deploying this information strategically by approving university funds for dual hiring only when a woman and underrepresented minority is the *first hires* and, in this way, seeks to address both diversity and equity issues across the institution. Again and this is important: Senior women first hires will, more often than men, seek to place partners who are their equals in terms of rank and status. Understanding how men and women think about, and value, their partnerships may help universities refine policies governing couple hiring in ways that promote greater gender equality.

4. University Programs, Policies, and Practices: How to Maximize Options?

Universities today are in the midst of major transitions in hiring practices. Couples comprise a significant proportion of the academic workforce, and couple hiring, when done properly, can support important institutional objectives.

Many universities are founding "Dual-Career Programs" to assist with the relocation of both academic and non-academic faculty partners (Figure 5).[5]

---

5   For model dual-career program guidelines, see: The University of Rhode Island (prepared in conjunction with National Science Foundation ADVANCE program funding): www.uri.edu/advance/work_life_support/dual_career_guidelines.html; The University of California, Berkeley: http://facultyequity.chance.berkeley.edu/resources/fsg_appendixh.html. In Germany, the Munich Dual Career Office, which is part of the Technical University Munich, assists partners of top-level scientists coming to TU Munich, Max-Planck-Society, the Helmholtz Zentrum München, the German Aerospace Center (DLR), the Fraunhofer-Gesellschaft, SÜD-CHEMIE AG, Infineon Technologies AG and the Munich University of Applied Sciences. See http://portal.mytum.de/dualcareer/index_html_en and http://www.en.uni-muenchen.de/institutions/admin/services/dual_career_en/index.html. For a list of German universities with Dual Career Offices, see http://portal.mytum.de/dualcareer/netzwerk/index_html/.

Both pathways are important – but space allows me to follow only that related to the hiring of academic partners.

Figure 5: Dual-career programs

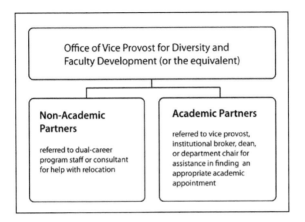

Couple hiring is a sensitive topic because it challenges cherished ideals of academic advancement, including open competition, fairness, and merit. The reality, however, is that the academic workforce has changed and that universities increasingly hire couples to attract top talent from the broadest range of applicants. A number of universities now take "great pride," as one administrator put it, in working collaboratively with departments across their institutions to address dual-career issues.

Universities are organized differently and, once the decision is made to consider partner hiring, there is no one best way to do so. All institutions that hire partners are quite clear that they do so on a case-by-case basis, looking carefully at the qualifications of each candidate set alongside institutional priorities. Some, however, have consistent procedures for initiating and seeing through that process, whereas others do not.

Universities across the U.S. offer a variety of solutions for dual-career academic couple hiring. All 13 universities in our study engage in couple hiring for recruitment or retention – with greater or lesser institutional support and success. This is quite different from a 2000 survey of 600 U.S. universities showing that only 20 to 24% of U.S. universities had some sort of dual-career academic hiring policy in place, while 15% of universities nationally did not support couple hiring (Wolf-Wendel / Twombly / Rice 2000: 294).

Five of the universities in our study (four public and one private institution) have written policies or principles guiding dual hiring. The others have no formal policies and rely instead on informal practices developed over the years. Two private universities, for example, have no written procedures but a centralized mechanism in the person of a "broker" – a distinguished member of the faculty who works university-wide (across all schools and colleges) to find the right departmental "fit" for a partner and simultaneously to find resources to seal a deal in a timely fashion.

Administrators with hiring guidelines in place argue that protocols help 1) clarify for all participants – administrators, faculty members, Equal Opportunity officers, and perhaps potential job candidates – the processes by which such hires are vetted in a timely fashion, and 2) facilitate clear communication between key players across the university. The hope is that clear and coherent protocols remove the sense of intrigue and favoritism that can adhere to partner hiring and bring greater fairness to the process. Universities who engage in dual-career academic hiring should treat all requests for a partner hire equitably; that is to say, requests for partner hires should trigger known and agreed-upon processes that work consistently throughout the institution. Survey comments also show a strong preference among faculty for transparent and consistent procedures for couple hiring.

Written protocols do not in themselves determine outcomes. Universities that have established dual-hiring protocols state openly (often on their websites) that these guidelines do not guarantee employment to any candidate. Department chairs, deans, and provosts emphasized that each dual hire is unique and must be considered on the merits of each case. Policies define the processes by which partners are considered for hire; they do not define departmental standards for such hires. Outcomes depend on the quality of a particular candidate's scholarship, the "fit" of a particular candidate's area of expertise with departmental priorities, and available funding.

A number of administrators worry that protocols might shut down the flexibility often required for finding the right "fit" for a partner within an institution. One department chair commented that he might be trying six different solutions for one partner hire at any moment. Another university, also without written protocols, mixes and matches approaches (sometimes using a university-wide faculty broker, sometimes following the chain-of-command from department chairs to the dean) in efforts to find potential tenure homes for partner candidates. Flexibility – for both administrators and departments – needs to be built into protocols. Written policies themselves, of course, do not solve everything. One search committee chair wrote that, although his university has the right policies, "They are not always backed up with action or even a (serious) explanation as to why there was no follow through."

Couple hiring involves several key issues that protocols should address. One of the thorniest is departmental autonomy versus university priorities. Even when candidates are excellent, partner hiring – in which open searches are often waived and provosts sometimes offer persuasive resources – can be viewed as violating the sacrosanct autonomy of departments to mold and shape their profiles through selective hiring. Given how much one hears about the need of departments to determine their own intellectual futures, it is significant that only 26 percent of survey respondents report that partner hiring disrupts the "intellectual direction" of their department (Figure 6).

Figure 6: Faculty perceptions of dual career academic couple hiring

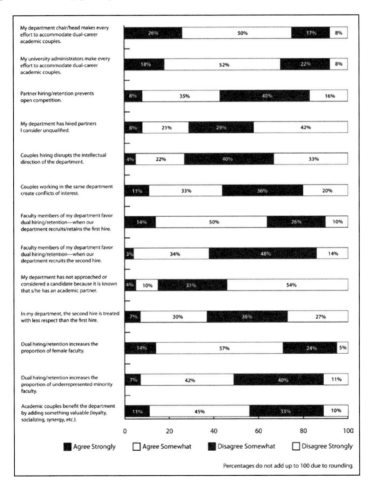

With couple hiring on the rise, many institutions encourage faculty to think of the university, not as a set of autonomous departments, but as an intellectual and corporate whole. Interdisciplinarity, for example, is fostered by an awareness of what departments and colleagues do across the university. One vice provost argued that academic couple hiring is another instance in which the total package may be greater than the sum of its individual parts. Another administrator continued that "what goes around, increasingly comes around" and that when asked to consider a partner hire, faculty need to bear in mind that their department may itself be on the requesting end of the partner issue in the near future. Agreed-upon protocols do not dictate solutions to departments but may ask them to cooperate in new ways.

Another issue protocols need to address concerns waiving open searches in order to move forward with a partner hire. Forty-three percent of survey respondents worry that couple hiring jeopardizes open competition (Figure 6). In other words, faculties are concerned that if a job is not advertised nationally and open to all comers, their department may lose the opportunity to make the best possible hire. The problem, of course, is that the candidate who emerges as the top pick of 300 applicants may choose not to take the job if his or her partner is not also accommodated. A few universities nationally continue to require an open search and encourage a partner to apply. Most universities, however, and certainly those in our study request a search waiver for partner hiring, which is typically vetted by the university's office of affirmative action/equal opportunity. In most cases, especially those in which a woman or underrepresented minority is involved as a first or second hire, a waiver is granted.

Many issues arise during the hiring process. In our published report, we detail the process by which partners are hired and the university policies governing that process. Part 3 of the larger report serves as a guide for administrators and universities seeking to develop procedures for academic partner hiring as well as for couples seeking to negotiate a couple hire. The issues involved include:

- Should universities have a written policy for partner hiring?
- When and how should job candidates raise the partner issue?
- Who brokers the deal?
- What funding models that work?
- What counts in hiring decisions?
- What types of positions are available for partner hires?
- How does geographic location impact universities couple hiring? How can universities collaborations in couple hiring?
- Are second hires as qualified as first hires?
- Why is it important for universities to evaluate their dual-hiring processes?

Based on the findings of our study, we offer the following top three recommendations:

Develop a dual-career academic couple hiring protocol. Universities have much to gain by developing agreed-upon, written protocols or guidelines for the processes whereby requests for partner hires flow efficiently through the institution. Each institution needs to develop policies that are right for it. Well-developed protocols increase the transparency and fairness as well as the speed with which departments can vet potential candidates. Written protocols may also help cultivate departmental reciprocity in partner hiring.

Budget funds for dual hiring. Couple hiring is now part of the cost of doing business. Universities need to budget funds for partner hiring to increase the speed and agility with which they can place qualified partners.

Use dual hiring to increase gender equality. Our data and practices at one of our participating universities suggest that recruiting women and underrepresented minorities as first (rather than second) hires may help universities address both diversity and equity issues. Women more than men tend to request positions for partners of equal academic rank.

References

Eick von Ruschkowski (2003): "Raising Awareness," Science (March 7, 2003). Available from http://sciencecareers.sciencemag.org/career_development/previous_issues/articles/2240/raising_awareness/.

Gramespacher, E. / Funk, J. / Rothäusler, I. (Eds.) (2010): Dual Career Couples an Hochschulen. Zwischen Theorie, Praxis, Politik. Opladen (forthcoming).

Schiebinger, L. / Davies Henderson, A. / Gilmartin, S.K. (2008): Dual-Career Academic Couples: What Universities Need to Know. Stanford.

Committee on Maximizing the Potential of Women in Academic Science and Engineering / National Academy of Sciences / National Academy of Engineering / Institute of Medicine (2006): Beyond Bias and Barriers: Fulfilling the Potential of Women in Academic Science and Engineering, Washington D.C., 5-5–5-6.

Wolf-Wendel, L. / Twombly S. / Rice S. (2000): Dual-Career Couples: Keeping Them Together. The Journal of Higher Education, Vol. 71 (2000), 291–321.

Wolf-Wendel, L. / Twombly, S. / Rice, S. (2003): The Two-Body Problem: Dual-Career-Couple Hiring Practices in Higher Education. Baltimore.

For more information:
1. Download the Stanford Report (free and online). This report includes a full description of our methodology: http://www.stanford.edu/group/gender/ResearchPrograms/DualCareer/DualCareerFinal.pdf

2. Enter our Dual-Career Portal where we provide resources for university administrators, faculty, and graduate students: http://www.stanford.edu/group/gender/ResearchPrograms/DualCareer/.
3. Enter our Video Portal where administrators, couples, and academics discuss dual-career at U.S. universities. http://www.stanford.edu/group/gender/ResearchPrograms/DualCareer/DualCareerVideos.html.
4. Read Gramespacher / Funk / Rothäusler (2010).

Work-Life Balance in Academia – Evidence from two Technical Universities

Sara Connolly, Stefan Fuchs, Claartje Vinkenburg

Persistent gender inequalities, together with expected shortages of talent, in Science, Engineering and Technology (SET) have made it an imperative to attract and retain female talent in technical universities. This paper considers the relationship between work-life balance (or the lack of it) and the careers of men and women in academia. Our focus is on what universities can do regarding work-life balance preferences and policies to stem any loss of talent through what has become known as 'the leaky pipeline'.

1. Women in Academic SET

In 2007 (p.1), the American National Academy of Sciences reviewed the situation of female scientists in academic Science, Engineering and Technology (SET) in the US to conclude that:

"Women are a small portion of the science and engineering faculty members at research universities, and they typically receive fewer resources and less support than their male colleagues. The representation of women in leadership in our academic institutions, scientific and professional societies, and honorary organizations is low relative to the numbers of women qualified to hold these positions. It is not lack of talent, but unintentional biases and outmoded institutional structures that are hindering the access and advancement of women. Neither our academic institutions nor our nation can afford such under use of precious human capital in science and engineering."

When compared to earlier statements on the issue, two notable changes are evident. First, the Academy refers to "unintentional biases and outmoded institutional structures" rather than discrimination or deficits to explain why women advance so slowly in SET. Among the institutional structures mentioned in the report, the lack of women-friendly work environments and arrangements figure prominently. Unintentional biases addressed in the report were seen to originate mainly from the male culture inscribed in academic work and careers in SET – a markedly hierarchical environment predominantly populated by men, where a tendency to reproduce existing structures in selection and recruitment procedures prevails, and where female colleagues and role models are scarce. In such circumstances, where women form a minority or 'token' position, Kanter (1977) argues that it makes women especially visible, thus prone to stereotyping and discrimination. Second, the Academy acknowledged that there are enough qualified women available for the upper realms today in academic SET. However, they don't make it to the top in equal proportions. Thus the situation of women in science could be described by "allowed in, but not to fully partake of science" (Etzkowitz et al. 2008).

The position of women in academic SET in Europe remains one charac-terised by vertical segregation, see Figure 1. Across all subjects, women account for 55% of all students and 59% of all graduates but only 44% of grade C academic staff, 36% of grade B academic staff and 18% of grade A academic staff, and the proportion of female academic staff in science and engineering are somewhat lower (SHE Figures 2009). However, the propor-tion of highly qualified women is growing, in 2006 women accounted for 45% of all PhD graduates - although the proportion is lower in science, mathematics and computing (41%), and engineering, manufacturing and con-struction (25%) – and the share of female researchers is growing even in SET. It is important to note that there are wide variations between these fi-gures across Europe – the situation in one country thus requires different and perhaps more drastic measures than that in another in order to prevent further leakage from the pipeline[1].

Figure 1: Proportions of men and women in a typical academic career, students and academic staff, EU-27, 2006

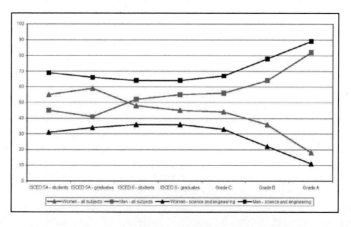

In this paper, the focus is on what men and women working in a technical university consider important regarding a productive and attractive academic work environment. From this perspective, we take a look at work

---

1   See Bismuth in European Commission (2009).

arrangements supporting work-life balance, and analyse how scientists manage to reconcile domestic responsibilities, family obligations, and their partnerships with the requirements and realities of a career in science.

2. Work-Life-Balance (WLB) in Academe

Today, there is widespread recognition that issues of work-life balance (WLB) are neither a private matter nor restricted to those with family obligations (Brough et al. 2008). To enable and achieve WLB has also become an imperative in attracting and retaining talent in both public and private organisations (Greenblatt 2002; Drew / Murtaugh 2005; Lewis / Campbell 2008). From the employees' perspective, WLB issues and the provision of flexibility regarding work-life arrangements are now important criteria in the search for jobs, with regard to satisfaction on the job and work commitment, and in its contribution to career success (e.g. Smith / Gardner, 2007; Roberts, 2008; Lyness / Judiesch, 2008). In academe, a considerable proportion of young academics experience the relationship between home and work in science as increasingly unsatisfactory and unhealthy (Sturges / Guest 2006).

While we observe these trends throughout the industrialised world, important cross-country variations in policies and practices regarding work-life arrangements persist, for example, the legal regulation of the length of maternity leave (Ackers 2003; Hantrais / Ackers 2005). Few studies have analysed the 'business case' of WLB policies empirically (Yasbek 2004), the net impact is difficult to assess and usually costs are easier to identify than benefits. Organisational awareness and management support are indirectly related to, but essential for, the positive relationship between WLB and productivity (Bloom / Van Reenen 2006). However, across sectors and organisations a 'long hour' working culture is still associated with career success in SET. It is also true, that in academe, scientists experience little or no difference between 'home' and 'work', and are expected to be available for 'the cause' at all time. Hence WLB has long been considered a purely private matter by academic organisations and career breaks are usually considered appropriate when scientists receive a fellowship, take a sabbatical or other forms of (paid) leave for their research. A general disinterest towards how scientists manage to reconcile domestic and family responsibilities with their career in science, together with other factors, has been found to contribute significantly to women's disproportionate attrition from the science pipeline (Fuchs et al. 2001). At universities and in SET in particular, working conditions and career structures may contribute to the already low numbers of men and women interested in the field.

3. WiST2 Study

The second WiST (Women in Science and Technology) working group was formed by the European Commission in 2007. Among its participants were representatives of European and multinational companies, university representatives, and academic and other experts on "women in science". The task of the working group was to consider what companies and universities can do to prevent the leaky pipeline in SET, and to assess the business case of WLB for companies and universities (European Commission 2009)[2].

To track these questions empirically, we have designed an online survey based on the Athena Survey of Science Engineering and Technology (ASSET) surveys – which were run in the UK in 2003, 2004, 2006and 2010[3]. The data analysed in the following were obtained from two prestigious European technical universities that granted access to their academic and administrative employees in 2008 and 2009 - University A is located in Germany and University B in the Netherlands. The online survey link was distributed via email with a response rate of just under 10%. These unique data not only allow us to shed light on the general significance of WLB policies at the intersection of gender and careers in science. It also provides an opportunity to assess the working of legal and institutional regulations and cultures on careers in science from a comparative perspective.

3.1 University A

The total number of students across departments at University A is approximately 27,000, of whom 35.2% are female (21% in engineering, 7% in electrical engineering, 10% in machine construction, 13% in information sciences but 40% in mathematics and chemistry). University A employs over 7,000 people, including student assistants, among these are roughly 2,300 academics and 2,000 persons working in the administration. In recent years the proportion of female academics employed at University A has increased slightly and is currently about 13% among all professors and 28% among the other research and teaching personnel with considerable variation between departments. In administration, the proportion female is around 58%.

---

2   Some of this research has been published in Connolly and Fuchs, European Commission (2009).
3   www.athenasurvey.org.uk.

3.2 University B

University B has a slightly smaller student body of 15,321, of whom 20% are female (8% in engineering, 11% in electrical engineering, math and computer sciences, 23% in applied sciences, 17% in civil engineering and geosciences, 33% in architecture, 37% in industrial design engineering, and 20% in technology, policy and management). University B employs 4,640 people – 2,762 academic and 1,878 support staff. Of the total academic staff, 22% are female; this number has risen steadily over the past 10 years. In 2008, of the academic staff at assistant professor level and at associate and full professor level, 22% and 7%, respectively, were female, while in other research (including PhD and post-doc level) and teaching positions about 25% are female. Of the administrative staff 40%, are female.

4. WiST2 samples - University A and University B

Of the employees that answered the WiST2 survey (404 at University A and 395 at University B), the administrative personnel are underrepresented in the sample from University A, while academics are slightly underrepresented from University B (Figure 2)[4].

Regarding the proportion of female employees, we find that more female academics answered our survey and that the response rate from female administrators was particularly high in University A (Figure 3). The sample at University B was a stratified sample, for which all female academic staff including PhD students, a matched sample of male academic staff, and all administrative staff at the professional entry level (i.e. requiring a higher vocational or university degree) were invited to participate.

---

4   Academic grades in University A and B: Level 1, Dean or Head of Department; Level 2, Full Professor; Level 3, Associate Professor; Level 4, Assistant Professor; Level 5, Teaching/Lecturing position (docent); Level 6, Contract researcher; Level 7, Post-doctoral position, Level 8, PhD student/ Doctoral candidate; Level 9, Student Assistant Teaching/ Research/Administration.
Administrative grades in University A: Level 1: Head of office/ Unit manager; Level 2: Scientific support staff; Level 3: Specialist; Level 4: Office clerk.
Administrative grades in University B: Level 1: VSNU level 15 or above; Level 2: VSNU level 13 or 14; Level 3: VSNU level 10, 11 or 12.

Figure 3: Proportion Female Employees at University A & B and in WiST2 Samples

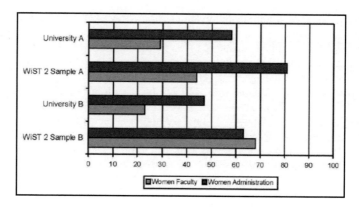

Figure 2: Proportion Faculty and Administrative Staff in University A & B and in WiST2 Samples

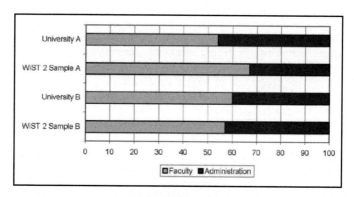

A closer look at the sample demography (Table 1) reveals that junior faculty and academics with fixed term contracts are heavily represented in both samples. This is not surprising given the high proportion of post-docs and contract research staff typically employed in scientific disciplines. Furthermore, this particular group provides us with data that is highly relevant to the research questions relating to career development and staff retention.

The majority of our samples, with the exception of male administrators, are currently engaged in some form of flexible work arrangement and just under a third of female employees work part-time. A significant proportion of women and a non-trivial number of men in University B have taken career breaks. The majority of the sample is married or has a partner, more than a third of academics and more than half of administrators are parents.

Table 1: The WiST2 Samples

		University A %	University B %
Junior faculty	Male academics	68	77
	Female academics	68	76
Office clerk	Male administrators	5	71
	Female administrators	40	85
Non-permanent contract	Male academics	85	55
	Female academics	80	60
	Male administrators	21	9
	Female administrators	36	25
Flexible work arrangement	Male academics	64	65
	Female academics	71	78
	Male administrators	21	37
	Female administrators	77	55
Part-time employment	Male academics	10	18
	Female academics	32	29
	Male administrators	4	5
	Female administrators	28	35
Partner	Male academics	78	72
	Female academics	75	83
	Male administrators	23	76
	Female administrators	73	81
Parent	Male academics	34	44
	Female academics	40	37
	Male administrators	62	55
	Female administrators	62	55
Career break	Male academics	5	20
	Female academics	39	33
	Male administrators	1	27
	Female administrators	35	54

Note: Figures are percentages of each university sample and do not sum to 100%

In the following, we present main results from our survey crucial to the challenges universities face today as described above. First, we consider what university employees believe are the most important features of their attraction to an academic workplace. Second, we analyze career breaks and dual careers before we address the particular importance of creating a "woman-friendly" work environment to both attract women to and retain them in academic SET. Finally, we shed light on the career aspirations and expectations of men and women working in a scientific environment.

5. Attraction of a career in University A and University B

Whilst some consensus might emerge over the factors which draw people to a particular occupation, for example, intellectual challenge or interest are likely be high on the list for an academic. It is likely that preferences in relation to what attracted them to a particular employer are likely to be quite diverse, particularly when we consider the heterogeneity which might exist across role (academic or administration), grade (senior or junior) and household status (married or single, parent or not). Therefore, it is interesting that when faced with a range of options that there should be two which stand out across two institutions. In both of our samples, the employer's *geographical location* and *flexibility* were the most important factors in their choice of employment (Table 2). Location was a particularly strong pull for academics employed at University A, which is located at the heart of a large German city. We also observe considerable differences between men and women in the university administration.[5] Geography is also of importance to academics and people working in the administration at University B. However, for academics in particular, flexibility is considered more important and - as with their counterparts at University A – highly valued by both male and female academics.

Table 2: Factors in choice of employment

		University A %	University B %
Geographical location	Male academics	52	38
	Female academics	45	30
	Male administrators	11	26
	Female administrators	32	30
Flexibility	Male academics	43	47
	Female academics	48	41
	Male administrators	20	30
	Female administrators	57	27

Note: Figures are percentages within each university sample and do not sum to 100%

When asked to pick from a detailed list of possible reasons why they have chosen their employment with this particular employer, *family reasons* and *WLB issues* were of some concern to all respondents. The top reason, however, is *flexibility of working hours* – a very important dimension of WLB related policies and practices.

---

5   We can rule out that 'geography' implies moving after one's partner: virtually no one in the sample reports to have taken up his or her employment because of partners' choices (2 – 3%; not shown).

At a first glance, addressing 'flexibility' in an academic context may seem odd because there is little that is not flexible. At the same time, flexibility is a prerequisite for the relentless and uninterrupted research activity expected from academics and scientists. In the WiST2 survey, we use a narrow definition of flexibility when we look at hours worked and the content of work contracts. A much wider definition of flexibility is used in the survey when we address careers and career structures in academe, where flexibility extends to issues such as deviance from the ideal linear career path or possibilities to come back after a career break. The scheduling and timely completion of meetings is a related issue which is also often identified in discussions of flexibility at work.

6. Work, Family, and Career Breaks

At both universities, a significant proportion of women have taken career breaks (43% and 42%; see Table 3), while this is a rare event in the case of male academics (5%) or administrators (6%) in University A, 24 % of the male respondents in University B report having had a career break (20% of male academics and 27% of male administrators). Those who have taken a career break – mostly for parental (usually maternity) leave – typically interrupt their career for less than a year and mostly for less than 6 months in University B. Some interesting differences in terms of the culture surrounding career breaks emerge.[6] Only 42% of those women who have taken career breaks at University A report that their boss and/or colleagues were supportive of their plans, whereas the equivalent figure for those at University B is 52% and even higher, 62%, for men. There are similar differences between the proportions who report that their manager or supervisor kept in contact during their career break. These differences may be due to differences in legal regulations, e.g. of parental leave, or differences in the organizational culture, for example regarding the provision of support.

After the career break, the vast majority returned to the same job or to a different job but at the same level. A significant proportion of men (14-19%) report that they experienced difficulties in returning to work after a career break, but, worryingly, this was true for over a quarter of the women who had taken career breaks. All respondents were also asked about which factors were likely to be most helpful in easing the transition back to work after a career break. There was clear agreement that flexible working and the guarantee of the same job when returning after the career break are key factors –

---

6   Some selectivity in response to the survey has to be taken into account (see figures 1 and 2), especially since WLB issues were a more appealing issue to women than to men.

particularly amongst women who also identified the availability of other care support, and building up from part to full time work and training as factors helping in the transition back to work.

Table 3: Experience of career breaks

	University A %		University B %	
	Male	Female	Male	Female
Taken a career break*	5	43	24	42
Type of career break	Not asked			
Paid maternal leave			6	5
Parental leave (full-time)			3	4
Parental leave (part-time)			38	10
Unpaid leave or sabbatical			13	10
Other			41	23
Length of career break				
< 3 months	27	13	23	15
3-6 months	27	8	32	56
7-12 months	13	27	13	14
Between 1 and 2 years	13	17	19	6
> 2 years	20	35	13	8
On your return				
Same job	62	72	77	71
Different job, same level	31	12	10	9
Same or different job, lower level	0	11	6	12
Did you experience any difficulties on your return?	14	26	19	29
Employer maintained contact during career break	13	36	55	60
Yes, regularly	Not asked		39	13
Yes, once or twice			15	47
Was your employer supportive of your plans?	19	42	63	52
Have you considered but not taken any career breaks?*	18	21	13	17

Note: * column %, remainder % of those having taken a career break by gender within each university

---

Box 1: Reasons why women in science did not take a career break

- Money
- Insecurity: "No permanent post"
  "Chain of non-permanent contracts for years"
  "Project work with no possible replacement"
  "Re-entry not safe or guaranteed"
- Career preference: "Career is too important to waste time"
  "I like research and teaching and work is attractive"
  "Career is great and fun – regarding family it is either or "
  "Career doesn't allow a break"
  "Career was more important, now it is too late"
- "Stupidity"

Source: WiST 2 university survey; selected answers to open-ended question

A significant proportion of female academics in both samples report having considered, but not taken, a career break offering explanations that underline the 'either-or' nature of the decision, its tight coupling to becoming a mother, and the anticipation that the decision is potentially harmful to career advancement (see Box 1).

7. Work-life Balance

Geography and flexibility are particularly important in the current employment choices of academics and employees of the university administration in our samples (Table 2). Aside from personal significance, flexibility is considered *the* major contributor to a good work-life balance in general by a majority of our respondents, regardless of their sex and affiliation (Table 4). In line with other research on this issue (see e.g. Corporate Leadership Council 2009), these results strongly suggest that work-life balance to a highly qualified workforce is first and foremost about contributions to a better 'workload management'. This includes the reconciliation of work and domestic or family issues but also facets beyond these, like allowance for absence on short notice or the provision of home offices. To universities, these results should underline the importance of elastic solutions to the preferences of their employees regarding work-life balance.

Table 4: Which are the most important contributors to a good work-life balance

	Academics %		Administrators %	
University A	Male	Female	Male	Female
- Flexibility in hours/days worked/ work pattern	49	76	64	75
- Senior management show awareness of issue	39	57	41	63
- Being able to ask for time off at short notice within leave allocation, without need to give reasons	48	43	36	48
- Enhanced maternity/paternity/other parental leave	34	60	23	54
- Important meetings/activities on a regular pattern or scheduled within core hours	37	9	44	57
- Home/remote working	41	52	14	33
University B				
- Flexibility in hours/days worked/ work pattern	85	86	77	88
- Being able to ask for time off at short notice within leave allocation, without need to give reasons	58	50	66	55
- Home/remote working	68	78	42	65

Note: Figures are a column % within each university sample

While other surveys found little or no impact of gender on work-life balance preferences (ibid.), female academics and administrators at University A consider awareness of senior management and enhanced possibilities concerning parental leave more important than their male counterparts while, perhaps in a reflection of differences in work cultures, the issue was not considered important by employees of University B.

8. Balancing Dual Careers

Over three quarters of our sample reported having a partner at the time of the survey and just fewer than 40% are in dual career partnerships – they have partners who work full-time. Of the respondents at University A, roughly half of the academics have partners working fulltime with slightly more female academics than male academics having partners working fulltime. At University B, the picture looks more 'traditional' with a majority of female academics and administrators in dual careers, whereas male employees tend to have partners working less than fulltime or not at all. A much higher proportion of the women in dual career couples are also parents (see Table 5).

From the larger proportions of female academics with children and dual careers it is also probable that female academics are much more likely to shoulder domestic and career responsibilities than male academics. We also find that a significant proportion of those academics who have taken a career break are also engaged in dual careers (54% of the female academics in University A and 75% of the female academics in University B).

Table 5: Dual careers

	Academics %		Administrators %	
University A	Male	Female	Male	Female
Dual careers (partners working fulltime)*	34	40	41	40
Dual career couples with kid(s)**	29	53	57	64
University B				
Dual careers (partners working fulltime)*	21	67	24	54
Dual career couples with kid(s)**	20	40	47	50

Note: * Figures are a column % within each university sample, ** figures are a % of dual career couples by gender and role within each university

Given the higher proportion of dual career couples in University B, it is perhaps not surprising that a larger proportion (over a third of academics and administrators) should report finding it difficult or very difficult to balance dual careers. For female academics at University B this reaches 44% (see Figures 4a and 4b).

Figure 4a: Sometimes, dual careers are hard to balance - how have you found this in your relationship? Academics

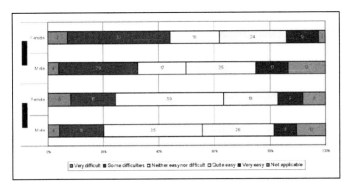

Figure 4b: Sometimes, dual careers are hard to balance - how have you found this in your relationship? Administrators

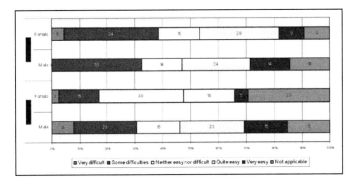

With the rise of dual couples in academe (see e.g. Schiebinger et al. 2008), the issue of whose career is more important has received increasing attention. In the U.S. for example a "relatively high premium on balance and equality" has been found in relationships between academic partners when compared to other dual career couples. Even in this group, however, men "privilege their careers over those of their partners at significantly higher rates than do women" (Schiebinger et al. 2008: 35).[7] In both WiST samples of academics almost half of the men (44% and 42%) but only 12% and 16% of the women consider their own career more important than that of their partners. In the other direction between 10% and 15% of female academics report that it was mostly their partners' career that was more important while male response to the same statement was negligible (see Figures 5a and 5b).

Figure 5a: During this relationship, whose career has been more important? Academics

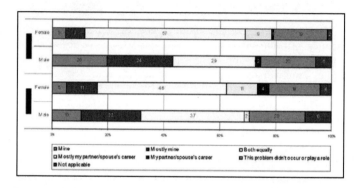

Figure 5b: During this relationship, whose career has been more important? Administrators

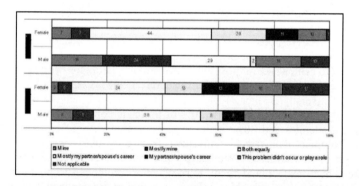

It is also interesting that, while we find about 20% of male and female academics reporting that privileging one career was not a problem to their relationship, female academics at University B tend to stress equality to a greater

---

7   Schiebinger et al. (2009: 35) report that 68 % of male survey respondents but less than one third of female respondents consider their own career more important than that of their partner.

extent than their male counterparts, and at University A, these differences are less pronounced, with a similar picture emerging regarding the administrative staff at both universities. Like the academics, men working in administration, to a large extent, consider their career to be more important than that of their partners, and especially so at University B.

9. Career Aspirations

Obviously, given the average age of our sample (44 for administrators and 37 for academics in both universities), the majority of our respondents retain further career ambitions – for example, only 36% of administrators and 25% of academics in university B report having already achieved their career ambitions. The vast majority of academics (over 90%) and administrators (between 70-80%) expect to remain working in a scientific environment and most envisage remaining in the University sector. However, perhaps unsurprisingly given the prevalence of fixed term contracts, a significant proportion expect that they will change employer in the near future. Over a third of male academics and a quarter of female academics expect to leave University A in the near future compared with less than 15% of administrators. At University B, just over 40% of academics and just over one-quarter of administrators expect to change employer in the near future. Therefore, there is much greater anticipated turnover amongst the academic workforce in both universities.

Some interesting differences emerge between the two samples when we compare the responses to the questions posed on career aspirations/expectations. In general those employed at University A are less likely to expect to achieve senior positions, for example less than a third of men and women expect to become a senior academic (~ 28%) compared with over 40% in University B (men: 47%; women 42%). Whilst men are more likely to already hold senior positions (20% of the male compared with 6% of the female academics and 30% of the male compared with 20% of the female administrators employed in University B already hold senior positions), amongst those who have not already been promoted women are much more likely to both 'expect' and 'want' to hold senior administrative positions.

Regarding work-life balance issues we find no evidence that those who have taken career breaks are in any way less ambitious - almost equal proportions of female academics who have and who have not taken a career break report not having fulfilled their career ambitions yet (roughly 80%). However, over 60% indicated that workplace factors had had a detrimental impact upon their career development. In both Universities, the three most important factors cited were "Lack of support or encouragement", "The attitude of senior colleagues" and "Lack of job opportunities". Women in both universities were much more likely to cite lack of support or lack of opportunities (see Table 6).

Table 6: Have any workplace factors had an especially detrimental impact upon your career?

	University A %			
	Academics		Administrators	
	Male	Female	Male	Female
Have any workplace factors had a especially detrimental impact upon your career?	63	70	64	78
- Lack of support / encouragement	25	34	18	33
- Attitude of senior colleagues	17	23	15	21
- Limited job opportunities	8	24	23	30
	University B %			
	Academics		Administrators	
	Male	Female	Male	Female
Have any workplace factors had had an especially detrimental impact upon your career?	57	68	47	58
- Lack of support / encouragement	18	28	16	17
- Attitude of senior colleagues	21	21	16	18
- Limited job opportunities	17	19	29	24

Note: Figures are a column % within each University sample

All academics are subject to fierce competition for scarce top positions in academe. Of the possible drivers that lead women to drop from the academic pipeline, we find some evidence that men and women are not equipped with "marketability" to the same degree and argue that small differences might accumulate to significant gender disadvantages over time. Young female academics are less likely to have given presentations at international (external) conferences – although the differences are more striking in University A (see Table 7).

Table 7: External profile/exposure of young academics

	University A %		University B %	
	Male	Female	Male	Female
Without a PhD	50	37	71	76
Post-doc	71	54	69	60

Note: Figures are a column % within each University sample

10.   Conclusions

In choosing an academic career, we find that a good work-life balance is clearly attractive to all respondents. At the same time, however, we find that working conditions are generally of more importance to women than to men, and particularly so to women who have taken a career break. Synchronizing the timing of career and family at a time of fierce competition remains a challenge for women in science. The importance of security of employment to employees sits in contrast with the prevalence of non-permanent contracts for young academics.

To potential employers, acknowledging the fact that dual careers are now widespread throughout the academic landscape is another important aspect of our work. If universities aim at creating a women-friendly work environment, it is important to acknowledge that dual careers are the rule rather than the exception among younger cohorts of academics and that, nonetheless, dual careers are hardly equal or balanced careers regardless of the surrounding rhetoric: across the board male academics still consider their own career of more importance than that of their partners.

We find that geographical location and the availability of flexible work arrangements are the two most important factors in the choice of employment of male and female academics alike. While we see few gender differences regarding work-life balance preferences, these are most pronounced in more traditional gender role institutional environments and male dominated academic milieus. Here, issues such as the role/views of senior management regarding work-life balance policies remain vital to women's position in particular. We also found a general skepticism among both male and female academics that taking leave would not harm one's career. Against this background, we may conclude that, first, policies to support the balancing of work and family are important but also have a potential to amplify existing gender inequalities. Second, our results lend support to the notion that work-life policies should not be of a 'one size fits all' nature but rather designed to meet the (ever changing) needs and preferences of heterogeneous employees. Third, academic employers can, and sometimes have to, address a variety of issues to show that they care for a female-friendly hence progressive work environment beyond a culture of 'long hours' and the reconciliation of work and family.

References

Ackers, P. (2003): The Work-Life Balance from the Perspective of Economic Policy Actors. Social Policy & Society 2, 221-229.

Bloom, N. / Van Reenen, J. (2006): Management practices, work-life balance, and productivity: A review of some recent evidence. Oxford Review of Economic Policy 22 (4), 457-482.

Brough, P. / Holt, J. / Bauld, R. / Giggs, A. / Ryan, C. (2008): The ability of work life balance policies to influence key social/organisational issues. Asia Pacific Journal of Human Resources 46, 261-274.

Corporate Leadership Council (2009): Driving Attraction and Commitment with a Work-Life Proposition. Special Focus on Science and Technology Employees. In: European Commission, Directorate-General for Research (Ed.): Women in science and technology. Creating sustainable careers, European Commission, 14-31.

Drew, E. / Murtagh, E. M. (2005): Work/life balance: senior management champions or laggards? Women in Management Review 20 (4), 262-278.

Etzkowitz, H. / Fuchs, S. / Gupta, N. / Kemelgor, C. / Ranga, M. (2008): The coming gender revolution in science. In: Hackett, E. J./ Amsterdamska, O. / Lynch M. / Wajcman, J. (Eds.): The handbook of science and technology studies. Cambridge, 403-428.

European Commission, Directorate-General for Research (2009): Women in science and technology. Creating sustainable careers. Brussels.

Fuchs, S. / von Stebut, J. / Allmendinger, J. (2001): Gender, science, and scientific organizations in Germany. Minerva 39, 175-201.

Greenblatt, E. (2002): Work/Life Balance: Wisdom or Whining? Organizational Dynamics 31, 177-193.

Hantrais, L. / Ackers, P. (2005): Women's choices in Europe: Striking the work-life balance. European Journal of Industrial Relations 11 (2), 197-212.

Kanter, R. M. (1977): Some Effects of Proportions on Group Life: Skewed Sex Ratios and Responses to Token Women. American Journal of Sociology 82: 965-990.

Lewis, J. / Campbell, M. (2008): What's in a Name? 'Work and Family' or 'Work and Life' Balance Policies in the UK since 1997 and the Implications for the Pursuit of Gender Equality. Social Policy & Administration 42, 524-541.

Lyness, K. S. / Judiesch, M. K. (2008): Can a manager have a life and a career? International and multisource perspectives on work-life balance and career advancement potential. Journal of Applied Psychology 93 (4), 789-805.

Roberts, E. (2008): Time and Work-Life Balance: The Roles of 'Temporal Customization' and 'Life Temporality'. Gender, Work and Organization 15, 430-453.

Schiebinger, L. / Henderson, A. / Gilmartin, S. (2008): Dual Career Academic Couples. What Universities Need to Know. Stanford University: Michelle   R.   Clayman   Institute.   Available   from: http://www.stanford.edu/group/gender/Publications/index.html.

SHE Figures 2009: Statistics and Indicators on Gender Equality in Science. Brussels: European   Commission.   Available   from: http://ec.europa.eu/research/science-society/index.cfm?fuseaction=public.topic&id=126.

Smith, J. / Gardner, D. (2007): Factors affecting employee use of work-life balance initiatives. New Zealand Journal of Psychology 36, 3-12.

Sturges, J. / Guest, D. (2006): Working to live or living to work? Work/life balance early in the career. Human Resource Management Journal 14, 5-20.

The National Academy of Science (2007): Beyond Bias and Barriers: Fulfilling the Potential of Women in Academic Science and Engineering. Washington, D.C.

Yasbek, P. (2004): The business case for firm-level work-life balance policies: a review of the literature. Labour Market Policy Group. Wellington: Department   of   Labour   [online].   Available   from: http://www.dol.govt.nz/PDFs/FirmLevelWLB.pdf>.

Gender-Oriented Human Resources Development in International Cooperation – The Mentoring Programme TANDEMplusIDEA as a Model of Best Practice

Elke Breuer, Carmen Leicht-Scholten

The article gives an overview on the project TANDEMplusIDEA that was conducted by the technical universities Imperial College London, ETH Zurich, TU Delft and RWTH Aachen between 2007 and 2010. Based on the mentoring concept of RWTH Aachen, the partner universities have in the course of TANDEMplusIDEA realised the first mentoring programme for female scientists in international cooperation. As a pilot scheme funded by the 6th Framework Programme of the European Commission, the project also contained the scientific evaluation of the programme and the development of a best practice model for international mentoring. A particular focus of the evaluation was on the professional and personal development of the mentees, on their satisfaction with the programme modules and on the international dimension of the programme. The article presents the programme in the context of gender-oriented human resources development, describes the results of this evaluation, and develops recommendations for future international mentoring schemes.

1. The starting point

If one considers the situation of women in science, two observations become obvious:

1. Although by now women account for half of the students and university graduates (51.8% in Germany), their numbers drop the higher one ascends the hierarchy. Women write 42.2% of all dissertations in Germany, but only 24.3% of all postdoctoral lecture qualifications. In top positions, their numbers decrease even more: Only 16.2% of all professors are female (Federal Statistical Office Germany 2009). Numbers for the European Union are similar: While there are 45% female PhD graduates, only 18% of women are in grade A academic positions (European Commission 2009).

2. Women are particularly underrepresented in science, engineering and technology (SET). In Europe only around 30% of all graduates in science, engineering and technology are female, and the number of women in top

positions drops even more to 14% (European Commission 2005). This observation is reflected in the data of the universities of the IDEA League, a network of renowned technical universities in Europe.[1] At Imperial College London 36.5% of all students are female, but only 12.5% of all professors. At ETH Zurich, it is 30.6% opposed to 10.4%; and at RWTH Aachen, there are 34% female students, but only 8.3% female professors (numbers for 2008, source: own data).

The reasons for this situation are manifold and have been analysed in various studies. There are several structural and systematic disadvantages for female scientists, especially in male-dominated scientific cultures: Many female scientists are less integrated into the scientific community and receive less career support than their male colleagues, while at the same time they have less access to professional networks and hardly find female role models in science. Another factor is the problem of the reconciliation of work and family life – which is still more relevant for women than for men – and which is opposed to the professional ethics of the ever-working scientist (cf. for example Allmendinger et al. 2000; Lind 2006; Zimmermann 2000). At the same time, studies have shown how important professional support systems are for a successful career development. Social scientists, but also the consultancy firm McKinsey & Company recommend: "Coaching, network-building or mentoring programs can be highly effective in raising women's awareness of the limitations they impose on themselves and enabling them to manage their careers in a male-centric environment" (McKinsey & Company 2007: 21).

2. Gender-oriented human resources development

These observations also influence human resources development at universities, especially against the background of foreseeable demographic changes and shortages of skilled personnel in the future. In order to stay competitive, universities (and companies) will have to attract and retain qualified personnel on all career levels. They will also in particular need to look for the potential of hitherto underrepresented groups, as it is strongly believed that more (gender) diversity among the staff makes a major contribution to the creativity and quality of research, and enriches the competences that are necessary to solve complex problems (cf. Wissenschaftsrat 2007).

---

1   The IDEA League is a network of five leading technical universities in Europe (Imperial College London, TU Delft, ETH Zurich, RWTH Aachen University and ParisTech). Since 1999 they cooperate in research and education. Through one of its central groups the network fosters equality and diversity within its institutions. For more information visit www.idealeague.org.

At RWTH Aachen University, these challenges should be met through the development of a coherent concept for gender and diversity management that establishes equality and diversity as fundamental principles throughout the university. It is developed by the scientific unit "Integration Team – Human Resources, Gender and Diversity Management (IGaD)" that is directly situated at the rector's office. The team works predominantly in the areas human resources and organisational development, work life balance, research and teaching. Because of the particular female underrepresentation in science and technology, it sees gender as one of the key diversity categories and uses mentoring programmes as a central instrument of gender-oriented human resources development. At RWTH Aachen University, seven mentoring programmes are tailored to the needs of the different target groups, ranging from school children to postdocs, in order to specifically attract and promote highly qualified female scientists on different career levels.[2]

Figure 1: The mentoring concept at RWTH Aachen University

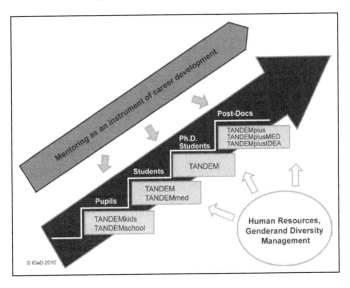

The programmes refer to findings on women in science and take them as a starting point for initiating individual and cultural change. They aim to support female scientists in their career developments and encourage them to stay in academia, for example through the promotion of network building which strengthens the participants' integration into the scientific community.

---

2   For more information please see http://www.igad.rwth-aachen.de/engl/mentoring-programmes.htm.

But at the same time the programmes want to stimulate change processes and long-term effects on the organisational culture of science by enriching the scientific and cultural climate through diverse role models and new perspectives on science (cf. Leicht-Scholten 2008a): The participating scientists will in the future be more sensitised for equality issues, but they will also serve as role models for following generations of female students.

3. The international mentoring programme TANDEMplusIDEA

In the context of the European network of the IDEA League, the mentoring concept of RWTH Aachen University has been expanded to the international dimension. In the project TANDEMplusIDEA, four technical universities of the network have cooperated in the first international mentoring scheme for female postdocs of natural sciences and engineering. Funded for three years between 2007 and 2010 by the 6th Framework Programme of the European Commission, the project TANDEMplusIDEA comprised the development and implementation of a mentoring programme for international female scientists as well as its scientific evaluation and the development of a best practice model for international mentoring. The objective of the programme was to support and encourage high qualified female research staff to apply for and obtain leadership positions. In doing so, it aimed to increase the number of female professors on an international level and, in general, to achieve a better balance of sexes in academia, science, and technology. This should ultimately lead to improved gender equality in science and more gendered research cultures at universities, enriching research and education in general.

The project was conceptualised and coordinated by IGaD at RWTH Aachen University. In addition, there were national contact persons at each partner university of the IDEA League, Imperial College London, TU Delft and ETH Zurich.[3] These national coordinators were responsible for the selection of mentees and for the organisation of the project events at their universities.

Addressees of the programme were female postdocs of natural science and engineering from the four participating universities. The mentoring programme was realised between February 2008 and March 2009 with 16 highly qualified female scientists. They took part in a programme based on three modules: one-to-one-mentoring, training and networking. In the mentoring part, the mentees were paired with a scientific mentor of international

---

3   ParisTech was an associated member in the project as the university joined the IDEA League after the project had been developed.

reputation. They were free to choose a male or female mentor, according to their needs and expectations. The other two instruments, networking and training, served as an introduction into the scientific community and as a further qualification for a career in science (Leicht-Scholten 2007). At both a Summer and Winter School, TANDEMplusIDEA offered training seminars that were conducted by external trainers and dealt with topics related to international careers in science and technology, e.g. intercultural communication, conflict management and leadership skills. They emanated from the demand of the mentees and offered background information and hands-on solutions for future situations. Networking events with international speakers complemented the programme and offered the participants the possibility to exchange and network among the group, as well as with external speakers and guests. The events were organised alternately at the four partner universities, each time offering new stimuli, and introducing new organisations and people. This international dimension made TANDEMplusIDEA extraordinary. It addressed issues that are important for worldwide careers, facilitated international exchange and networking among scientists, and fostered further collaborative working in Europe. In this regard, the programme also benefited the participating universities, not only because of increased employee retention among the project's participants, but also because of potential scientific collaborations.

Figure 2: Project structure TANDEMplusIDEA

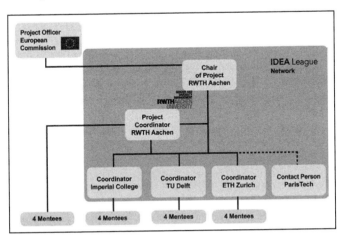

4. International mentoring: Results and experiences

4.1 Evaluation method

The scientific evaluation of a mentoring programme is an important aspect for its quality management and future development. As mentioned by Löther (2003), it is useful to collect qualitative and quantitative data, and to interview the participants at each stage of the programme. The evaluation of TANDEMplusIDEA was based on two aspects: The mentees filled in three written standardised questionnaires, one at the beginning, one in the middle, and one three months after the end of the programme. The questionnaires tracked the personal and professional development of the participants, their expectations towards the programme and their experiences and satisfaction with the different modules. In addition to this written survey, there were informal interviews with all participants throughout the course of the scheme. To ensure the adaptation and customisation of the programme to the needs of the participants, they were also asked to evaluate each training and networking event. The data contrived allows an evaluation of the overall success of the programme TANDEMplusIDEA, but also enables the development of quality criteria for international mentoring programmes in general.

4.2 Sociodemographic data

As mentioned above, the participants of the mentoring programme TANDEMplusIDEA were female postdocs of the four participating universities. The group was composed of 16 mentees altogether, four from each university. Beyond their affiliation to the four European universities, the group was very international, hailing from eleven nations altogether. Many of them had already been very flexible in their careers and moved a lot. The composition of the group, therefore, shows how important mobility and international careers are for this generation of scientists. The mentees also represented various fields of science and technology. 38%[4] of mentees worked in engineering, 44% in natural sciences, and 19% in medicine (at medical faculties, respectively). The majority had already been – or still was – working with an interdisciplinary focus.

---

4   The numbers of the following evaluation results are rounded for reasons of better readability.

On average the mentees were 32 years old. In the course of the programme, the number of mothers increased from 19% to 44%, but, interestingly, none of them left academia; all started working again after a short period of maternity leave. For the group of academics whose birth rate is usually exceptionally low, this number is very surprising.[5] We take it as a hint that the mentees of TANDEMplusIDEA felt encouraged – maybe even by one another – to combine a career in science with children.

4.3 Professional situation of the mentees

92% of all mentees were employed in non-permanent positions; a situation very common in academia. At the end of TANDEMplusIDEA, 69% of all mentees said that their situation had changed in one way or the other since the beginning. The career steps mentioned most frequently were: "I have presented my work at conferences and symposia" (75%) and "I have published in important scientific journals" (75%). Individual mentees had also received prices and awards. Interestingly, no mentee said that she had not taken any career step at all. When questioned about the contribution of TANDEMplus-IDEA to these developments, mentees stated, for example, that they had formed collaborations with other universities or that their mentor had invited them to conferences or encouraged them to write a particular paper. These results illustrate that the programme had indeed concrete effects on the career planning and development of the mentees. In the course of the programme, their overall evaluation of their professional situation did not change significantly. Among the factors most impeding their careers were: job insecurities where funding was not guaranteed, their unclear position within their institutes, and difficulties with male colleagues and superiors.

4.4 Expectations towards the programme

The mentees were asked for their expectations towards the programme modules mentoring, training and networking in the first questionnaire as well as in the selection interview before the start of the programme. From the programme, the mentees mainly expected support in the development of their personal and strategic skills, support in their career planning and useful new

---

5   A recent study on the correlation between childlessness and employment relationships in science has again revealed that in general women on all levels of the academic hierarchy tend to be more often childless than their male colleagues (Metz-Göckel et al. 2009).

contacts and networks in the scientific community. They were less interested in concrete topics like publishing or academic committee work. Asked for important topics for the training seminars, the majority of mentees chose "Analysis of potential capacity and career planning" and "Communication & negotiation techniques", as well as "Leadership skills" and "Conflict management". Seminars on these topics were later conducted. The particular wish towards the mentors was that they would be able to give suggestions for the achievement of career goals and support the mentees in their self-reflection. Before the beginning of the mentoring relationship, 69% of all participants said they would prefer a female mentor, 6% preferred a male mentor, and 25% had no preference. Considering the expectations towards the programme and its modules, there were no overly significant deviations with regard to the four universities.[6]

4.5 Satisfaction and profit of the mentees

In the course of the programme 56% mentees were matched with female mentors and 44% with male mentors. As with the mentees, the mentors were very international. The distances between mentee and mentor ranged from under 100 km up to 3.000 km, but it was not significant that distance would have an impact on the mentees' satisfaction with their mentors. The vast majority (81%) had met 1-3 times in person, as recommended by mentoring experts. Meetings mostly took place at the office of the mentor, followed by encounters at conferences, meetings or events. In the final evaluation, mentees were especially content with the personal support they had received by their mentor, although satisfaction with this module was not as high as that with the other two programme modules: 69% of the mentees said they were satisfied or very satisfied with their mentors. At the same time is has to be noted that only 44% of all mentees were satisfied with their *own* performance in the mentoring relationship. In individual comments various mentees noted that they had experienced their mentor as very friendly and helpful but that they could have put more effort into the relationships themselves. Reasons for this (partly) hesitant behaviour were lack of time, in particular as several mentees were pregnant or had babies during the time of the programme. Another role may have played by the fact that some participants were unsure about the role and importance of the mentor in the beginning of TANDEMplusIDEA. In general, however, the mentoring module was very

---

6   In general it has to be noted that the case numbers of the evaluation are very small as they go back to just 16 participants. We can therefore make statements for our project and observe general tendencies but cannot claim to be representative for the mentees' universities, faculties, or age groups as a whole.

much appreciated. After all, 88% of the mentees were still in touch with their mentor after the programme had ended.

Regarding the second programme module, 100% of all mentees were satisfied or very satisfied with the seminars. They felt particularly supported in the topics "Self-confidence", "Career planning" and "Conflict management". Also the networking received high approval rates of 88%. In this module the mentees were particularly satisfied with the exchange of information and experiences with scientists from different disciplines and in similar life situations. These results underline the findings we gathered at conversations and interviews with the mentees. An important success of the programme was that the participants were – often for the first time – able to exchange and network with other women in similar situations. Already after the first programme event, several mentees mentioned how much they appreciated this opportunity of the programme:

- "It was a joy for me meeting so many excellent women in the same situation and with similar interests (...)."
- "I would do it again! It was very motivating / stimulating to meet other women in similar situations!"
- "This is a very special group of people and opportunity. I have found support and advice that is not available elsewhere, so this has been an invaluable experience. The things I have learnt will be of use to me for many years. Also very enjoyable - we have formed a great community of friends!"

In this regard the programme was able to achieve one of its most prominent objectives: To establish a network of female scientists who feel better integrated into the scientific community.

The mentees also very much appreciated the international dimension of the programme and the new insights into different scientific cultures they had gained:

- "It was in particular the international focus of the programme that appealed to me. Academia is very different in each of the four countries, and the mentees are very international. This gives us an insight into career opportunities in different countries. The project helps me to consider various career paths, offers orientation on my scientific way and enables me to share experiences and network with other international female scientists."
- "This is an excellent initiative. Its international basis shows us that women scientists everywhere face similar challenges. Most of us have clear ideas of what we want from our careers, but the scheme is helping

us to clarify the steps needed to achieve those goals and to define strategies for maintaining a good work life balance. (...)"

It is, therefore, not surprising that the overall satisfaction with the programme
was 100% - 69% of the mentees were satisfied, 31% were even very satisfied.
Asked for their subjective perception of what they profited from most, a majority mentioned a strengthening of their personal and strategic skills, support
of their career planning and motivation for professional advancement. Also
the insights into the different scientific cultures were considered as very valuable.

Figure 3: Personal benefit of TANDEMplusIDEA

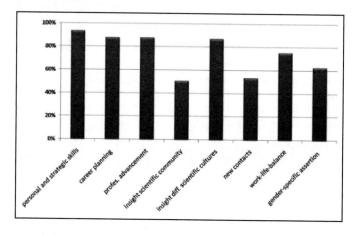

When comparing the rates of satisfaction between participants from the different universities, there are no significant statistical differences. However,
the tendency can be observed that the satisfaction with the mentoring part
was particularly high among Swiss and German mentees; that the British
participants were especially satisfied with the seminars, and the Dutch mentees with the networking module. These differences may be due to peculiarities of the different scientific cultures, but it should also not be neglected that
the benefit from a particular programme component extensively depends on
the personality of the mentee and her current situation. In general, it could be
noted that not all participants profited equally from all three modules. As
Leicht-Scholten (2008b) points out in her comparative study on mentoring
programmes with disciplinary focus, usually those mentees who are not as
satisfied with one of the instruments take much more advantage of one or the
two others.

In addition to these answers, we were able to observe results of the programme in different key areas. The participants have started to cooperate, both with their mentors and among the group. The initiative came from the participants themselves. As one mentee wrote:

- "My research is gradually involving more and more techniques and methods which are traditionally used in other sciences and vice versa. (...) The difference mainly lies in the value of the parameters. But even the possible techniques to determine the parameters are often similar. (...) A future scientific collaboration would certainly ensure our continued relationship, which all of us would greatly value."

We believe that these collaborations, and in particular the proactive approach of the mentees, are a very positive indicator that TANDEMplusIDEA has been successful in establishing a functioning network of female scientists throughout Europe.[7] Other factors that influenced the success of the mentoring programme were a good cooperation structure among the partner universities and a strong structural affiliation: The programme had the support and commitment of the top executives of all four partner universities. Each event was opened by the rector or president of the host institution. Additionally, the coordinators from all partner universities held influential positions in the fields of human resources and/or gender mainstreaming. Their model of cooperation (see also Figure 2) guaranteed a direct contact person at each of the four universities, which allowed a close supervision of all participants. Also, the organisation of the events in the four cities benefited a lot from the presence of a coordinator on-site.

In the course of the evaluation, it turned out how important it is to inform all participants extensively on the objectives and outline of the programme. Although during the programme TANDEMplusIDEA information was given through personal conversations, a detailed mentoring brochure and an introductory session on mentoring in the first training seminar, the feedback of the mentees indicated that even more information would have been desired. In particular, they would have needed more guidance with regard to the mentoring relationship.

Other comments by the mentees suggested that because they appreciated their exchange so much, they wished there would have been even more time for reflections and networking within the group. It was also mentioned that "it could have been clearer what a 'network' and a 'training' event was". This confusion was due to organisational reasons. As the mentees travelled to each event it made sense to combine a networking session with training input. In the future this could be communicated clearer. Another recommendation,

---

7   This evaluation focused on the point of view of the mentees. It should not be forgotten, however, that also the mentors and even the host institutions benefit from the programme.

expressed directly after the first Networking Event in London, was that a two-day meeting was too short. The second Networking Event in Zurich was extended to three days accordingly. Interestingly, there was a strong negative response among the participants toward discussing career-related topics too much from a gender-perspective. Although several participants of TANDEM-plusIDEA reported that they had felt excluded in their scientific careers at one point or another, their attitude was a very pragmatic one, all mentees being successful in their careers in (male) scientific cultures. At the same time, the programme – in some cases for the first time – raised the participants' awareness on certain structural disadvantages women in science face, thus facilitating a stronger sensitisation and potential action in the future.

5. Conclusion

TANDEMplusIDEA has been the first mentoring programme conducted in an international cooperation between four universities. Its approach focused on the individual support of single scientists, but also on long-term effects on the scientific cultures at technical universities. At the end of the programme the mentees were asked what they think made the success of the programme. Some representative comments included:

- "The combination of mentoring, trainings and networking. The networking in the female group with the same 'education standard' and comparable aims."
- "The TANDEMplusIDEA programme embraces several different life aspects. It puts a stress on the work-life-balance which is not done in many other training programmes. Moreover, from my point of view the international networking and trainings increase the value of the programme a lot."
- "The combination of the four universities, travel to other countries where one has no distraction and can focus for 1-2 days on career/personality etc. and the training."
- "First of all the relationship between girls within the group was great. All the girls were very motivated during the program. Second, the program was very well organized and tailored for the mentees needs (mentoring, training and networking parts). During the whole program there was a very pleasant atmosphere (...)."

Our evaluation results, therefore, point towards four critical aspects for the success of (international) mentoring programmes:

1. A very good introduction of the concept and information, especially on the mentoring module.
2. An excellent framework programme that is targeted specifically to the needs of the participants and that leaves enough time for exchange and networking among the peer group of mentees.
3. A good selection of participants, in the group of mentees, as well as in the matching with the mentors.
4. The international dimension as it offers extra benefits, introduces new people, institutions and scientific cultures at every meeting. The mentees get acquainted with different approaches to science, broaden their international networks and become prepared for the demands of international careers, such as flexibility and mobility.

Other studies (e.g. Leicht-Scholten 2008b) had already confirmed that it is a prerequisite for the success of a mentoring programme that they have a strong structural affiliation at the host institution(s), a very clear structure and dedicated programme coordination.

TANDEMplusIDEA was able to prove the success of an international mentoring scheme as it supported individual scientists in their career planning and initiated effects on the gender balance in academia. In the course of the programme it also became apparent how important the engagement and commitment of all players (the mentees, the mentors and the institutions) are. TANDEMplusIDEA has been a successful pilot project that should, according to the participants and the coordinators, be continued in the future.

References

Allmendinger, J. et al. (2000): Should I stay or should I go? Mentoring, Verankerung und Verbleib in der Wissenschaft. Empirische Ergebnisse einer Studie zu Karriereverläufen von Frauen und Männern in Instituten der Max Planck Gesellschaft. In: Page, J. / Leemann, R.J. (Eds.): Karriere von Akademikerinnen. Bedeutung des Mentoring als Instrument der Nachwuchsförderung, Bern, 33-48.

European Commission (2005): Women and Science. Excellence and Innovation – Gender Equality in Science. Working Document. Brussels.

European Commission (2009): SHE Figures 2009. Statistics and Indicators on Gender Equality in Science. Brussels: European Commission. Available from: http://ec.europa.eu/research/science-society/document_library/pdf_06/she_figures_2009_en.pdf.

Federal Statistical Office Germany (2009): Hochschulen auf einen Blick. Wiesbaden.

Lind, I. (2006): Wissenschaftlerinnen an Hochschulen. Analyse der aktuellen Situation. In: Dahlhoff, J. (Ed.): Anstoß zum Aufstieg – Karrieretraining für Wissenschaftlerinnen auf dem Prüfstand, Bielefeld, 142-189.

Leicht-Scholten, C. (2007): Challenging the leaky pipeline: Cooperation scheme between technical universities and research institutions for excellent female researchers. First results. In: Welpe, I. et al. (Eds.): Gender and Engineering: Strategies and Possibilities. Frankfurt a. M., 175-189.

Leicht-Scholten, C. (2008a): Exzellenz braucht Vielfalt – oder: wie Gender and Diversity in den Mainstream der Hochschulentwicklung kommt – Human Resources, Gender and Diversity Management an der RWTH Aachen. Journal Netzwerk Frauenforschung NRW, 23, 33-39.

Leicht-Scholten, C. (2008b): Where is the Key to Success? A Comparative Evaluation of Mentoring Programmes for Outstanding Female Scientists in Natural Science, Engineering, Social Sciences and Medicine. In: Grenz, S. et al. (Eds.): Gender Equality Programmes in Higher Education. International Perspectives, Wiesbaden, 163-178.

Löther, A. (Ed.) (2003): Mentoring-Programme für Frauen in der Wissenschaft, Bielefeld.

McKinsey & Company (2007): Women Matter. Gender diversity, a corporate performance driver. Available from: http://www.mckinsey.com/locations/paris/home/womenmatter/pdfs/Wo men_matter_oct2007_english.pdf .

Metz-Göckel, S. et al. (2009): Wissenschaftlicher Nachwuchs ohne Nachwuchs? Zwischenergebnisse des Projekts „Wissen- oder Elternschaft? Kinderlosigkeit und Beschäftigungsverhältnisse an Hochschulen in Deutschland" (conference presentation, final report forthcoming in 2010).

Wissenschaftsrat (2007): Empfehlungen zur Chancengleichheit von Wissenschaftlerinnen und Wissenschaftlern [online]. Drs. 8036-07. Berlin. Available from: http://www.wissenschaftsrat.de/texte/8036-07.pdf.

Zimmermann, Karin (2000): Spiele mit der Macht in der Wissenschaft. Passfähigkeit und Geschlecht als Kriterien für Berufungen. Berlin.

JUNO Code of Practice: Advancing Women's Careers in Higher Education

Jennifer Dyer, Peter Main, Saher Ahmed, Katharine Hollinshead

The Institute of Physics has a longstanding interest in diversity issues. In 2003, the Institute introduced a Site Visit scheme, in which selected panels visited physics departments and produced a dedicated report on their "gender inclusiveness". After two years, the results of these visits were condensed into a general report: Women in University Physics Departments: a Site Visit Scheme. Building upon the best practice identified in this influential report, the IOP has established the JUNO Code of Practice that aims to advance the careers of women in higher education physics. The Code gives departments specific actions to improve the participation and retention of women, based on five core principles. The main aims of the scheme are to develop an equitable working culture in which students and staff, men and women, can achieve their full potential; to allow assessment of gender equality performance against a robust framework; and to promote open discussion of gender and other equality issues. Over half the physics departments in the UK have now signed up to support our JUNO scheme. It shows how professional bodies can have a major impact in promoting gender equality.

1. Introduction

The Institute of Physics has a longstanding interest in diversity issues. Its *Women in Physics Group*[1] is a self-organising network group of members with interests in gender issues. Partly due to the existence of this Group and in response to the first International Conference on Women in Physics in 2002, the Institute established a *Women in Physics Program*, which, in 2004, became its *Diversity Programme*; there are two members of staff dedicated to this work.

In this article, we describe Project JUNO, which emerged from the Institute's Diversity programme and which builds upon a series of university site visits. This voluntary scheme for university physics departments aims to improve their gender friendliness and the career progression of women, by setting out practical advice and guidance. We also reflect on how projects

---

1   http://www.iop.org/activity/groups/subject/Women_in_physics/index.html

such as this contribute to the recruitment and retention of women within UK university science departments.

In common with many countries, the UK has difficulty in attracting women into physics and engineering. Only a little over 20% of the students who study physics beyond the age of 16 are female. In 2005, for example, although Physics was the 12th most-popular A-level in the UK overall, it was the sixth most-popular A-level subject for boys but only 19th most-popular for girls; almost 78% of those taking A-level Physics were boys. Only 14% of girls who were awarded an A* or A for GCSE Double Award Science or Physics (the UK's pre-16 qualification) went on to sit A-level physics. In other words, there is a very substantial number of girls who have the ability to do well at physics but who are choosing not to study the subject post-16.

The Institute of Physics commissioned a review to try and understand the causes of this problem (Murphy / Whitelegg 2006). They found that, as students progress through school, their interest in science overall declines, particularly for girls and particularly for physics. They also found that girls tend to develop the perception that "they can't do physics," even when this is not the case. Drawing on this review, a teachers' guide for action (Institute of Physics 2006a) and two videos[2] were produced to help teachers to find ways of encouraging more girls to study physics.

The Institute has continued its *Girls in Physics* work and has worked with the UK's National Network of Science Learning Centres, funded by the Department of Children, Schools and Families (DCSF), on an action research program to share information on successful teaching and learning strategies to engage girls with physics. The second phase, in 2008, enabled teachers from 100 schools to participate. The DCSF published two further reports from the Girls into Physics: Action Research evaluation. The Research Brief (Daly / Grant / Bultitude 2009) contains recommendations from the project and highlights the key findings of the evaluation. The full Research Report (Grant / Bultitude 2009) contains the theory of change model developed for the evaluation, rich data from teachers and students and further analysis of key issues, which is useful for informing continuing professional development (CPD) using action research approaches with teachers and students.

The gender of undergraduate and postgraduate physics students in UK universities mirrors that of A-Level students: just over 20% of these students are female. However, there is a more general problem, which is shared by almost all academic subjects: the proportion of women becomes successively smaller as they move from lecturers, to senior lecturers/readers and through to professors, as shown in Figure 1.

---

2   Institute of Physics: Girls in the Physics Classroom videos. Available from education@iop.org.

Figure 1: Percentage of female academic staff in UK physics departments

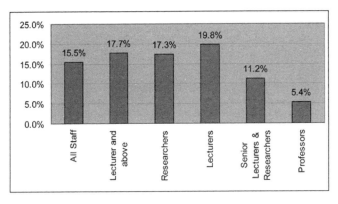

Source: HESA 2007/08

Although there has been improvement in the numbers of female staff in physics departments in recent years, as shown in figure 2, the situation still remains that women become increasingly under-represented as seniority rises.

Figure 2: Percentages of female academic staff in UK physics departments 1996-2008

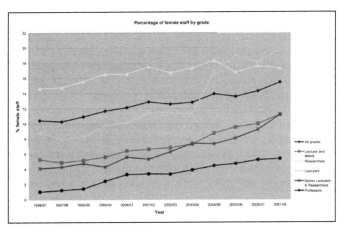

Source: HESA 2007/08

2. University Site Visits

The *American Physical Society*[3] has been offering a site visit scheme for many years. Following a visit to the US, a senior woman physics professor made a presentation about this scheme to the heads of UK physics departments at one of their twice-yearly meetings held at the Institute. The response of the largely male audience was interesting, varying from the supportive, through the skeptical to the downright hostile. One major perception that needed to be overcome was that this was not even an issue. However, the most powerful argument put forward was the clear loss of talent of women in the academic pipeline.

Following this meeting, the Institute wrote to all heads of physics departments in the UK offering a visit; ultimately, all 16 departments that requested it were visited. Visits were, therefore, by invitation only and involved an external panel of between four and six people, which always included at least one man to ensure that the visits were not seen as being biased from the outset. The panel spent a whole day on site, mainly talking informally and confidentially to senior management, undergraduate students, and all levels of academic and research staff, including post-docs and postgraduate students, holding discussions with male and female staff separately. By and large, both the visiting teams and the departments regarded these visits as friendly, constructive events, reflecting an important theme in this work: because the panels were physicists themselves, they were seen less as an external auditing team and more as a group of friends offering advice because they were from an impartial and professional organisation. As an obviously neutral friend, known and respected by both the management and the staff, and without any aim other than to help, the Institute was able to gather information in a manner that would be difficult for an unknown outside body, and essentially impossible for an internal audit.

At the end of each visit, a semi-formal report was agreed by the panel and given confidentially to the relevant head of department. Items of good practice were highlighted as well as any issues to be addressed, with positive suggestions on how the situation could be improved. Since the visits were by invitation only, the Institute was not able to impose any requirements. However, in almost every case, the reports were discussed openly and six departments sent a response to the Institute, stating how they were addressing the issues raised. Indeed, one of the most important legacies of the visits was that gender issues were raised and discussed in physics departments, in many cases for the first time. Similarly, departments realised that they were not monitoring disaggregated statistics, for staff or for students, and had, therefore,

---

3   http://www.aps.org/programs/women/sitevisits/

missed some important differences between the numbers of men and women in their department.

The visits themselves uncovered some serious issues. Although infrequent, several cases of sexual harassment were reported. Some of these were quite unknown by the department management, although every university visited had an explicit HR mechanism for dealing with such cases. Even more worryingly, in one incident, where the management did know about the harassment, the matter had not been dealt with properly.

The panels also found evidence that women frequently felt excluded by cultural issues. For example, at the postgraduate level, in some departments the social interaction revolved around football and drinking, to the exclusion of women; in one case, a woman from an Islamic background felt completely isolated. At higher levels, many women expressed the view that senior university management was 'unnecessarily aggressive' and confrontational and, for that reason, they were reluctant to become involved in such activities.

The visits managed to unearth information that was previously unknown to the department and also demonstrate serious problems with procedures that were thought to be working well. One of the recurring themes that emerged from almost all of the visits was the discrepancy between what departmental and HR managers asserted was the situation, what was the real state of affairs that emerged when the visiting panel spoke to the various members of the department, and what the perceptions of the staff were. A typical example might be that someone in management would say that all staff at all grades were appraised every year. Then the panel would speak to the research staff and find someone who been in employment for more than five years and had never been appraised, and another member of staff who would say that the appraisal scheme was not compulsory. Another example was a head of department saying that promotion procedures were fair and transparent only for it to emerge that some women thought that male candidates were being favoured. Such discrepancies were occasionally severe and, in a few cases, led to animated debates in the departments following the visit.

At the end of the site visit scheme, a report (see Institute of Physics 2006b) was published by the Institute highlighting the good practice that was found across the physics departments that we visited and making recommendations for improvement across the whole sector. These recommendations were focused around improving practice for undergraduate and postgraduate students, research staff, and academic staff. This report was widely distributed, to all physics departments, professional bodies in the UK, and other relevant women in SET organisations, and has influenced other professional bodies in other subjects, both in the UK and in other countries. In addition, we are aware that even departments that were not visited read the report carefully and many of them instituted change on that basis.

3. Project JUNO

The report on the site visits was a major step. By coincidence, in 2005, there was an international review of physics research in the UK by the EPSRC, PPARC, IOP and RAS (2006); the report drew attention to the low proportion of female academics and called upon the Institute, among others, to try to remedy the shortage. To take the recommendations from the review, as well as to build on the site visit work we had already undertaken, we decided to develop a code of practice (see Institute of Physics 2009a), based around five principles, which were identified through the good practice already acknowledged in our site visit report. The five principles are:

1. A robust organisational framework to deliver equality of opportunity and reward
    *   Establish organisational framework
    *   Monitoring and evidence base
2. Appointment and selection processes and procedures that encourage men and women to apply for academic posts at all levels.
    *   Ensure processes are fully inclusive
    *   Take positive action where necessary
3. Departmental structures and systems that support and encourage the career progression of all staff and enable men and women to progress and continue in their careers
    *   Transparent appraisal and development
    *   Transparent promotions processes
4. A departmental organisation, structure, management arrangements and culture that are open, inclusive and transparent and encourage the participation of all staff
    *   Promote an inclusive culture
    *   Transparent work-allocation model
5. Flexible approaches and provisions that enable individuals, at all career and life stages, to maximise their contribution to SET, their department and institution.
    *   Support and promote flexible working practices.

For each principle, there are also key actions and a set of assessment criteria covering all of the good practice areas identified. For example, for the first key action of Principle 2, we have

*   Ensure career breaks are taken into consideration
*   Gender awareness training for all staff who interview
*   Provide induction for all new staff, including research assistants

A full list of the assessment criteria can be found in the JUNO code of practice (see Institute of Physics 2009a).

An action plan setting out how the department plans to progress in the future is also a requirement. This action plan is expected to cover all five JUNO principles, and should demonstrate clearly how the department plans to resource its actions, when it expects to undertake them and who has responsibility for ensuring that they happen.

One important facet of the combined assessment criteria is that, they define a benchmark of good practice, which is useful even if departments go no further with the scheme. Although Project JUNO is specifically for physics departments, the criteria would be applicable to almost any subject, particularly in the science area. For those who do wish to go further, in order to become a JUNO Supporter, departments affirm their support for the principles and commit to working towards Juno Champion by sending a letter to the Institute signed by university senior management confirming this commitment. In the original formulation of the scheme, they then had two years to submit an application for Champion, outlining how they met the five principles of the scheme and their action plan. The JUNO Assessment Panel would then assess their application and decide whether to award JUNO Champion (for Champion logo see Figure 3). Champion status is awarded for three years, when departments must re-apply by submitting a further action plan, demonstrating progress made since Champion was awarded and future actions to be addressed. The Institute makes available the list of supporters and champions to prospective students and job applicants.

Figure 3: JUNO logos

IOP Institute of Physics
Juno Supporter

IOP Institute of Physics
Juno Champion

Following the first few applications for Champion status, it was obvious that the step from Supporter to Champion was too great for most institutions, given the demands of embedding the five principles throughout the department. Many departments found that they simply did not have sufficient time or resources to fully embed the principles or achieve the necessary goals in their action plans within two years. For example, a change in Head of Department or key personnel in the administrative staff could often delay plans for a few months. Therefore, in November 2009 we introduced a new intermediate step, JUNO Practitioner, for which a department must show that it has set up processes to move towards meeting the criteria, such as putting together a 'JUNO Committee' and formalising an action plan and methods of measuring impact. For Practitioner we expect departments to have started to collate a solid evidence base on which to build. We have designed a

Practitioner good practice benchmarking checklist (see Institute of Physics 2009b) that departments can use as a starting point for discussion within their committees and to assess where departments currently are in terms of their own equality good practice. Departments are encouraged to use this checklist in a positive way, to benchmark progress already made.

Currently 29 physics departments are signed up as JUNO Supporters, with many more showing strong interest. This represents over half of the physics departments in the UK, and we are hoping that this alone will provide an impetus for other departments to sign up and join the scheme. Only 4 out of the original sixteen departments that participated in the site visit program have not signed up. One university in the latter category said that the reason was because of the 2-year deadline for Champion.

We are hoping that the introduction of Practitioner will ease the daunting task of implementing and embedding, and then evidencing, the five principles. The JUNO Practitioner level is designed to not only be a stepping stone on the way to Champion but also a way of the Institute and the department recognising and rewarding progress being made on the way to becoming Champion. Indeed, at the most recent JUNO Assessment Panel meeting in March 2010, the Panel awarded Practitioner to three physics departments, proving this to be a welcome step on the way to becoming Champion.

Our aim, ultimately, is for all UK physics departments to be part of the scheme. In the summer of 2009, the first two physics departments, University of Warwick and Imperial College, London achieved JUNO Champion status. Both Champions have commented on how useful participating in the scheme has been for embedding good practice in their departments. Professor Malcolm Cooper, Head of Physics at the University of Warwick, said,

"At Warwick we have tried to create flexible and transparent processes which encourage everyone, male and female, to achieve their ambitions. We have been fortunate to have female role models in all areas and at all levels who demonstrate that gender is no bar to success."

4. Working with others

Recent legislation in the UK, such as the Gender Equality Duty (see The Sex Discrimination Code of Practice 2007), which came into force in 2007, has tended to insist that public institutions have to be *pro-active* rather than *reactive* in dealing with issues such as gender, ethnicity, disability etc. Therefore, it is not sufficient to react to a particular issue, one needs to anticipate it, and to have procedures in place that ensure fairness and remove discrimination. Consequently, universities take these matters seriously, not least to avoid potential challenges in a court of law.

In dealing with gender issues, the *Athena SWAN Charter*[4], which is aimed at all SET departments and not just physics, has very similar principles to JUNO and has a similar set of levels, in their case, Bronze, Silver and Gold. However, the Bronze award is a university-level award and this must be achieved before a department can then progress individually to Silver or Gold. As a result, the scheme tends to be organised in a top-down approach, with central university administration, usually the HR department, leading the way. While this is an excellent way of ensuring the essential commitment from senior university management, it does have the major drawback of not being owned by staff in the department, who can perceive this is an imposition. In addition, it is also subject to the discrepancy between management assertions and the reality in the department that was so visible in our site visits. The JUNO award is seen as equivalent to Athena SWAN silver and we have developed 'fast-track' routes between the two schemes. JUNO has a specific advantage for physics departments in that, as it is solely a departmental award, physics departments are not reliant on their universities achieving a general Bronze award first. Nevertheless, the Institute is keen for physics departments to use JUNO as leverage for encouraging their universities to participate in the Athena SWAN initiative and ultimately achieve Athena Gold.

The Royal Society of Chemistry (RSC) has also set up a similar scheme (see Royal Society of Chemistry 2008) to JUNO, as have the London Mathematical Society, who has recently established their own Good Practice Award for women in mathematics (see The London Mathematic Society 2009). Both the Institute and the RSC are working closely with the Athena SWAN team to ensure that universities see what we are doing as coherent and complimentary, and that there is no confusion between the particular schemes. Together we have formed the *Athena Partnership*, along with the UK Resource Centre for Women in SET[5], not only to promote the various specific programs, such as JUNO, but also to offer resources to help departments make progress in this area. For example, one of the major problems for a department is to be able to compare its environment and performance with those of other institutions; therefore, we offer benchmarking tools to allow that comparison to be made. The tools might just be statistical, say on the number of female professors, or more qualitative, for example, the way one deals with career breaks.

The *Athena Partnership* also offers site visits, but, whereas the original Institute site visits, as described in section 2, tended to identify good practice and any problem areas, these serve more as advisory, working with the staff in the departments, possibly taking them forward towards JUNO or some other form of accreditation. The hope is that, over time, other professional

---

4   http://www.athenaswan.org.uk/html/athena-swan/
5   http://www.ukrc4setwomen.org/

bodies will join the partnership, possibly using the JUNO brand. Although many of them do not have the resources enjoyed by the RSC and the Institute, the Partnership allows them to build upon all the existing work and to offer support to their member groups at relatively little cost.

As a final point, we have also tried to transfer the elements of our work in universities to private companies by initiating a similar site visit scheme in industry, jointly with the UK Resource Centre for Women in SET. Although there has been one very successful visit, in general it has been too difficult to persuade companies to take part, because, although they do see the value of the scheme, it is believed that the management culture is so different, often with the added complication of trade unions, that they may be worried that the visits would raise expectations of change that they would not be able to fulfill, and that they might then be vilified for having poor practice.

5. Summary

There is frequently a large difference between what universities claim to be the case with equal opportunities and what is actually happening in the departments. Externally based schemes can be an excellent way of monitoring real behaviour, provided the external body has the trust of both management and staff. Genuine culture change needs both commitment from senior management, that is, someone championing the cause at a high level, and support from all levels of staff and students of the department. Direct impact of these schemes can often be difficult to measure, given the time lag between raising awareness and changing practice and this then feeding through to increased numbers of female physicists. Nevertheless, taking part in such schemes and implementing good practice benefits everyone, not just female members of staff. And by raising the profile of gender issues, we can ensure they are discussed both formally and informally at the departmental level. There are drawbacks, however, in that the scheme has no real carrot or stick as departments are free to choose whether they participate in it at all. In addition, there are ramifications on workload and resources; departments must find staff willing to take on the additional work of progressing the JUNO agenda and resource the resulting activities accordingly. It is also difficult to quantify and measure success; culture change is not always tangible. However, recent national statistics do show positive trends in the recruitment and retention of women and that at every grade of staff in UK physics departments in recent years, the percentage growth of female staff is significantly higher than that of male staff.

Therefore, the steps needed to change the culture of physics departments, so that they are more inclusive, need to be developed from inside the profession and professional bodies, such as the Institute of Physics, are ideally placed to deliver such schemes. They are well known to everyone in the departments, from the heads to the undergraduate students, most of whom are members. In addition, they have a reputation for independence and trust.

References

Daly, A. / Grant, L. / Bultitude, K. (2009): Girls into Physics: Action Research. Department for Children, Schools and Families. Research Brief DCSF-RB103. Available from: http://www.dcsf.gov.uk/research/data/uploadfiles/DCSF-RB103.pdf

EPSRC / PPARC / IOP / RAS (2006): International Perceptions of UK Research in Physics and Astronomy, 2005. Available from: http://www.iop.org/activity/policy/Publications/file_21581.pdf

Grant, L. / Bultitude, K. (2009): Girls into Physics: Action Research. Department for Children, Schools and Families. Research Report DCSF-RR103. Available from: http://www.dcsf.gov.uk/research/data/uploadfiles/DCSF-RR103(R).pdf

Institute of Physics (2006a): Girls in the Physics Classroom: A Teachers' Guide for Action. Available from: http://www.iop.org/activity/education/Policy/Policy%20and%20consultations/page_22210.html

Institute of Physics (2006b): Women in University Physics Departments. A site visit scheme 2003-2005. Research Report. Available from: http://www.iop.org/activity/diversity/iop-resources/wip/file_31789.pdf

Institute of Physics (2009a): Project JUNO Code of Practice. Available from: http://www.iop.org/activity/diversity/initiatives/juno/documentation/file_38486.pdf

Institute of Physics (2009b): JUNO Practitioner Good Practice Checklist. Available from: http://www.iop.org/activity/diversity/initiatives/juno/documentation/file_38489.doc

Murphy, P. / Whitelegg, E. (2006): Girls in the Physics Classroom: A Review of the Research on the Participation of Girls in Physics. London, Institute of Physics. Available from: http://www.iop.org/activity/education/Policy/Policy%20and%20consultations/page_22191.html

Royal Society of Chemistry (2008): Planning for Success - Good Practice in University Science Departments. Available from: http://www.rsc.org/ScienceAndTechnology/Policy/Documents/PlanningforSuccess.asp

The London Mathematical Society (2009): Good Practice Awards: Advancing women's careers in university mathematical sciences departments. Available from: http://www.lms.ac.uk/activities/women_maths_com/good_practice_award.pdf

The Sex Discrimination Code of Practice (Public Authorities) (Duty to Promote Equality) (Appointed Day) Order 2007. Available from: http://www.opsi.gov.uk/si/si2007/uksi_20070741_en_1

Preparing students of science, technology, and business for a culturally diverse workplace: Practical approaches and best practise recommendations in transferring key intercultural communication skills

Alexia Petersen, Stephan Petersen

In this paper, the authors identify some of the special challenges of transferring key intercultural communication skills to the specific target groups of science, engineering, and business students, by: 1) introducing those concepts and components the authors have found to be most effective in teaching skills transfer within a compact 2-day workshop format, 2) identifying what target group-specific training can achieve, and 3) proposing best practices recommendations for a balanced approach containing both conceptual and practical elements in intercultural communication skills training, based on the author's Cultural Paradigm Shift Model. The paper also identifies the potential risks for internationally-oriented universities in relying on uncoordinated awareness and skills training at different faculty, institute, or special program levels, and, thereby, also postulates in the conclusion a new but seminal question for international universities at large *after* target-group specific training has been carried out: *who* should or must "paradigm shift" to harness the potential in cultural diversity?

1. Introduction: Aims and approach

As a network of leading universities of technology and science, the IDEA League's goal is not only to attract the best young science and engineering specialists and train them for the urgently needed technological breakthroughs in Europe, but also to develop standards and best practices in the process. One reality this must address is the culturally diverse environment in which today's university graduates – especially in the scientific, engineering and business fields – will work. In preparing this special target group for the challenges they will face in the international field, the experiences of the authors, as trainers of applied intercultural communication, attest to a real need for universities to recognise intercultural communication skills as key skills that should be taught as early and systematically as possible during post-secondary education.[1]

Feedback received in the last eight years from participants and organisers of such intercultural training workshops for professionals, in both commercial and academic sectors, has consistently 1) indicated that sustainable skills transfer training requires the provision of a conceptual framework that functions effectively to explicate specific cultural impacts on workplace communication, and as a structural tool for reassessing different culture-specific perceptions of "problems" and culture-appropriate "solutions"; and 2) expressed the need to introduce intercultural training to the primary target group of science, technology, and business students as early on as possible during their university education, especially as resources, company policy, and other situational factors may later all conspire to overlook cross-cultural awareness and skills on the job. This is a clear indication from the industry that, applied intercultural communication skills need to be developed as a key skills package for internationally working professionals, and, thus, must be acquired *before* one enters the work force. Therefore, how can primary student target groups be equipped with suitable, sustainable intercultural communication skills that are valid in interaction with the widest spectrum of cultures, in a short amount of time?

In response to this expressed need from the industry, the authors developed a values-based Cultural Paradigm Model, which draws from three well-known descriptive models of culture in the academic literature (Hofstede 2001; Trompenaars 1993; Hall 1976).[2] The model is used initially in a workshop to illustrate two dominant communication styles and their points of conflict interface, which arise between two divergent sequences of "cultural logic" that follow from a context of our own assumptions and expectations about how people *should* think and act, thereby, engendering misunderstandings the target group often encounters in such daily workplace interactions as cross-cultural problem-solving, conducting meetings, making decisions, distribution and completion of tasks, working in teams, providing leadership and supervision, communicating instructions, communicating about and

---

1   The authors – an intercultural communication trainer from Canada and a German engineer and manager working for a high-technology spin-off of RWTH Aachen University – were initially commissioned in 2002 by RWTH Aachen University to develop a course in applied intercultural communication that could be offered to students of all faculties. As of 2010, workshops have been conducted regularly for undergraduates, graduate/PhD students, post-doctoral fellows, DAAD scholarship student groups, non-scientific administrative staff, RWTH alumni and professors on a regular basis. The observations and recommendations discussed here by the authors are based on over 100 trainings for RWTH Aachen University and other academic institutions in primarily the 2-day workshop format, but also including seminars of various lengths and focus.

2   Only four dimensions – power distance index, individualism, masculinity, uncertainty avoidance index – were initially published in Culture's Consequences – International Differences in Work Related Values (1980). The fifth, time dimension, was added later in the 2nd Edition (2001).

responding to problems in emails, and resolving conflicts. Therefore, the authors adhere to Trompenaars' (1993) and Schein's (2004) working definition of culture as "the way in which people solve problems"[3]. However, the authors will illustrate how the Cultural Paradigm Model can also be used prescriptively to define a 4-step diagnostic tool to identify new strategies for cross-cultural action, thereby, directly responding to the target group's very straightforward questions: How will this help solve concrete problems? Accurately assess culture-appropriate solutions? Identify potential risks and potentials in a cross-cultural work situation? Several other key teaching components used in a 2-day introductory workshop will also be cited.

2. Extending the Research to Applications and Skills Training

2.1 The Cultural Paradigm Model: Combining Hofstede, Trompenaars, and Hall

This descriptive model of the two dominant communication paradigms (Figure 1) combines Hofstede's five cultural dimensions (2001) with Trompenaars' "Cultural Onion" model (1993), to illustrate the "organisation of meaning" into patterns of "effective social interactions"; and Hall's low context/high context communication paradigms (1976), to describe patterns of verbal and non-verbal behaviour in communicating meaning in social interactions.

---

3   The authors acknowledge that there are critics of Hofstede's 5-dimensions model, and Hall's contexting model (P. W. Cardon 2008). For example, the Schwartz Value Survey (SVS), with its seven cultural values orientations, is commonly acknowledged to as contributing significantly to developing and extending the discourse in comparative intercultural research. However, for the purpose of this paper's best practices training experiences and recommendations, it is not the aim here to engage in a meta-analysis of the literature of intercultural communication, but to focus on the transferability of one particular cultural values framework model into usable tools for problem-solving. While acknowledging the interpretative discourse that does exist in the field of theoretical intercultural communication, the authors as trainers point out that models which are over-sophisticated on an abstract level are generally viewed suspiciously by this target group in a skills training context. A manageable and usable structure needs to not only elucidate the patterned behaviours and conflict interfaces resulting from a few key concepts developed in intercultural literature, and focus on providing diagnostic tools for skills training. For this reason, the author's Cultural Paradigm Model limits its focus to a variation of these five values orientations drawn from Hofstede and Trompenaars: hierarchy (Hofstede's "power distance"), fact vs. relationship, individual vs. group; how these three dimensions interrelate to shape a culture's attitudes toward time and perception of risk; and how all these shape the cultural logic assumptions pertaining to channels and contents of information flow.

224 Alexia Petersen, Stephan Petersen

It defines 1) how a system of cultural values priorities impacts communication channels and information flow, and 2) how they link to create two distinct communication dichotomies (e.g. fact/truth-driven, individually assertive low context communication vs. face/harmony-driven, leader-mediated high context communication), which in turn engender dissimilar and divergent paths of "cultural logic". "Paradigm shifting", an ability to *reasonably accurately* assess the cultural logic path driving an unfamiliar cultural behaviour, is the key skill to identifying different alternative, culture-appropriate behaviour.

For example, it is unnecessary, at the initial stages of skills training, for a learner to acquire an especially complex and abstract understanding of hierarchy. Rather, it is important to learn to translate an intellectual understanding of the hierarchy (e.g. Hofstede's power distance) imperative into an ability to deal with the rules governing information flow through either closed or direct communication channels between a superior and a subordinate in various work communication scenarios. Understanding hierarchy in terms of a cultural logic pertaining to status-appropriate information flow enables the learner to develop different strategies for problem-solving in either a moderately hierarchical culture or strongly hierarchical culture, in terms of who can provide what information, where, when, and how. From this, a German Ph.D student, for example, can learn to "Paradigm Shift" by identifying the communication dichotomy that emerges between communication behaviour that follows a *factual* "red thread" as the driving force of individually assertive problem-solving discourse, and that approach, which prioritises the *hierarchical* "red thread", through which factual information must appropriately travel in order to be resolved. Having identified this basic dichotomous assumption, and subsequent chain of expectations-action-interpretation-reaction pertaining to teamwork behaviour and leadership or supervision style, "Paradigm Shifting" enables one to distinguish between two sets of questions that define culture-appropriate behaviour: first, questions pertaining to the nature of communication channels and information flow (What is the hierarchical "chain of command"? How open or closed/mediated are public communication channels for me? How many channels of communication must be opened to transfer the *total* amount of information? Where? How? By whom?); and only then those questions defining factual content (Argue the factual "red thread" oneself, or tell a story and leave space for the "caring father" to instruct the "red thread"? Expect mediation from a third party, or address the specific problem directly to a specific person? Abstractise the problem or a criticism to the group "onstage"? Or address a specific issue to a specific person "off-stage"? Create a thicker "sandwich" around the criticism, or go straight to the "meat", or create a thinner "sandwich"?). Such differentiated questions, which reflect paradigm shifting, enable the learner to better prepare for different styles of leadership, teamwork, task completion, decision making, conducting meetings and discussions, giving critical feedback, dealing with deadlines, and negotiating conflicts.

Figure 1: Descriptive Cultural Paradigm Model of two dominant communication styles

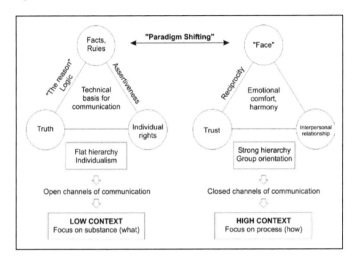

Figure 2: An adaptation of Trompenaars' (1993) "Cultural Onion" as a prescriptive tool

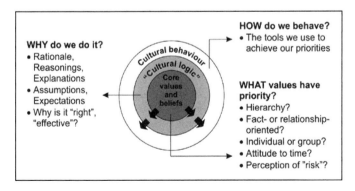

To train "Paradigm Shifting", Trompenaars' model of the "Cultural Onion" provides an optimal complement to the Paradigm Model framework. Originally, Trompenaars utilises the "Cultural Onion" mainly as a descriptive model to distinguish between the visible (behaviour) and invisible (logic and core values dimensions) layers of culture. However, the authors have found these layers can easily be translated into the distinct outward-moving steps of an analytical process (Figure 2), which 1) identifies dominant operative core values priorities at the heart of a miscommunication or conflict, 2) engenders a cultural logic path of assumptions-expectations-actions-interpretations; and 3) shapes distinctive culture-specific patterns of behaviour, such as that described above, when talking about and solving problems.

2.2 The 4-step "Cultural Paradigm Shift" Model

In combining the descriptive value of two well-established models of culture, the authors have adapted and extended them into a 4-step diagnostic tool to deconstruct and re-assess cross-cultural miscommunication:

1. Identify dominant operative core values priorities, or assumptions (in the Cultural Paradigm framework)
2. Map out subsequent divergent "cultural logic" path sequences (e.g. from culture-specific perception of "problem" to "solution")
3. Identify key conflict interfaces at points between divergent paths of "cultural logic" (identification of other's expectations become possible options for new action)
4. Conclude culture-appropriate action (distinction between corrective and prescriptive solutions)

This approach is highly effective and elucidating for learners because it:

- provides a systematic clarity, at the end of which learners can draw for themselves quite logical conclusions of culture-appropriate actions that they were not able to before; students realise that, quite apart from someone being "stupid", "incompetent", "crazy", or "uncooperative", it is largely a question of not understanding the rationale behind one's own and the other's expectations, and where they diverge;
- better distinguishes between personality-specific issues and fundamentally culture-driven behaviour;
- creates a comparatively simple and accessible base-line assessment, which learners can continue to enrich or even modify through their own future experiences;
- provides students with functional tools to independently create transparency, assess the impact of culture (among other factors) on workplace interaction, predict potential misunderstandings or more serious conflicts, and proactively plan alternative, culture-appropriate strategies and steps to avoid miscommunication or prevent dangerous escalation when they do occur;

- enables students to learn from mistakes before they happen in the "safe" context of a workshop; an entire analytical process that can be practised over 90 minutes in the controlled conditions of a case study activity will have to translate into an independently fluent (re)action in real life circumstances with relative certainty and confidence.

2.3 Other key teaching components in the workshop

Having introduced and established the conceptual "red thread" of the 4-Step Cultural Paradigm Shift Model, the workshop draws on several different applications to train "Paradigm Shifting":

- Case study analysis
  - practise identifying different operative cultural values priorities, which engender divergent cultural logic sequences
  - create "Cultural Onion analyses" by "mapping out" key dichotomous cultural logic sequences of assumptions-expectations-misinterpretations of action, and where conflict interfaces are likely to occur
  - identify alternative culture-appropriate action through understanding what was expected
- "Paradigm Shifting" on the level of language
  - identify native patterns of verbal communication, which carry over into one's foreign language patterns, thereby engendering hidden conflicts in "international English", despite a common technical vocabulary and correct grammatical usage
  - how to use language to create balanced Face + Fact solutions
- Role-play simulation using synthetic cultural role prescriptions
  - a cultural awareness training exercise that enables learners to consolidate what they have hitherto learned on an intellectual level at an immediate, experiential level
- Assessment and response to tricky, high context emails requires learners to "Paradigm Shift" simultaneously on the levels of conceptual analysis and technical use of language to create a balanced Face + Fact solution

2.4 What target group-specific training achieves

An overview can be given of some of the typical problems encountered by the four primary university target groups defined in this paper. An introductory 2-day workshop on applied intercultural communication that is regularly taught to all of these groups at RWTH Aachen University, with the exception of professors, who attend a very condensed workshop format, is designed to teach those skills that enable an independent and proactive response to the issues listed below, *as perceived from each group's perspective*:

a) Professors and teaching staff
- many foreign students expect more academic supervision and guidance than what the professor has time to offer, is willing to offer, or perceives is necessary
- many foreign students' native communication behaviour appears to be incompatible with the expected academic discourse style of the institute
- foreign students from certain cultures exhibit a "passive" academic behaviour, such as not signalling a lack of conceptual understanding of course material, with consequences in final examination results
- expectations by foreign students from some cultures that German professors become a "father figure" substitute

b) Non-academic administrative staff
- foreign students from certain cultures do not appear to acknowledge the finality of university administrative rules
- foreign students from certain cultures continue to seek out an individual colleague even if he/she is not the appropriate contact person for the technical issue
- how to reach certain foreign student groups if they do not proactively approach or respond to university initiatives
- how to deal with male foreign students who do not acknowledge female authority positions
- how to deal with female foreign students who are represented by a male authority figure from within their cultural and family hierarchy

c) Doctoral students in supervisory roles
- in underestimating or failing to react preventively to cultural impacts on teamwork dynamics (e.g. fundamental incompatibilities in academic learning and communication styles), professors expect doctoral students to "deal with the situation", but who are limited in what they can do correctively once a problem has arisen
- German doctoral students: perceived inability of certain foreign student groups to participate proactively in teamwork ("how do I get them to tell me they don't understand?")
- foreign doctoral students: perceived unwillingness of German professors to provide the full support considered necessary for students to perform well ("why can't the professor read my signals that I need help?")

d) Undergraduate students

- what kind of behaviour will get the student into trouble abroad (e.g. perceived as disrespectful)?
- what skills will make the student more competitive in the commercial or academic sector?
- how can the student improve his interaction (socially and academically) with other students, or during foreign exchange programmes abroad?

Scenario-specific issues such as these can be satisfactorily addressed and resolved within the framework of the 2-day workshop described above. The authors' Cultural Paradigm Shift Model is a 4-step diagnostic model by which to better measure *how* or *how much* "Paradigm Shifting" is necessary for culture-appropriate action. Consistently positive participant feedback across all university target groups, especially from those in leadership roles such as non-scientific academic staff, graduate/PhD students, and professors, is an important indication that such intercultural communication courses achieve as much as they can outside of a larger integrative policy framework.

3. Conclusions

3.1 Best practices recommendations for target group-specific training

The authors conclude that a solid conceptual knowledge base, derived from Hofstede et al., can be combined, adapted, and extended into a 4-step diagnostic tool to deconstruct and re-assess cross-cultural miscommunication. In fact, feedback from the primary target groups of science, technology, and business students, and including participants of the widest range of cultural backgrounds, has repeatedly confirmed the effectiveness and sustainability of teaching skills transfer in this way.

In summary, an effective skills and applications-based training programme for the primary target group defined in this paper should meet the following criteria:

1. Provide from the outset a clear, concrete definition of "culture" and how it directly impacts patterns of behaviour in authentic workplace scenarios; avoid drawing heavily from theoretical research or statistics.

2. Avoid limiting focus to the level of superficial etiquette (this is a relatively straightforward topic that is thoroughly covered by any number of books).

3. Focus consistently on a limited number of key conceptual ideas and how such culturally different values contexts can engender divergent assumptions and expectations in the behaviour in various work scenarios.

4. Provide a culture non-specific approach that encompasses the widest spectrum of cultural *groups* and renders them accessible.

5. Draw on authentic prototypical scenarios, that learners from all professional sectors and cultural backgrounds can immediately relate to in the form of case studies; then consistently consolidate how these Key Learning Points refer back to new perspectives and solutions for learners' own cross-cultural situations and questions.

6. Ensure that the conceptually descriptive model being taught can be translated into a usable prescriptive model for diagnosing culture-specific perceptions of a "problem" in order to re-assess culture-appropriate "solutions".

7. Include a module to introduce the hidden conflicts in "international English", and to highlight the often under-developed, inherent potential in using English as an intermediary tool.

8. Enable learners to visualise what the intellectual explanations and conclusions of the research actually look and sound like in such concrete entities as emails, contracts, re-negotiated deadlines, problem-solving techniques, leadership and supervision style, teamwork, decision making, etc.

9. Include as much cultural diversity in the workshop group as possible; this imparts a degree of immediacy and authenticity to the discussions, as participants' own experiences confirm and add dimension to what the trainer introduces.

10. Optimally, be as compacted as possible in structure rather than spread out over several lectures or an entire semester. (The 2-day format taught to the primary target group at RWTH Aachen University has proven to be effective precisely because it is both highly compact and intensely focussed, allowing students to be maximally immersed in skills training for two consecutive days and to continue consolidating their skills through further reading, learning, and experience. The sustainability of the intercultural communication fluency acquired is confirmed by the contacts the authors maintain to many students who are now working professionals in both academic research and the commercial sector.)

3.2 After the training: New questions

Until now, while courses taught at RWTH Aachen University to the target groups defined in this paper have been many and varied throughout the university, they have all been individually organised at the request of these groups themselves. In other words, despite the quantity of training being offered, none of it has been part of a truly concerted and integrative philosophy defining university policy at large. This is offset by a frequent but seminal question posed by participants in the workshops (as well as the authors themselves) *after* completing training: *who* should or must paradigm shift to both minimise the risks and synergise the potentials inherent in the cultural diversity at an international university at large?

Universities like RWTH Aachen University cannot only aim to pass on the specialised skills necessary for graduates in a globalised scientific and commercial community; in order to attract the best students, instructors, and professors internationally and create a work environment that benefits from its cultural diversity, intercultural communication skills must be a priority formulated explicitly by the university leadership.

A look at the manner in which courses are typically set up indicates that, many universities lack a coordinated approach to fostering and harnessing the intercultural skills that are being nurtured at various levels of the university. For example, as with commercial companies, "soft skills" courses are typically requested by an administrative body similar to a company's human resource department, which reacts to the needs of key groups of people within the institution. This results in individual, stand-alone courses being set up throughout the university. However, unlike in commercial companies, individual institutes and special programmes often finance their extracurricular course programmes with their own institutional funds. This leads to a situation where intercultural communication awareness is seemingly ever present and growing throughout the university, but the university leadership itself remains largely unaware of, 1) the larger implications of its growing need in the university, 2) what issues are being addressed in the courses, 3) what training alone can achieve and what it cannot achieve without more large-scale systematic policy changes, 4) what these changes should be, 5) by whom should they be made, and 6) how they should be made.

To begin to answer the above questions, the university itself must undergo a fundamental paradigm shift on at least three levels: 1) recognition that a long-term solution to these problems lies in a large-scale, coordinated policy change that requires a cross-group perspective, and not merely patchwork solutions at individual group-specific levels; 2) re-assessment of policies that embody an integrated intercultural vision that is comprehended and supported by all groups involved; and 3) change that must be initiated by university leadership and propagated iteratively and systematically from the top down. These conclusions bring into sharper focus the necessity for universities to recognise the limitations and potential risks of taking merely a piecemeal approach to awareness or skills training at the faculty, programme, or institute levels. In other words, the university itself cannot simply propagate intercultural communication skills training in its various populations; it must have the foresight and courage to exercise primary leadership in recognising and embracing "Cultural Paradigm Shifting" as an institutionalised vision.

References

Cardon, P. (2008): A Critique of Hall's Contexting Model: A Meta-Analysis of Literature on Intercultural Business and Technical Communication. In: Journal of Business and Technical Communication, 2008, 22(4), 399-428.

Hall, E.T. (1976): Beyond culture. Garden City, New York.

Hofstede, G. (2001): Culture's Consequences: Comparing values, behaviors, institutions, and organizations across nations. 2nd ed. Thousand Oaks, CA.

Schein, E. (2004): Organisational Culture and Leadership. 3rd ed. San Francisco, CA.

Schwartz, S. H. (1992): Universals in the content and structure of values: Theoretical advances and empirical tests in 20 countries. In: Advances in Experimental Social Psychology, 1992, 25, 1-65.

Schwartz, S. H. (1994): Beyond individualism/collectivism: New cultural dimensions of values. In: Kim, U. / Triandis, H. C. / Kâgitçibasi, Ç. / Choi, S. / Yoon, G. (Ed.): Individualism and collectivism: Theory, method, and applications. Thousand Oaks, CA, 85-119.

Trompenaars, F. (1993): Riding the waves of culture: Understanding cultural diversity in business. London.

About the authors

Elke Breuer studied Political Science, War Studies, English and German at RWTH Aachen University and King's College London, and finished her studies with a Magister degree and the State Examination for Teaching Practice. During and after university, she gained practical experiences in international relations, human resources development and education. Between 2005 and 2006 she worked as a student assistant for public relations at RWTH Aachen's office for equal opportunities. Since 2007 she has been a research assistant at the department Integration Team – Human Resources, Gender and Diversity Management at RWTH Aachen University. Her work focuses on gender, further education and science management. She was the coordinator of the international mentoring programme and EU-project TANDEMplus-IDEA.

Verena Bruchhagen holds an MA in Educational Science. Since 1996 she has been head of the women´s studies at the department of Educational Science and Sociology at the Technical University Dortmund/Germany. Together with Iris Koall, she has founded DiVersion – Managing Gender & Diversity, a professional education and training program. She works on teaching and training professionals as well as on supervision and coaching programs. She has written numerous publications on the issue of adult education in women studies, managing gender & diversity, learning and teaching diversity.

Sara Connolly is Senior Lecturer in Economics and Associate Dean in the Social Sciences Faculty at the University of East Anglia. She is a labour economist with particular interest in educational attainment, training and pay. Her recent research includes a study (with Mary Gregory) of the long-term consequences of part-time work for women on their future job prospects and an investigation into the career patterns of research scientists in the UK to investigate gender differences in pay and promotion. In 2007 she joined the EU Commission's second expert group on Women in Science and Technology (WiST 2) and is currently studying academic and scientific careers across the EU. Recent publications include: "The part-time pay penalty: earnings trajectories of British Women", Oxford Economic Papers (2009) and "Moving down: Women's part-time work and occupational change in Britain 1991-2001", Economic Journal, (2008).

Jennifer Dyer has recently joined the Institute of Physics as the Diversity Programme Leader. In this role, she manages the Institute's Diversity Programme, working on projects on women in physics, good practice for disabled students and for students from ethnic minorities and advising the Institute internally on good practice in equality and diversity issues. Prior to working at the IOP, she was Policy Director at Skill: National Bureau for Students with Disabilities (from 2002-2009), responsible for national policy and planning on issues of disabled students in higher and further education in the UK. She has also been Faculty Administrator at The University of Bristol and Policy Officer at the Higher Education Funding Council for England (HEFCE).

Stefan Fuchs is head of the Regional Research Network at the Institute for Employment Research (IAB) in Nuremberg, Germany. He is a sociologist and in his time at Munich University (LMU München) has conducted extensive research on women in science. In 2007 he joined the EU Commission's second expert group on Women in Science and Technology (WiST 2). Among his recent publications is a chapter in the Handbook of Science and Technology Studies co-authored with Henry Etzkowitz, Namrata Gupta, Carol Kemelgor and Marina Ranga on "The coming gender revolution in science" (2008, pp. 403-428; edited by E. J. Hackett, O. Amsterdamska, M. Lynch & J. Wajcman. Cambridge).

Sabrina Gebauer, pedagogue, studied at the University of Augsburg with focus on organisational and work psychology. She is a research assistant at Gender Studies in Science and Engineering at TU Munich, Germany. Her main research fields are diversity in teams and organisations, personnel development and innovation research. In her present project she examines gender related issues of methods of user integration in sustainability innovation processes.

Julia Hahmann received her Magister degree at RWTH Aachen University in 2006 in communication science, sociology, and psychology. In January 2008 she joined Prof. Heather Hofmeister's team at the Department of Sociology at RWTH Aachen University, where she focuses her research on Aging and the Life Course, Social Network Analysis, and the field of Gender and Science. While working at the Chair of Sociology with specialty in Gender and Life Course Research, Julia Hahmann researched Gender Inequality within Science by studying the situation of women professors at RWTH Aachen University, focusing on structural inequality concerning the distribution of resources. In April 2009 Julia Hahmann joined the Human Technology Centre (HumTec) of RWTH Aachen University, where she is working on the project City2020+, which explores climatic and demographic change and their impact on the citizens of Aachen. She also researches gendered evaluation of telemedical applications within the project AC-TEC.

Victoria Hantschel, sociologist, studied at the LMU Munich with focus on sociology of economics and organisations, as well as social psychology. She is research assistant at Gender Studies in Science and Engineering at TU Munich, Germany. Her main research field is the evaluation of the change process at TU Munich due to the gender issues of the German Excellence Initiative. She recently worked on a study concerning the lack of people with migration background in engineering sciences.

Heather Hofmeister is Professor of Sociology with the specialty Gender and Life Course Research at RWTH Aachen University. Her research focuses on work, family, gender, leadership, and social change considering geographic context and life course perspective. Her Ph.D. from Cornell University (USA) in 2002 focuses on couples' paid and unpaid work and commuting in life course perspective. She began work at Bamberg University, Germany in 2002 to research gendered career pathways in international comparative life course perspective. In 2007 she joined RWTH Aachen University, and in 2008 she became the first female vice-president at RWTH, responsible for Human Resources Management and Development, and the leader of the Center for Doctoral Studies. She currently leads or works as part of a team on a number of research projects. Hofmeister leads the Virtual Project House for Gender and Technology Research (VPH) and the Aachen Research Commission for Equity (arce).

Susanne Ihsen, sociologist, studied at the RWTH Aachen, Germany. She was scientific assistant at the Centre for Research and Development in Higher Education/Department of Informatics in Mechanical Engineering in Aachen where she got her PhD in 1999. From 1999 till 2004 she was Manager at the Association of German Engineers (VDI). In December 2004 she became the first professor for Gender Studies in Engineering at the Technical University Munich (TUM). Her main research fields are sustainability in the engineering profession, the development of a changed image of the engineering professions, career perspectives of female engineers, gender and diversity in companies and university and engineering education with regards to gender and diversity.

Iris Koall holds a PhD in Business Administration. She is working in the field of diversity, especially gender studies & disability studies at the University of Dortmund/Germany. Contemporarily, she holds the position as research director for ForTe (Forschungstelle Teilhabe) at the Faculty of Rehabilitational Sciences. She has published numerous publications about Managing Diversity as change process, cultural framework and equal opportunities, connecting theory of social systems with gender in organizations and questions of heterogeneity, and paradox system construction towards a theory of complex diversity management. Together with Verena Bruchhagen, she has founded DiVersion – Managing Gender & Diversity, a professional education and training program. She also works as a coach (DGSv) and consultant in the field of Diversity and Career Development.

Thomas Köllen did his PhD degree in business administration at Vienna University of Economics and Business. He conducted studies in Jena/Germany, Turin/Italy and Vienna/Austria. He was research assistant at the Research Institute for Gender and Diversity in Organisations in Vienna. Thomas Köllen received a doctoral fellowship from the Austrian Academy of Science including a research fellowship at the Johann Wolfgang von Goethe University, a. M., Germany. His research focuses on the diversity dimensions "sexual orientation/sexual identity" and "gender".

Carmen Leicht-Scholten holds a visiting professorship in "Gender and Diversity Management in engineering" at Technical University Berlin from July 2010 until April 2011. Coevally, all research projects of the scientific unit "Integration Team – Human Resources, Gender and Diversity Management" at RWTH Aachen University remain under her direction during her leave of absence. In 1998 she received her PhD in political science at the University of Hamburg. Subsequently, she worked as a scientific consultant, focusing on gender in social politics and implementation strategies of gender concepts. Carmen Leicht-Scholten joined RWTH Aachen University at the Department of Sociology in 2004, where she was assigned the coordination and scientific management of all mentoring programmes in 2005. Since 2007 she has been a member of the WIST II Group (Women in Science and Technology) of the European Commission. She has developed the gender and diversity management concept of the Institutional Strategy of RWTH Aachen University. Her research focuses on gender and diversity in natural and engineering sciences.

Alexia Petersen who is a native of Toronto, Canada holds degrees in English and comparative literary studies from the University of Toronto and Queen's University, Kingston, Canada, and has been living in Aachen for 20 years, where she works as an international trainer and consultant in the field of applied intercultural communication. Working equally within the commercial and academic sectors with the primary technical, scientific, and business target groups at all levels of the organisations, her seminars and workshops focus on skills transfer and solutions-focussed applications, particularly within the framework of leadership skills. In addition to her many teaching activities at RWTH Aachen University, Alexia Petersen contributes to the extracurricular course programs at several international research and graduate schools, and Executive MBA programs taught at RWTH and University of St. Gallen, Switzerland.

Stephan Petersen studied engineering at RWTH Aachen University and afterwards conducted research for his PhD thesis at Forschungszentrum Jülich. For over 15 years, he has been with a high-technology spin-off of RWTH Aachen University that is active worldwide. Together with Alexia Petersen, he developed a training concept to teach intercultural communication skills for technical and management professionals, based on his daily multicultural experiences with staff, customers, and research partners from around the world. This concept has been used for the last 10 years to teach applied intercultural communication in companies and universities alike, in particular at RWTH for target groups at all levels. Stephan Petersen regularly teaches seminars for professors at RWTH and holds teaching assignments at other academic institutions.

Teresa Rees CBE BA PhD FRSA AcSS is Pro Vice Chancellor (Research) at Cardiff University, a member of the Russell Group of UK research-intensive universities and the 9th largest UK University. She is a Professor in the School of Social Sciences and her research interests are in women and science, gender mainstreaming and knowledge economies. She was an expert adviser to the European Commission's Research Directorate-General for 12 years, on women and science and gender mainstreaming. She was the rapporteur for the European Commission's ETAN report on women and science and the Helsinki Group review of national policies on women and science.

Londa Schiebinger is the John L. Hinds Professor of History of Science and the Barbara D. Finberg Director of the Clayman Institute for Gender Research at Stanford University. She received her Ph.D. from Harvard University and is a leading international authority on gender and science. Over the past twenty years, Schiebinger's work has been devoted to teasing apart three analytically distinct but interlocking pieces of the gender and science puzzle: the history of women's participation in science; the structure of scientific institutions; and the gendering of human knowledge. Her current work, "Gendered Innovations," explores how gender analysis, when turned to science and technology, can spark creativity by opening new questions and fields for future research. Schiebinger is the recipient of numerous prizes and awards; her work has been translated into ten languages, including German. She speaks and consults nationally and internationally on issues concerning women and gender in science, medicine, and engineering.

Katharina Schiederig works as a research assistant at the Center of Gender and Diversity at Free University Berlin. In her PhD thesis she deals with gender relations in transnational corporations, with a special focus on International Framework Agreements. Katharina holds a Master's degree in Political Science from Free University Berlin and in Development Studies from

Sciences Po Paris. She has worked for the ILO's Global Labour University and UNESCO Zimbabwe. Her research interests centre around work, gender and development issues.

Karin Schlücker is currently working on a research project on diversity in academic career paths. She taught at the J. W. Goethe-University Frankfurt a. M. and the Fern University at Hagen (both Germany), and participated in several research projects developing a special interest in qualitative inquiry. In 2008, she published her dissertation in sociology on methods and methodology of qualitative text analysis (Vom Text zum Wissen. Positionen und Probleme qualitativer Forschung. Konstanz: UVK). Publications in English up to now: Interpreting the needs of homeless men: Interviewing in context. In: Chamberlayne, Prue et al. (Eds.): Biographical methods and professional practice. An international perspective. Bristol: Policy Press, pp. 251-261; and forthcoming in 2010: Performance is ...? Short Cuts - On Voice and Other Metaphors. In: International Review on Qualitative Inquiry.

Martin K.W. Schweer graduated in psychology in 1988. From 1990 he conducted doctoral studies and received his postdoctoral lecturing qualification in Germany at Ruhr-University Bochum in 1995. Since 1998 he has been the Holder of the Chair of Educational Psychology at the University of Vechta; Head of the Centre of Trust Research and Head of the sport psychological centre Challenges. Prof. Dr. Martin Schweer has long-time experience in consultation of top-level athletes and in business consultation. His research focuses are school and organisation, sport psychological consultation and support especially considering the trust phenomenon.

Junko Takagi is Associate Professor in the Management Department ESSEC Business School in France and co-chair of the Chair of Diversity and Performance, partnered by Air France, Deloitte and L'Oréal. She received her PhD in sociology from Stanford University, a MA in sociology from the University of British Columbia and a BA in international relations from Tokyo University of Foreign Studies. Her teaching activities include courses in numerous programmes at ESSEC as well as in-company training programmes. It comprises intercultural management, diversity management, personality and group dynamics, leadership, and the self and identity. She also carries out team-building seminars in different programmes with up to 300 participants. Her research interests focus on multicultural identities and their impact on behaviour in organisations, the impact of culture on interpersonal relations and management practices, the meanings of "diversity" and their consequences, how to incorporate diversity into management, and reciprocity in interpersonal interactions. She has published on gender issues, ethnicity, the medical profession and healthcare for the elderly.

Ann-Kathrin Vaske graduated in gerontology at the University of Vechta in 2005. From 2005 till 2008 she was project coordinator of mentoring programmes for students at the Equal Opportunities Office as well as research assistant at the Department of Gerontology and Research Methods (both at the universities of Vechta). Since 2008 she has been a research assistant at the Chair of Educational Psychology at the University of Vechta.

Claartje Vinkenburg is associate professor of organisational behaviour and development at the VU University Amsterdam. She studied social psychology at the University of Groningen, after which she worked in management consulting and as a visiting scholar and adjunct lecturer at Northwestern University (USA). As managing director of the Amsterdam Center for Career Research (www.accr.nl), Claartje's research and publications focus on gender, leadership and career advancement, including the effects of normative beliefs about parenting on women's career patterns and outcomes. Claartje acted as rapporteur for the second Women in Science & Technology working group (WiST2) commissioned by the EU DG Research, of which the final report entitled "Creating Sustainable Careers" was published in 2009.

Asli-Juliya Weheliye is a research assistant at the scientific unit "Integration Team – Human Resources, Gender and Diversity Management" at RWTH Aachen University. She has a background in business administration, human resources management and cultural studies and holds a masters degree from Free University in Berlin. Her research focus is on gender and diversity in organisations, organisational development, intersectionality and diversity in higher education. Prior to her employment at RWTH Aachen University, she worked at Heinrich Boell Foundation in Berlin and as a consultant in the field of diversity, migration and integration. As a certified diversity trainer of the "A CLASSROOM OF DIFFERENCE™" training programme, Asli Weheliye is also engaged in awareness raising projects all over Europe.

Andrea Wolffram has been associate director of the scientific unit "Integration Team – Human Resources, Gender and Diversity Management" at RWTH Aachen University since 2008. She has a background in sociology, political science, gender and diversity studies and received her doctorate in philosophy at the Brunswick University of Technology in 2002. Afterwards she was postdoctoral fellow at the scientific unit "Work-Gender-Technology" at the Hamburg University of Technology, where she carried out research projects in the field of motivation and retention of women for science and engineering studies. In her research she focuses on gender and diversity in higher education and science, migration/mobility of scientists and gender technology studies.

The Holocaust and its Aftermath

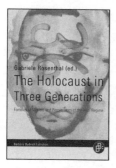

GABRIELE ROSENTHAL (ED.) The Holocaust in Three Generations Families of Victims and Perpetrators of the Nazi Regime. 2nd edition 2010. 393 pp. Pb. 39,00 € (D), 41,10 € (A), 67,00 SFr, US$58.00, GBP 36.95 ISBN 978-3-86649-282-0 ISBN 978-3-86649-282-0

What form does the dialogue about the family past during the Nazi period take in families of those persecuted by the Nazi regime and in families of Nazi perpetrators and bystanders? What impact does the past of the first generation, and their own way of dealing with it have on the lives of their children and grandchildren? What are the differences between the dialogue about the family past and the Holocaust in families of Nazi perpetrators and in families of Holocaust survivors?

Spiral of Time – Making Women's History Visible Vol 4 – 2010 ISSN 1864-5275

The bilingual journal is published biannually with many colourful photographs. Annual subscription rate (two issues with 64 pages each) plus postage. Subscription rate 29,90 €, plus postage single issue: 16,80 € plus postage.

The editors have tried to make their mothers' and grandmothers' history tangible. Older survivors as well as younger academics reflect the experiences, distress and visions of dead and living women during the years 1938 to 1958. They tell us about two decades of German history whose future political power needs to be discovered yet.

In your bookshop or order directly from

Verlag Barbara Budrich • Barbara Budrich Publishers
Stauffenbergstr. 7. D-51379 Leverkusen Opladen
Tel +49 (0)2171.344.594 • Fax +49 (0)2171.344.693 • info@budrich-verlag.de
US-office: Uschi Golden • 28347 Ridgebrook • Farmington Hills, MI 48334 • USA •
ph +1.248.488.9153 • info@barbara-budrich.net • www.barbara-budrich.net

www.barbara-budrich.net